Luther's View of Purgatory

Luther's View of Purgatory

An Examination of His Theological Understanding
of Suffering as the Cross

Min Hwan Kim

Foreword by Robert Kolb
Afterword by John R. Stephenson

☙PICKWICK *Publications* · Eugene, Oregon

LUTHER'S VIEW OF PURGATORY
An Examination of His Theological Understanding of Suffering as the Cross

Copyright © 2025 Min Hwan Kim. All rights reserved. Except for brief quotations in critical publications or reviews, no part of this book may be reproduced in any manner without prior written permission from the publisher. Write: Permissions, Wipf and Stock Publishers, 199 W. 8th Ave., Suite 3, Eugene, OR 97401.

Pickwick Publications
An Imprint of Wipf and Stock Publishers
199 W. 8th Ave., Suite 3
Eugene, OR 97401

www.wipfandstock.com

PAPERBACK ISBN: 979-8-3852-2309-1
HARDCOVER ISBN: 979-8-3852-2310-7
EBOOK ISBN: 979-8-3852-2311-4

Cataloguing-in-Publication data:

Names: Kim, Min Hwan, author. | Kolb, Robert, 1941–, foreword. | Stephenson, John R. (John Raymond), afterword.

Title: Luther's view of purgatory : an examination of his theological understanding of suffering as the cross / Min Hwan Kim ; foreword by Robert Kolb ; afterword by John R. Stephenson.

Description: Eugene, OR: Pickwick Publications, 2025. | Includes bibliographical references and indexes.

Identifiers: ISBN 979-8-3852-2309-1 (paperback). | ISBN 979-8-3852-2310-7 (hardcover). | ISBN 979-8-3852-2311-4 (ebook).

Subjects: LSCH: Purgatory. | Luther, Martin, 1483–1546—Theology.

Classification: BR333.3 K56 2025 (print). | BR333.3 (ebook).

VERSION NUMBER 07/18/25

Unless otherwise indicated, Scripture quotations are from the ESV® Bible (The Holy Bible, English Standard Version®), copyright © 2001 by Crossway Bibles, a publishing ministry of Good News Publishers. Used by permission. All rights reserved.

Scripture quotations marked NRSVCE are taken from the New Revised Standard Version Bible: Catholic Edition, copyright © 1989, 1993 the Division of Christian Education of the National Council of the Churches of Christ in the United States of America. Used by permission. All rights reserved.

The Latin Vulgate (VUL) was translated from the original languages into Latin by Jerome in A.D. 405. For over a millennium, it remained as the preferred translation of the church. This version of the Bible is in the public domain.

Dedicated to
Kyung (Kay), Paul, and Gloria

Contents

Foreword by Robert Kolb | ix
Preface | xiii
Acknowledgments | xv
Abbreviations | xvii

1 Reasoning Behind the Subject | 1
2 Brief Overview of the History of Purgatory | 11
3 Luther's View of Purgatory | 37
4 Luther's Perception: *Simul Purgatorium et Iustificatio Sola Fide* | 91
5 Purgatory as the Cross: Luther's Theological Interpretation of Suffering | 142
6 Reflection on the Subject | 188

Afterword by John R. Stephenson | 197
Appendix: Responses to the Doctrine of Purgatory | 199
Bibliography | 209
Subject Index | 219
Scripture Index | 227

Foreword

MARTIN LUTHER'S MATURE THEOLOGY coalesced slowly as he pursued the route to his "Doctor in Biblia" degree and then began his professorial career in the office of teacher of the church in the 1510s. Like most of us, he experienced flashes of new insight on occasion, but most of his thinking, as we see it in his own lecture notes, the notes taken by students, and his published writings, took shape in jerks and starts. He tested ways to best make clear what he was finding in Scripture for the people to whom he was preaching and whose confessions of sin he was hearing. By 1521 or 1522 the central core of his understanding of the gospel of Christ had taken shape in the way in which he would preach and teach for the rest of his life. Nonetheless, he never ceased to practice his trade as "teacher of the Bible" in the manner he had formed as student and young instructor, in a laboratory located in pulpit and lecture hall. He continued to test, adopt, adapt, and reject formulations of his ever-growing insights into God's message for his human creatures.

Luther's religious formation took place in his parent's household, in schools in Mansfeld, Magdeburg, Eisenach, and finally Erfurt's university and Augustinian cloister. In somewhat different ways, each built on the basic framework of medieval Christianity that laity, clergy, and theologians had constructed in the wake of the conversion of the Germanic tribes. The conversions of individual groups often took place under political sponsorship and were not followed up with extensive catechesis or preaching to develop an understanding of the biblical message in its own terms. Adequate educated personnel could not be marshalled in most cases. Thus, the popular faith of the common people, largely unable to read the Scriptures and to find access to good preaching, prayed to Christianity's newly labeled divine beings and altered some religious practices. But they retained the structure of their traditional religion.

Germanic religions had relied on human effort, mostly in the performance of sacred rites, to establish and maintain a good relationship with divine power. That power lay in a number of gods or goddesses, whose aid could be marshalled with properly executed sacrifices. In the new religious system, the mass that developed around the Lord's Supper took most prominent place as such a sacrifice. Theologians, of course, rose above the level of popular belief, but their religious instincts acquired in their childhood moved all too easily into the legal framework of thinking of the Roman Empire and Greek culture that formed the seedbed and structure for the theology German teachers of the faith inherited from Mediterranean predecessors. In both, the Creator God had often appeared as a demanding and angry judge rather than a loving father who sought communication with his human creatures and loved them as his creatures and children. Human performance of the law and conformity to the principles governing all reality constituted the vital element of holding the world in order.

Luther's gradual weaning away from this medieval foundation for his theological thinking took place under the influence of his training in the philosophy and theology of William of Ockham. He took from Ockham and his late-fifteenth-century follower Gabriel Biel certain fundamental principles including the ultimate almighty power of the Creator and the essential goodness of the created order. At the same time, he fiercely rejected Ockham's assertion that believers must do "what is in them"—the best they can—to earn the initial grace that enables them to please God in a saving way.

A vital component in this system of salvation from sin, the role of purgatory in reconciling sinners with their Creator, formed the context for Luther's falling into the role of public reformer. Purgatory, a place where pious Christians work off the temporal punishment for their sins that have been absolved of eternal guilt in the confession of sin to the priest and his absolution, claimed a prominent place in the popular faith and practice of late medieval believers. It was the sale of indulgences to relieve purchasers from the weight of purgatorial suffering that compelled the Wittenberg Augustinian friar Martin to compose ninety-five theses in search of a pastorally responsible approach to such indulgences. This led to the controversy that propelled Luther and his colleagues into leadership of their call for reform.

Foreword

Min Hwan Kim has produced a perceptive analysis of how this important element of Luther's early thinking underwent a transformation of definition and finally largely disappeared from his active vocabulary. Kim's study of Luther's changing definition and use of the concept of purgatory reveals how the Wittenberg reformer struggled to transform or leave behind fundamental features of his childhood and monastic faith. This took place inevitably as the implications of his realization that God's unconditional grace and believers' trust in the work of Christ for their deliverance from sin and death took hold of his thinking. Kim sketches how purgatory shifted from being a place for satisfying God's requirements to a designation for the spiritual attacks and struggles (*Anfechtungen*) that Satan throws at believers. Slowly "purgatory" understood in either sense waned in the reformer's active vocabulary.

Kim's careful tracing of these developments provide us with an important contribution to understanding how Luther continued to experiment with how best to express the faith—when possible, in continuity with what the people had known and said, but also in radically new ways. Thus, Kim also provides a model for the study of the reformer's thinking and his application of his ever-growing insights gained from his study of Scripture to the lives of his people.

Robert Kolb,
Professor of Systematic Theology emeritus,
Concordia Seminary Saint Louis USA
Mainz, the seventeenth Sunday after Pentecost 2023

Preface

IN THE EARLY PHASE of my doctoral program in Toronto, Ontario, I assumed that Martin Luther might have denied purgatory at least soon after the composition of his *Ninety-five Theses* of 1517 since his theology of justification by faith alone cannot be, I supposed, compatible with the notion of purgatory. Researching the subject of eschatology in Luther's works, however, I noticed that Luther's formal rejection of the doctrine of purgatory appeared much later with the publication of *A Recantation* in 1530. This finding bewildered me with questions: "Why did it take so long for Luther to reject the doctrine of purgatory? Does this mean Luther kept the notion of purgatory all along when writing his sermons, lectures, tracks, and booklets, etc., until then? More importantly, how could he hold *both* the doctrine of justification by faith alone and that of purgatory in his way of thought?" These puzzling questions kept me searching for the answer and became the research topic of my doctoral dissertation.

Challenges were encountered in almost every corner of the chapters. Luther's view of purgatory, being a minor subject in Luther scholarship, has not been treated fairly as a research subject, on the one hand, and the quantity of Luther's writings surpass what might be expected among the writers, on the other. A series of challenges played a critical role in raising further questions and seeking answers in the given limitations, and turned out to be, retrospectively speaking, the guiding posts in completing this project. Adding certain sections that could not be included in my doctoral dissertation due to a word limit, and eliminating what seems unnecessary for this publication, this book now presents my study on Luther's view of

Preface

purgatory. I wish readers would find this book useful to understanding Luther and his works.

Min H. Kim
St Albert, Alberta
Commemoration of Martin Luther,
Doctor and Confessor, February 18, 2024

Acknowledgments

"QUI SEMINANT IN LACRIMIS, in exsultatione metent" (Psalmi 125:5, VUL; 126:5 in English). I can speak only retrospectively that in seeking answers to my research questions on Luther's view of purgatory, I felt being in a tormenting condition or a "purgatory" in an *emotional* sense—the notion to which Luther referred as *Anfechtung*. My doctoral dissertation took longer than expected from researching, drafting, and editing due to working full-time in the Canadian Armed Forces since early 2014 where I supported soldiers most of time in the combat army units that are "always" in high tempo. I resumed my research, I recall, only after fall 2017 when I returned from my deployment to Ukraine.

All my labor for the research would have been nullified without several people to whom I am deeply indebted. Without the encouragement, advice, and research direction of Professor John Stephenson—my dear spiritual and theological father since my Master of Divinity program, and co-director for my doctoral dissertation, as well as the author of the Afterword of this book, it would have been almost unlikely that I enrolled in a doctoral program. Nor would it have been successful without his scholarly advice and guidance in completing the dissertation and now publishing it as a book. My acknowledgments would only be words devoid of sense without addressing the immense support and exceptional leadership of Professor David Neelands—Dean Emeritus of Faculty of Theology, Trinity College in the University of Toronto, and director of my doctoral dissertation and highly respected advisor of the doctoral program—with his thought-provoking and editorial comments. My heartfelt appreciations are indebted to Professor Robert Kolb, the external examiner of the oral defense of my dissertation, for his highly encouraging comments and advice to my research as well as his willingness to write the Foreword of this book. Moreover, this section cannot fulfill its purpose without acknowledging Holly Vogel, librarian at Newman Theological College in Edmonton, Alberta, who was always interested in the progress of my research and kindly accommodated my requests.

Most of all, I am greatly indebted to my dear wife, Kyung (Kay), who always journeyed with me, accommodating my needs to complete this project, attentively listening to my research arguments and thoughts, and sharpening my perspectives. This also extends to my son, Paul, and my daughter, Gloria, who readily supported me, including reading each chapter and sharing their thoughts while studying in their university programs.

Abbreviations

AE   *Luther's Works*. American Edition. Volumes 1–30. Edited by Jaroslav Pelikan. St. Louis: Concordia, 1955–1976. Volumes 31–55. Edited by Helmut T. Lehman. Philadelphia/Minneapolis: Muhlenberg/Fortress, 1957–1986. Volumes 56–75. Edited by Christopher Boyd Brown. St. Louis: Concordia, 2009–

BC¹   *The Book of Concord: The Confessions of the Evangelical Lutheran Church*. Translated and edited by Theodore G. Tappert. Philadelphia: Fortress, 1959

BC²   Robert Kolb and Timothy J. Wengert, eds. *The Book of Concord: The Confessions of the Evangelical Lutheran Church*. Minneapolis: Fortress, 2000

CCDD   Heinrich Denzinger, ed. *Compendium of Creeds, Definitions, and Declarations on Matters of Faith and Morals*. 43rd ed. Edited by Peter Hünermann. San Francisco: Ignatius, 2012

CCML   Donald K. McKim, ed. *The Cambridge Companion to Martin Luther*. Translated by Katharina Gustavs. Cambridge: Cambridge University Press, 2003

Dial   Gregory the Great, *Dialogues*

OHMLT   Robert Kolb, Irene Dingel, and Ľubomir Batka, eds. *The Oxford Handbook of Martin Luther's Theology*. Oxford: Oxford University Press, 2014

ST   Thomas Aquinas. *Summa Theologiae*. Matriti: Biblioteca de Autores Cristianos, 1952

ABBREVIATIONS

WA   *D. Martin Luthers Werke. Kritische Gesamtausgabe.* 73 vols. in 85. Weimar: Böhlau, 1883–

WA Br   *D. Martin Luthers Werke. Briefwechsel.* 18 vols. Weimar: Böhlau, 1930–

WA Tr   *D. Martin Luthers Werke. Kritische Gesamtausgabe. Tischreden.* 6 vols. Weimar: Böhlau, 1912–1921

1

Reasoning Behind the Subject

"The theme of justification is not one theme among many. It has principal significance. It touches on every theme. Justification concerns not merely one's own history, not only world history, but also natural history. It has to do with everything. Hence sanctification is not something that follows justification. Instead, its theme is also none other than justification."

—Oswald Bayer

INTRODUCTION

FOR OVER FIVE CENTURIES historians and theologians have examined numerous subjects with which Martin Luther dealt in their historical, political, cultural, social, economic, and theological contexts. The five-hundredth anniversary of the commencement of the Reformation was another significant landmark to address various subjects in Reformation study in general, and in the theology of Luther in particular. With all the inundations of publications on Luther and the Reformation in the sixteenth century alike, there is a particular subject that has not yet been addressed in comparable depth and scope, namely, Luther's view of purgatory. Under the plausible conjectures that for Luther the doctrine of purgatory was not an important subject, and that his doubts about purgatory began to appear in 1518, it seems to have been generally assumed that as soon as Luther claimed the theology of justification by faith alone, his theological stance became irrelevant to the subject of purgatory; or, in its development his theology had no room for discussion on the subject.

LITERARY REVIEW

Amid a scarcity of publications that treat the subject of Luther's view of purgatory by itself, there are four books that deserve a brief review as they partly address the subject in their books, if not in a full scope, except for the second book in the following list. In *The Theology of Luther*, Julius Köstlin addresses the subject of purgatory under the section on the *Explanations of the Ninety-five Theses* of 1518 (hereinafter *Explanations*) and for other subsections such as the Leipzig Debate and Luther's sermons in early 1520s. Published over one and a half centuries ago, *The Theology of Luther* still stands out as it provides a succinct and salient orientation on the subject.[1]

In *Luther vs. Pope Leo: A Conversation in Purgatory*, Paul Hinlicky stresses that at the time of composing the *Ninety-five Theses*[2] Luther already interprets purgatory in an existential perspective. With a slogan: "Purgatory without delay! Purgatory now!" echoing repetitively throughout the book, he claims that in the *Ninety-five Theses* Luther makes an argument "against a purely postmortem purgatory."[3] Behind the claim stands the sub-title of the book—"a conversation in purgatory." Published on the occasion of the five-hundredth anniversary of the Reformation, the book whimsically constructs a context of imaginative ecumenical dialogues between Luther and Pope Leo X, and signifies the contemporary ecumenical relations in line with the *Joint Declaration on the Doctrine of Justification: by the Lutheran World Federation and the Catholic Church* (October 31, 1999). *Luther vs. Pope Leo* does not necessarily concentrate on Luther's view of purgatory

---

1. This publication is a set of two volumes with three editions in German entitled "Luthers Theologie in ihrer geschichtlichen Entwicklung und ihrem inneren Zusammenhange dargestellt" (1st ed., 1863; 2nd ed., 1883; 3rd ed., 1901; and reprint in 1968). The second edition was translated into English in two volumes by Charles E. Hay in 1897. Köstlin, *The Theology of Luther*, 1:273–76, 1:323–24, 1:353, and 1:361, respectively.

2. It is also called the *Disputation on the Power and Efficacy of Indulgences (Disputatio pro declaratione virtutis indulgentiarum)*. AE 31:25–33; WA 1:233–38.

3. Hinlicky, *Luther vs. Pope Leo*, 6–7.

Reasoning Behind the Subject

in a research style, nor does it claim to treat the subject for that purpose. Nonetheless, this book deserves attention since it addresses Luther's view of purgatory, particularly his *existential* perspective.

Craig Koslofsky discusses the subject in some detail in *The Reformation of the Dead* with a specific timeline of Luther's denial of postmortem purgation and the formal doctrine. Under the sub-section of "Luther and Purgatory: Separating the Living and the Dead" in chapter 2, Koslofsky claims that Luther still held his belief in postmortem purgation in 1528, but denied both postmortem purgation and the corresponding doctrine with the publication of his *Recantation of the Doctrine of Purgatory* (*Widerruf vom Fegefeuer*, 1530; hereinafter *Recantation*). Koslofsky argues that the sixteenth-century Reformation is in essence a Christian ritual and social movement that separates the living from the dead (e.g., a funeral rite), which coincides with Luther's view of purgatory itself. Koslofsky's assertion will be revisited later with discussions on the timeline of Luther's denial of the doctrine of purgatory.[4]

Finally, in his PhD dissertation "Gerhard Westerburg[5]: His Life and Doctrine of Purgatory and the Lord's Supper," Russell Woodbridge briefly touches on the subject in chapter 3 entitled "Westerburg's Theology of Purgatory." Woodbridge's dissertation addresses a specific timeline of Luther's rejection of the doctrine of purgatory. In reference to Luther's *Notes on Ecclesiastes* 9:5–6 (1526), Woodbridge claims, unlike Koslofsky, that Luther's rejection of the doctrine occurs at the time of his annotation on Ecclesiastes in 1526.[6]

REASONING, INQUIRIES, AND SIGNIFICANCES

If Luther in 1517 already made an argument against the notion of "a purely postmortem purgatory," as Hinlicky proposes, and if Luther did not deny the notion of postmortem purgation until his rejection of the formal doctrine of purgatory in 1530, as Koslofsky claims, here arises a question: "Why did it take so long for Luther to deny purgatory?" In response to

---

4. Koslofsky, *The Reformation of the Dead*, 34–39.

5. Gerhard von Westerburg (d. 1558), brother-in-law of Andreas Bodenstein von Karlstadt, was a pastor of an Anabaptist congregation in Cologne in 1534, and afterwards ministered to a Reformed congregation in East Freisland until his death. Woodbridge, "Gerhard Westerburg," 1–2.

6. Woodbridge, "Gerhard Westerburg," 99–104, and 102 respectively.

Koslofsky's claim that Luther still maintained in 1528 the notion of postmortem purgation, but denied it in 1530 in a polemical circumstance of rejecting the formal doctrine of purgatory,[7] I raise a further question: "Does Luther's statement in 1528[8] indicate his *willingness* to maintain the notion of postmortem purification or his *acknowledgement* of God's power in hidden will?" Whether Luther's rejection of the doctrine of purgatory occurred in 1530 or in 1526 (Koslofsky and Woodbridge, respectively), the research question remains valid, regardless. Furthermore, any answers to these questions would not be substantially satisfying unless the following critical question is answered: "How could Luther hold *both* purgatory and justification by faith alone?" Finally, returning to the general assumptions mentioned above, imperative is an answer to the next questions: "Why is it significant to examine Luther's view of purgatory despite his denial of purgatory, after all? What was Luther's intention and purpose in treating the subject of the punishments of purgatory in the *Explanations*, and how did he maneuver it?"

These questions are significant in consideration of the following aspects: first, challenging the assumption that until his 1530 *Recantation* Luther did not deny the notion of postmortem purgation, nor did he reject the formal doctrine of purgatory, these questions seek clarification on Luther's view of purgatory and its development; second, they require a theological investigation on the subject of Luther's view of purgatory in general, and the subject in relation to the development of his theology of justification (i.e., his Reformation breakthrough)—compatibility of both subjects in Luther until his denial of the formal doctrine of purgatory, in particular; and third, they propose to treat the subject both in broad and narrow spectrum, and seek explication as to in what particular way Luther articulates in the *Explanations* of 1518 the notion of postmortem torment in purgatory.

BRIEF ACCOUNT

In the *Explanations* of 1518, Luther articulates the subject of postmortem punishments in purgatory with his theological interpretation of suffering as the cross and a foretaste of hell in two frameworks—his theology

---

7. Koslofsky, *The Reformation of the Dead*, 37.

8. "... although all things are possible to God, and he could very well allow souls to be tormented after their departure from the body." AE 37:369; WA 26:508.8–9. *Confession* (1528).

of justification and his theology of the cross. This statement can be explicated with respect to the three questions raised above. Concerning the first question: "Why did it take so long for Luther to deny purgatory or reject the doctrine of purgatory?" a twofold point of reference holds a key: first, Luther distinguishes his notion of purgatory from the doctrine itself, and second, there are two turning points in Luther's view of purgatory: one in 1521/22 when he rejects the formal doctrine, and the other in 1525/26 when he dismisses the notion of postmortem torment. Luther's denial occurs in 1521/22 when he attacks the doctrine of purgatory as received as lies and deceit. This is the first turning point where he redefines purgatory as a foretaste of hell rather in this life while still maintaining the notion of postmortem torment yet for few souls only. The second turning point occurs in 1525/26 when he dismisses the notion of postmortem torment, while keeping the notion of God's power in hidden will to torment the departed souls,[9] and accepts instead the notion of postmortem peaceful rest of the soul. Subsequently, in 1530 Luther affirms his denial with publication of his *Recantation*.

The relation of faith and suffering in Luther's theological perspective holds a clue for the second question: "How could Luther hold both purgatory and justification by faith alone?" Luther perceives purgatory as the cross of souls, and in his theology of justification, faith and the cross are not opposed to each other, nor are they to be separated. In other words, while one is certainly saved by faith alone, both faith and the cross are complementary with respect to the Christian life here below and in purgatory. Luther's notion of the alien (i.e., external) righteousness of God explains this. Concerning the notion of the alien righteousness of God, Luther articulates a twofold effect: the instantaneous effect (i.e., forgiveness in baptism) and the continual effect (i.e., the removal of sin whenever one is repentant). In this framework, Luther's articulation of suffering as the cross of souls in purgatory corresponds to the continual effect of justifying grace for the growth of faith and love in Christ until souls' entry into the final destination.

Furthermore, Luther's theological interpretation of suffering as a foretaste of hell and the cross signals a clue for the third question: "What was Luther's intention and purpose in treating the subject of the punishments of purgatory in the *Explanations*, and how did he maneuver it?" In the *Explanations*, Luther articulates his view of purgatory in light of the theology

---

9. AE 37:369; WA 26:508.8–9.

of the cross, and explicates the subject of the punishments of purgatory as the cross of suffering imposed by God who can only be found in suffering, as opposed to the theology of glory that avoids and disdains the cross. In so doing, Luther not only interprets suffering as the cross as well as a foretaste of hell in this life, but also reinterprets it with reference to postmortem torment of souls in purgatory. Significant is Luther's twofold purpose highlighted in his interpretation: with the *Anfechtung* account in reference to John Tauler, as well as to his biblical reference, Luther defends from the accusations of heresy the Wittenberg theology and his propositions on purgatory, claiming that they correspond to Scripture and a tradition of German theology, on the one hand, and criticizes his opponents' claim that their biblical references prove the doctrine of purgatory, as well as their tradition of scholastic theology which promotes indulgences, the center of negligence and avoidance of suffering in purgatory, on the other.

BASIS OF THE APPROACH

Framework of Development and Relation

In a broad spectrum, two aspects are to be considered in examining Luther's view of purgatory: its development and its relation with other major subjects. No single subject in Luther's thought remains unchanged or undeveloped, nor does any single subject exist in isolation from other subjects. We thus investigate the subject of Luther's view of purgatory and its development in relation to other major subjects such as Luther's theology of justification and the theology of the cross. This *modus operandi* also implies that within the boundary of a theological perspective—although theological perspectives do not exist in isolation from socio-political, historical, psychological perspectives—Luther's theological concept cannot be fully understood even in its own theological context *unless* it is examined in view of the two conjoined methodological frameworks: development and relation, which complement the point that Bernhard Lohse makes regarding the weakness and strength of the systematic and historical approaches.[10]

---

10. Lohse, *Martin Luther*, 140–44.

A Comparative Study

The research topic involves a wide range of Luther's view of purgatory between 1517/18 and (post-) 1530, and a comparative study will be conducted in examining his works, drawing particular attention to the following period—between 1518 and 1519: the *Explanations* (1518) and the *Leipzig Debate* (1519); between 1520 and 1522: the *Defense and Explanation of All the Articles* (March 1521; hereinafter *Defense*), Luther's *Letter to Nicholas von Amsdorf* (January 13, 1522), two sermons on *the Christmas Day* (Titus 2:11–15; 3:4–8, early 1522), and a sermon on *the Gospel for the Epiphany* (Matthew 2:1–12, early 1522; hereinafter *Epiphany*); between 1523 and 1530: *the Adoration of the Sacrament* (published April 1523; hereinafter *Adoration*), *Personal Prayer Book* (1524), *A Meditation on Christ's Passion* (1525; hereinafter *Meditation*), *Notes on Ecclesiastes* (delivered in 1526; hereinafter *Ecclesiastes*), *Confession Concerning Christ's Passion* (1528, hereinafter *Confession*), and the *Recantation* (1530); and after 1530: *Sermons on the Gospel of St John* (1531–32) and *Sermon Annotations on St Matthew* (1534–35, published in 1538; hereinafter *Sermon Annotations*).

In exploring the development in Luther's theology of justification, we will conduct a brief comparative study on selected writings of the period between 1513 and 1517: *First Lectures on the Psalms* (1513–15; hereinafter *Dictata*), the *Lectures on Romans* (1515–16), three sermons with the theme of three stages (1516–17: October 5 and 12, 1516, and January 1, 1517); between 1518 and 1520: the *Sermo de Poenitentia* of 1518, the *Sermon on Two Kinds of Righteousness* of 1519, and the *Freedom of A Christian* (1520); and after 1521: *Against Latomus* (1521), the *Lectures on Galatians* (1531/35), and the *Disputation Concerning Justification* (1536).

Context of Continuity and Discontinuity

With regard to the issue of continuity and discontinuity between Luther's earlier and later thoughts, I concur with Steinmetz' viewpoint that there is no "abrupt shift" between Luther's earlier and later thoughts but rather "growth and development" as the process of adopting new ideas and denying old ones continued throughout his whole life.[11] Furthermore, as far as Luther's theology of justification is concerned, I consider Luther's Reformation breakthrough or discoveries, not as a special event that occurred in a

---

11. Steinmetz, *Luther and Staupitz*, 140.

specific timeline, but as a process in a series of gradual discoveries from early lectures onward (e.g., Oberman,[12] Beutel,[13] Kolb,[14] Lohse,[15] Hamm,[16] and Leppin[17]).

PROCEDURE

Chapter 2 sets a brief historical background prior to discussing Luther's view of purgatory. The chapter claims that the tradition of prayers for the dead does not imply or prove the existence of purgatory. On the basis of Isabel Moreira's assertion that it was Bede (d. 735) who combined both the notion of postmortem purgation and prayer for the dead,[18] it establishes the major premise that purgatory defined as a postmortem place for purgation and consolidated with prayer for the dead is a theological orientation introduced in the Western Church in Late Antiquity. With Jean-Claude Larchet's viewpoint, the chapter establishes the minor premise that the doctrine of purgatory was a theological construction of the Latin Church in the post-Augustinian epoch.[19] Within these premises, the chapter addresses two elements that remained in the background of the development of the notion of purgatory (i.e., pastoral and theological inquiries and speculations, and prayers for the dead), and three components chiefly involved in the development of the doctrine of purgatory (i.e., penance, churchly relations between West and East, and indulgences). Finally, it undertakes a quick appraisal of research relevance prior to discussing Luther's view of purgatory. Attached to the Appendix is the review of responses to the doctrine of purgatory from recent scholarship of Roman Catholic circles (e.g., Pope Benedict XVI and Karl Rahner), two reformers (e.g., Luther and Calvin) of the Protestants, and the Orthodox Church (e.g., Mark of Ephesus).

The three questions raised above serve as a blueprint for the structure of this book, particularly for the subsequent three chapters from chapter

---

12. Oberman, *Luther*, 164–66. The *Dictata*, for instance, was the occasion of Luther's theological breakthrough. Oberman, *Reformation*, 95.
13. Beutel, "Luther's Life," 7.
14. Kolb, *Martin Luther*, 42.
15. Lohse, *Martin Luther's Theology*, 30.
16. Hamm, *Early Luther*, 109.
17. Leppin, "Luther's Transformation," 116.
18. Moreira, *Heaven's Purge*, 96–97.
19. Larchet, *Life After Death*, 176.

3. In answering the first question (chapter 3: "Why did it take so long for Luther to deny purgatory or reject the doctrine of purgatory?"), Luther's articles and sermons published in 1521/22 will be compared with the *Recantation* of 1530 with particular attention to terminology employed in the context of Luther's attacks on the formal doctrine of purgatory, which will prove how identical Luther's terminology is both in 1521/22 and 1530. Findings from the comparative study demonstrate that Luther's rejection of the doctrine of purgatory occurred in 1521/22, which coincide with his two discoveries in early 1520—that the gospel had been condemned and burned with John Huss' death at the stake, and the *Refutation of the Donation of Constantine* (hereinafter *Refutation*) by Lorenzo Valla (d. 1457)—and his conviction that the papacy is the Antichrist, followed by the papal accusation and condemnation of Luther for heresy under the bulls *Exsurge Domine* (June 10, 1520) and *Decet Romanum Pontificem* (January 3, 1521).

Concerning the second question (chapter 4: "How could Luther hold both purgatory and justification by faith alone?"), the chapter claims that in the *Explanations* Luther integrates the notion of suffering as the cross of souls in purgatory into his theology of justification with respect to the soul's continual growth in faith and love in Christ. With the examination of Luther's theology of justification in a chronological order, selectively between the *Dictata* (1513–15) and the *Disputation Concerning Justification* (1536), the chapter will establish a major premise that Luther's theology of justification encompasses both the instantaneous effect and the continual effect of the alien righteousness of God. Furthermore, with four significances drawn from the continual effect, I will propose as a minor premise that until 1521/22 Luther perceived a postmortem tormenting condition of purgatory in line with the notion of a continual effect. In examining Luther's view of purgatory in his theology of justification, the chapter will examine the *Explanations* prior to discussing his view of purgatory in accordance with the four significances of the continual effect of the alien righteousness of God. In the conclusion, the chapter will address the significance of this claim with respect to *before* and *after* the dismissal of the notion of postmortem torment (e.g., 1525/26) with particular aspects in terms of *continuity* and *discontinuity*.

Concerning the third question (chapter 5: "What was Luther's intention and purpose in treating the subject of the punishments of purgatory in the *Explanations*, and how did he navigate it?"), with the proposal that in the *Explanations* Luther articulates his theological interpretation of suffering as a foretaste of hell in the framework of the theology of the cross, the chapter will examine in comparison the *Dictata* and the *Explanations*, concentrating on the notion of tasting hell in this life, and establish the major premise that Luther's view of suffering as a foretaste of hell precedes his acquaintance with John Tauler's sermons. As for the minor premise, the chapter will argue that Tauler's role in Luther's disputation is to *represent* a tradition of German theology in order to *defend* the Wittenberg theology and Luther's propositions on the subject of the punishments of purgatory, and to *dispute* his opponents' scholastic tradition and their biblical reference to purgatory, as well as their criticism on Luther's propositions. Subsequently, after a review of the *Heidelberg Disputation* concerning the subject of the theology of the cross, the chapter will revisit the *Dictata* and the *Explanations* to address Luther's notion of a foretaste of hell in the framework of the theology of the cross.

Chapter 6 recapitulates the main points by underlining the research claim and its significances, briefly notes in what respect Luther's view of purgatory buttresses his Reformation breakthrough as a gradual process, highlights the image of pastoral Luther on the notion of purgatory, and finally addresses questions for further research.

2

Brief Overview of the History of Purgatory

"Fire, when applied to wood, first dehumidifies it, dispelling all moisture and making it give off any water it contains. Then it gradually turns the wood black, makes it dark and ugly, and even causes it to emit a bad odor. By drying out the wood, the fire brings to light and expels all those ugly and dark accidents that are contrary to fire. Finally, by heating and enkindling it from without, the fire transforms the wood into itself and makes it as beautiful as the fire itself."

—John of the Cross

INTRODUCTION

The purpose of the current chapter is not to offer a comprehensive review of the subject of purgatory, but to lay out a succinct historical background prior to discussing Luther's view of purgatory. This chapter proposes that the tradition of intercessory prayer for the dead does not prove the existence of purgatory as such. As a point of departure, it sets out as its major premise that the notion of purgatory defined as a place of postmortem purgation and consolidated with the tradition of prayer for the deceased is a theologoumenon for the learned (or a pious opinion in more common parlance) that originated in the Western Church in Late Antiquity. The major premise is established on the basis of Isabel Moreira's assertion that in the seventh century Bede (d. 735) incorporated both the notion of postmortem purgation and the practice of prayers for the dead, and gave birth in his theological narratives to what is commonly depicted as "purgatory."[1] As for the minor premise, I concur with Larchet that "the doctrine of purgatory can be seen as being in agreement with the post-Augustinian orientation of Latin Theology,"[2] and claims that purgatory as defined in the Western Church is rooted in the post-Augustinian theological interpretation.

In this framework, the chapter will address what was situated in the background—but not as a determinant—in the development of the doctrine of purgatory, and what contributed to the development. Concerning the former, two elements will be discussed: first, the necessity of responses to pastoral and theological inquiries and speculations; and second, the relationship between the living and the dead associated with the traditions of both East and West regarding prayers for the deceased. Concerning the major players involved in the development of the doctrine of purgatory in the Western Church, the following three components will be discussed: first, with a new form of penance (i.e., the Celtic or tariff penance) introduced in Late Antiquity along with a frequent, auricular confession, and with the notion of purgatory as a *place* for postmortem purgation, which was also consolidated with the tradition of prayers of the dead, the notion of purgatory developed as a formal doctrine in the penitential system of the High Middle Ages; second, the official definition of purgatory and its doctrine emerged concurrently with the Latin Church's attempt to resolve the inner-churchly issue of the Great Schism with the Orthodox Church; third, indulgences associated with the authority of the pope played a key role in the further development of the doctrine. Those components will provide a broad contextual background in which Luther addressed the subject.

---

1. Moreira claims that the incorporation of "prayers for the dead with a fully developed view of purgatory was first accomplished by Bede who finally brought together the parallel discourses of prayers for the dead and the fires of purgatory." Moreira, *Heaven's Purge*, 96–97.

2. Larchet, *Life After Death*, 176.

Brief Overview of the History of Purgatory

DIVERSE NOTIONS OF POSTMORTEM PURGATORIAL CONDITIONS

No such term as "purgatory" (*purgatorium*) is found in the works of the early church fathers. Jacques Le Goff claims: "Until the end of the twelfth century the noun *purgatorium* did not exist: *the* Purgatory had not yet been born."[3] The statement does not imply that a pious belief in postmortem purgation did not appear until the end of the twelfth century. By "*the* Purgatory," he refers to the particular concept defined as the postmortem intermediary *place* in the *other* world.[4]

While no such definite term as purgatory existed in Antiquity—precisely until Late Antiquity—except the notion of *promptuaria* (i.e., storeroom),[5] the subject of postmortem purgation was already discussed, but not necessarily in combination with prayers for the dead. In the third century, the term "*purgare*" (i.e., to cleanse) appeared with respect to postmortem conditions,[6] and Tertullian of Carthage (d. 220) understood it with respect to "a time of imprisonment."[7] Cyprian of Carthage (d. 258), on the other hand, addressed the subject in the context of Christian persecutions with an emphasis on purification both in this life and hereafter, and claimed that souls would undergo "full, universal retribution immediately after death"[8] as a "penitential way of purification."[9]

Both purificatory and punitive characters imply no different nature of postmortem conditions than that which essentially involves sufferings and pains. That is to say, the postmortem conditions are in essence painful ordeals. Thomas Aquinas (d. 1274), for instance, citing Augustine of Hippo (d. 430),[10] asserted that sufferings in purgatory exceed any imaginable pains and ordeals that anyone can undergo in this life.[11] Augustine's statement

---

3. Le Goff, *Birth of Purgatory*, 3; italics in the original. See also its Appendix II, 362–66.

4. Le Goff, *Birth of Purgatory*, 89–90.

5. Bartmann, *Purgatory*, 97.

6. Bartmann, *Purgatory*, 105.

7. Ratzinger, *Eschatology*, 223–24.

8. Pozo, *Theology of the Beyond*, 450.

9. Ratzinger, *Eschatology*, 223–24.

10. Augustine of Hippo (*Aurelius Augustinus Hipponensis*), a native North African, Bishop of Carthage, was the author of *Confessions* and the *City of God*. "Augustine," in Cross and Livingstone, *Oxford Dictionary*, 128–30.

11. O'Callaghan, *Christ Our Hope*, 305. See also Bartmann, *Purgatory*, 183–86; Salkeld, *Can Catholics and Evangelicals Agree?*, 28.

concerning the postmortem state of the soul, on the other hand, particularly the tormenting condition in hell, contains both pastoral and theological objectives, and it aimed to warn against Origen's notion of *apokatastasis* (i.e., restoration to the original condition, entailing the final salvation of all), and provide pastoral advice for those who under its influence did not seriously discern the critical effect of sin in this life.[12]

Postmortem purgatorial conditions were also believed as a *joyful* state. During the late medieval era, the purgatorial sufferings and pains were sometimes perceived in such a way that the pains were reckoned as a *near joy*.[13] In her *Purgation and Purgatory: the Spiritual Dialogue*, Catherine of Genoa (d. 1510) understood purgation as part of being in union with God who sheds the light of mercy, and the souls in purgatory enter a peaceful state.[14] She describes, "Both Body and Soul waited to see the workings of God, which increased their joy and suffering. They did so patiently; and this was another sign that this Soul was in the furnace of burning love in which, as in purgatory, it was being purified."[15]

These diverse notions of postmortem purgatorial conditions can perhaps be formulated in an analytic fashion as types or models (e.g., satisfaction and sanctification), as Jerry Walls attempts. In *Purgatory*, the last book of his trilogy, Walls as a Protestant philosopher, who maintains the Protestant logic of the economy of salvation, rejects the satisfaction model of purgatory (i.e., debt of the punishment of sin to pay in purgatory).[16] He proposes instead that purgatory can be considered in relation to the completion of *sanctification*, which is feasible not only for the Roman Catholics, but for the Protestants and the Orthodox alike. If the satisfaction model reflects the judgment-oriented concept of postmortem purgation, asserts Walls, the sanctification model depicts the purification-oriented perception of God's salvation.[17]

Despite this generalization within a type or model, the notion of postmortem conditions is, in fact, primarily subjective and characteristically

---

12. Le Goff, *Birth of Purgatory*, 68–69; see also Bartmann, *Purgatory*, 187.

13. The examples are Dante Alighieri (d. 1321), Bernardine of Siena (d. 1444), Francis de Sales (d. 1622), and Catherine of Genoa (d. 1510), quoted in Bartmann, *Purgatory*, 228–29.

14. Genoa, *Purgation and Purgatory*, 34–35.

15. Genoa, *Purgation and Purgatory*, 139–40.

16. Walls, *Purgatory*, 68–71.

17. Walls, *Purgatory*, 59–91.

diverse, partly due to the nature of access to eschatology that "offers no guided tour of the afterlife."[18] On this account, any obtainable analogies and imaginations including visionary accounts in Antiquity and the Early Middle Ages[19] became *sources* in depicting the postmortem conditions. This phenomenon was similar, to a certain extent, to the subject of eschatology in a broad sense. Daley observes that "the content of eschatological teaching was usually drawn from a variety of sources: biblical and apocryphal traditions; popular, semi-Christian beliefs about the fate of the human person after death; the myths and the reasoned convictions of Hellenistic philosophy; and a good deal of simple speculation."[20] Partly, for this reason, a symbolic and allegorical interpretation is often taken to conceive purgatory, as Zachary Hayes comments that "[p]urgatory is seen primarily as a symbol of the need for further maturation."[21] In the same vein, N. T. Wright notes, "The myth of purgatory is an allegory, a projection, from the present on to the future. This is why purgatory appeals to the imagination."[22]

BACKGROUND

Pastoral and Theological Inquiries and Speculations

"What I want to know is, where is he now?"[23] The question posed by a young widow coping with the loss of her husband raises pastoral and theological responses and inquiries. From a pastoral point of view, a parishioner is affected in uncertainty concerning the whereabouts and destiny of her deceased husband, and thus requires a pastoral response that can assist her amid a spiritual *tentatio*. From a theological point of view, the same question underlines the need of clarification about the state of the soul between death and resurrection. To meet the need of pastoral care, N. T. Wright, then a newly appointed Bishop of Durham in England, wrote a book to

---

18. Kelly, *Eschatology and Hope*, 121–23.

19. Moreira provides various vision accounts with respect to postmortem conditions including the visions of Barontus, Drythelm, Fursey, Paul, the Monk of Wenlock, and Wetti. Moreira, *Heaven's Purge*, 152–56, 132–30, 132–34, 149–52, 106, and 202, respectively. Moreira notes a succinct introduction in the section of "Visions of the Afterlife," 99–101. See also Delumeau, *History of Paradise*, 27–28.

20. Daley, *Hope of the Early Church*, 3–4.

21. Hayes, "Afterlife," 72–75.

22. Wright, *For All*, 35.

23. Wright, *For All*, xi.

provide pastoral advice and guidelines regarding the afterlife in which the above-mentioned story of the young widow is included.

The young widow's question is not a unique inquiry, nor is it a quest in a matter of spirituality that only emerged in the twenty-first century. The question concerning the afterlife is one of the primordial, universal queries regardless of religious or ethnic backgrounds—whether they be Christianity, Hinduism, Buddhism, Confucianism, or ancient Egyptian religion.[24] Traditionally within Christendom, except for Origenism, the final destiny of the fully good, or that of the entirely evil, is unequivocal, but the common question raised in this regard concerns those who fall into the middle group between the two. Heaven requires perfection, and hell is the perpetual destiny of the reprobate, but it is uncertain what happens to those who are at death neither fully good nor entirely evil. This inquiry raises a further question as to whether there is a posthumous remission of sin.

In response to these inquiries and speculations, the early church fathers provided pastoral advice and catechetical guidelines. Augustine of Hippo (d. 430), for instance, wrote as a new bishop his *Confessions* (c. 397) not only for the purpose of self-reflection in the style of an autobiography but also for pastoral guidance concerning various subjects including prayers for the dead.[25] Gregory the Great (d. 604) was another example in offering pastoral care and instructions regarding hereafter. Le Goff comments on the significant role that Gregory played in this regard and in contribution to the later development of purgatory:

> In his zeal as a pastor, Gregory the Great understood two psychological needs of the believers to whom he ministered: the need for authentic testimony delivered by witnesses worthy of belief and the need for details about the location of purgatorial punishments.
>
> Gregory's stories are particularly important because they served as the model for anecdotes that the Church used to popularize the belief in Purgatory in the thirteenth century, once that belief was officially sanctioned and defined.[26]

---

24. Le Goff, *Birth of Purgatory*, 17–51.

25. Augustine's prayers for his deceased mother, Monica. Brown, *Augustine of Hippo*, 158–81; Chronological Tables B and C. 73–78, 182–87.

26. Le Goff comments that Augustine is considered as the true father of purgatory and Gregory the Great as the last father of purgatory. Le Goff, *Birth of Purgatory*, 61–85, 93.

In a similar vein, the early church fathers addressed the subject of the afterlife in reference to the judgment and retribution of God, on the one hand, and faith and hope, on the other, and how the present life is indispensably relevant to the future after death. In doing so, various images and visionary accounts were employed to explicate the subject in a suggestive yet authoritative manner. Variations in thoughts and opinions, however, did not foresee the portent of disputes and controversies that came to emerge (e.g., Origenism),[27] nor was it anticipated that the subject of postmortem purgation could be addressed as a *dogma* in the later development in the Western Church even though uncertainty and ambiguity to a certain degree still remained.

Prayers for the Dead

Another element to be discussed as the background is the relationship between the living and the dead (also called "*ecclesial continuum*") in general,[28] and in the practices of prayers for the deceased in particular.[29] The nature of this relationship is essentially that of the communion of saints in the body of Christ—the church.[30] The subject of suffrages also falls into this category; however, it will be discussed later as it is closely associated with the penitential practice of satisfaction of the Latin Church in the High Middle Ages.

A twofold motif of prayers for the dead is noteworthy: first, a pious act of commemoration of the deceased, and second, a devoted act of assisting the dead regarding the remission of sins through litany (called "*ectenia*"[31] in the Eastern Church). The Eastern Church retains and practices the communal relationship by lighting two candles with a liturgical prayer, symbolically one for the living and the other for the dead, which signifies "the perpetuity of the prayer and its integration with that of the community and the entire Church."[32] An ancient Coptic liturgy notes:

---

27. In *The Hope of the Early Church*, Daley discusses the subject in Patristics.
28. Ombres, *Theology of Purgatory*, 64.
29. Walls, *Purgatory*, 155. See also Bartmann, *Purgatory*, 160.
30. Thiel, *Icons of Hope*, 48–55.
31. Larchet, *Life After Death*, 213–16.
32. Larchet, *Life After Death*, 211, 226–27. See also Kelly, *Eschatology and Hope*, 118–20.

> To these, O Lord, and to all those of whom we make remembrance, and to those also of whom each one thinks in his own heart, give rest in the bosom of Abraham, Isaac, and Jacob. Give them refreshment (*refrigerium*) in the smiling fields of the paradise of peace where there is neither sorrow nor pain ... O Thou, who art a God of goodness and the friend of man, deign to pardon them, for there is no man on earth, even if his life were but of one day, who is not stained with sin.[33]

In the Latin Church, which practices the Eucharistic Sacrifice for the dead,[34] Ambrose hoped that prayers for the dead could help the souls who suffer punishment, and offered intercessions for the deceased Emperor Theodosius.[35] Concerning prayers for the dead, Augustine commented that their efficacy is limited more or less to pious souls.[36] Gregory the Great adopted Augustine's view of a limited efficacy of these prayers,[37] and advanced in consideration of the Eucharistic Sacrifice by claiming it as "a real repetition of Christ's sacrifice."[38]

In the Middle Ages, prayers for the dead are also found in the liturgical prayers. The emphasis, particularly in Gallican prayers, is laid on the first resurrection with the notion of the other world.[39] Also, during the tenth and the eleventh centuries the Mass for the dead comes to be officially

---

33. Bartmann, *Purgatory*, 100–101.

34. Several church fathers who recommended offering the Eucharistic Sacrifice include Cyprian of Carthage (*Letters*, 1. 2) and Gregory the Great (*Dial* 4. 57–60). Unlike the Latin Church, the Eastern Church's theological understanding of the liturgy stands on the principle that "it is Christ Himself 'who offers and is offered'"; no liturgy can be offered "specifically for the deceased" as both the living and the dead are in one holy Catholic and Apostolic Communion; the liturgy cannot be used as a means. Larchet, *Life After Death*, 207n12. See chapter 9 "Relations between the Living and the Dead," 205–39 where the author also addresses the subject of the prayers for the remission of sins for the deceased, 212–16.

35. Ambrose, *Funeral Orations*, 322–23.

36. "For some of the dead, indeed, the prayer of the Church or of pious individuals is heard; but it is for those who, having been regenerated in Christ, did not spend their life so wickedly that they can be judged unworthy of such compassion, nor so well that they can be considered to have no need of it." Augustine, *City of God*, 21:24. 795.

37. The story of Gregory the Great's prayer for the late Emperor Trajan (ruled in the late first century and the early second century), who was also known as a non-Christian, appeared around a century after Gregory's death. *Dial* 4.46. It is uncertain, however, whether the story has a historical validity. See Trumbower, *Rescue for the Dead*, 141–46.

38. Schwarz, *Eschatology*, 357.

39. Le Goff, *Birth of Purgatory*, 122–24.

Brief Overview of the History of Purgatory

part of the liturgy. In the Carolingian era, mortuary registers entitled as the "Books of Life" were kept in commemorating the dead, and by the eleventh century (e.g., the Gregorian Reform) names of the departed Christians are gradually introduced to the liturgy. At Cluny during 1024–1033, for instance, there was the commemoration of the dead (i.e., All Souls' Day) once a year on November 2, the day after All Saints' Day, which signifies the solidarity between the living and the dead.[40]

Both East and West agree on the communal relationship of the living and the dead in the communion of saints in general, and prayers for the dead, in particular. Benedict XVI highlights this particular aspect of Christendom:

> The possibility of helping and giving does not cease to exist on the death of a Christian. Rather does it stretch out to encompass the entire communion of saints, on both sides of death's portals. The capacity, and the duty, to love beyond the grave might even be called the true primordial datum in this whole area of tradition—as II Maccabees 12, 42–45 first makes it clear. Furthermore, this original "given" has never been in dispute as between East and West. It was the Reformation which called it into question, and that in the face of what were in part objectionable and deformed practices.[41]

Despite the congruity of both East and West in this regard, both are yet distinctive to the extent that while in the latter a pious belief in postmortem purgation developed to be a systematized doctrine particularly during the High Middle Ages, the former keeps the tradition of prayers for the deceased in the liturgy, not necessarily developing it to a formal doctrine as in the West. It was Bede (d. 735) in the eighth century in the West who is first known to integrate both the notion of postmortem purgation and the practice of prayers for the dead into "a system that is fully recognizable as purgatory."[42] In the *Homily for Advent*, Bede addresses what takes place in purgatory:

> But in truth there are some who were preordained to the lot of the elect on account of their good works, but on account of some evils by which they were polluted, went out from the body after death to be severely chastised, and were seized by the flames of the fire of purgatory [*flammis ignis purgatorii*]. They are either made

---

40. Le Goff, *Birth of Purgatory*, 124–27.
41. Ratzinger, *Eschatology*, 233.
42. Moreira, *Heaven's Purge*, 161.

clean from the stains of their vices in their long ordeal up until Judgement Day, or, on the other hand, if they are absolved from their penalties by the petitions, almsgiving, fasting, weeping, and oblation of the saving sacrificial offering by their faithful friends, they may come earlier to the rest of the blessed.[43]

Bede's narrative exhibits two significant, interrelated aspects: first, the notion of postmortem purgation is articulated as a temporary *place* differentiated from that of hell;[44] second, the process of painful purgation is conjoined with the petitions of the living in such a way that the latter can possibly shorten the duration of the former.[45] While Bede references Augustine in this regard, it is Bede's own interpretation of Augustine, combined with the visionary accounts in the *Dialogues* of Gregory the Great.[46]

Theologians in the seventh century addressed the subjects of postmortem purgation and prayers for the dead; however, until Bede's time no immediate conjunction of the two subjects was made explicitly.[47] More importantly, this finding further remarks that the practice of prayers for the deceased does not necessarily imply or prove the existence of purgatory.[48] A direct correlation of the two subjects developed from Late Antiquity onwards, particularly during the High Middle Ages, in response to pastoral and theological inquiries and speculations.

Noticeable are particular components directly associated with the development of the doctrine of purgatory during the High Middle Ages: first, the medieval penitential system as the foundation following the new form of penance in Late Antiquity; second, the emergence of the definition and

43. Bede, *Homilies*, 17, quoted in Moreira, *Heaven's Purge*, 156. See *Bede's Ecclesiastical History*, Bk 5. Chap 12.383–390.

44. Moreira, *Heaven's Purge*, 161.

45. Moreira, *Heaven's Purge*, 160.

46. "[I]t is evident that Bede's description owed much to Augustine. But Augustine did not believe that there was a *place* [emphasis added] of extended purification in the afterlife or that human intercessory activities could expunge post-baptismal sin. It is clear, then, that Bede drew not only on Augustine but on other sources also, including scripture, visions of the afterlife, and claims for the efficacy of the Mass championed by the clergy and colourfully expressed in the *Dialogues* of Gregory the Great and in other clerical writings of the period. What is clear from the passage cited above is that Bede was not tentative in his opinion; he outlined the purpose of purgatory in an authoritative way, and his strong dependence on Augustine's phrasing suggests that he believed he had the authority of Augustine to guide him." Moreira, *Heaven's Purge*, 17–18, 160–61.

47. Moreira, *Heaven's Purge*, 95–96.

48. Moreira, *Heaven's Purge*, 96–97.

doctrine of purgatory amid the inner-churchly dialogues (e.g., the Second Council of Lyons, 1274, and the Council of Florence, 1439); and third, the practice of indulgences that played for further development in this regard.

THREE CORE COMPONENTS OF THE DEVELOPMENT

Penance

Canonical penance involving fasting and abstinence developed a great deal from the second and third centuries.[49] The extended process of the canonical penance in the early epoch aimed to admonish, exhort, and edify pastorally in order to restore the relapsed after baptism in the "process of transformation and integration."[50] Penance, practiced publicly and as frequently as once a year (i.e., public penance in Lent) administered by the bishop,[51] was concerned with what ought to be done in this life, and absolution was granted *only* upon the completion of penance.

In the sixth century, a different form of penance, known as "tariffed penance,"[52] was introduced in the Celtic monasteries where each sin was taxed with an appropriate penance.[53] Upon the penitent's confession, the confessor prescribes penance, upon the acceptance of which, the pronouncement of absolution follows without a formal procedure of completing penance.[54] The spread of adaptation to the tariff penance was

---

49. Rausch, *Systematic Theology*, 236.

50. Phan, *Eternity in Time*, 125n38.

51. Knowles, "From Gregory," 238–39.

52. Stephenson, "Reformation of Repentance," 60, 62. See also Dudley, "Sacrament of Penance," 56–59.

53. The seemingly "new" type of penance was in fact originated from the East in the fourth century. Price notes, "The tariffed penance which is conventionally attributed to the original of Celtic monks derived in fact from eastern practice developed in the fourth century, notably in the penitential epistles of Basil of Caesarea, which lists specific offenses with a set period of penance for each, and make no reference to any need for formal reconciliation at the end of the process." Price, "Informal Penance," 32–33, quoted in Moreira, *Heaven's Purge*, 135. See also Palmer, *Sacraments and Forgiveness*, 145–47.

54. Frantzen, *Literature of Penance*, 5–6. See also Tentler, *Sin and Confession*, 10. It has been the subject of scholarly debate as to whether there is a certain formula of absolution in the Celtic penance. See Connolly, *Irish Penitentials*, 143–48. Palmer notes that the term "absolve" or "absolution" rarely appears in the absolution formulas in Antiquity. Palmer, *Sacraments and Forgiveness*, 175.

noticeable from Iona to Luxeil in France, as well as to the European continent, through the wide pathways of the Celtic emigrants and missionaries.[55] In the meantime, Bede, who consolidated the notion of postmortem purgation and prayers for the dead,[56] also approved tariff penance with the document entitled "Penitential."[57] Practices of the two different systems of penance—canonical and tariff—continued throughout the ninth and tenth centuries. In the early ninth century, for instance, Charlemagne's reform of the church included the revival of canonical penance administered by the bishop, while in the late tenth century Archbishop Wulfstan of London and York maintained both systems.[58]

The advantage of tariff penance with respect to the *frequency* of confession and absolution engendered unexpected pastoral and theological issues, however. In the system of taxing each sin with penance at a proportional level, the accumulation of frequent penance often exceeded the capability of completing penance before death. To remedy the situation, a table of instruction was provided to assist the living and the dead alike in a communal aspect.[59] "An Old Irish Treatise *De arreis*" of the eighth century,[60] for instance, is the earliest document in this respect, and treats what is "equivalent" or "substitute" for commutation of penance. The table states a specific prescription of *arreum*,[61] with regard to "saving a soul out of hell."[62] The document exhibits theological articulations in response to

55. Knowles, "From Gregory," 239.

56. Moreira, *Heaven's Purge*, 161.

57. Moreira, *Heaven's Purge*, 161. As for the authorship of the *Penitentials* attributed to Bede, see Frantzen, *The Literature of Penance*, 69–71. As for the question whether the tariff penance in the sixth century is directly linked to the conception of purgatory, Moreira notes that there are significant differences between the two subjects. See Moreira, *Heaven's Purge*, 134–39.

58. Frantzen, *Literature of Penance*, 6.

59. Palmer, *Sacraments and Forgiveness*, 145.

60. Meyer, "Old Irish Treatise," 485–98, quoted in McNeill and Gamer, *Medieval Handbooks of Penance*, 142. See also Palmer, *Sacraments and Forgiveness*, 145.

61. The term "*arreum*" is the Latin form of the Irish term "*arra*" or "*arre*" meaning "equivalent, substitute, commutation." McNeill and Gamer, *Medieval Handbooks of Penance*, 142. See also Meyer, "Old Irish Treatise," 486.

62. Here are some examples: "1. The *arreum* for saving a soul out of hell, viz. 365 paternosters and 365 genuflexions and 365 blows with a scourge on every day to the end of a year, and fasting every month saves a soul out of hell. For this *arreum* for redeeming the soul that deserves torments in the body has been made according to the number of joints and sinews that are in a man's body. 2. Another *arreum*, viz. the three fifties [the

pastoral concerns and issues in the eighth century that the living can assist the dead with prayers and other acts if the penitents could not complete penance prior to death. By the time that theology in the "scholastic systematization" treats the subjects of sin and penance in a juridical formation,[63] the two components—postmortem purgation and prayer for the dead—in the form of tariff penance had long been part of the ecclesiastical tradition of Western Christendom. Penance, as a sacrament, consists in contrition, confession, and satisfaction; its effect reaches beyond death; and purgatory as a place for postmortem purgation is considered as "a continuation of earthly penance."[64] In this penitential system, what has *not* been completed in this life can be achieved during the afterlife, not only with indulgences but also through suffrages of the living.[65]

Suffrages[66]

Suffrages, as "an appeal for mercy,"[67] play a key role in maintaining the relationship between the living and the dead. In the Eastern Church, John Chrysostom (d. 407) and John Damascene (d. 709) affirmed the Church's custom of praying for the dead and the usefulness of individual and corporate suffrages made on behalf of the deceased. In principle, the communion of the one Body of Christ is reckoned to bind a moral and spiritual responsibility in giving an aid to the weak (e.g., 1 Corinthians 12:12–26). The intercessory prayer of the living for the dead is in this respect considered as an aid since souls in postmortem conditions are believed to be unable

---

one hundred and fifty psalms] every day, with their conclusion of the Beati [Psalm 118] to the end of seven years, saves a soul out of hell . . . 14. An *arreum* of pure prayers for seven years of hard penance to save a soul from the tortures of hell, viz. one hundred offerings, hundred and fifty psalms, one hundred Beati, one hundred genuflexions at every beatitude, one hundred paternosters, one hundred soul-hymns." McNeill and Gamer, *Medieval Handbooks of Penance*, 142–43, 145.

63. Salkeld, *Can Catholics and Evangelicals Agree?*, 44.

64. Le Goff uses the term "the continuation of the earthly penance" in reference to the paradigm shift of penance in the twelfth century. Le Goff, *Birth of Purgatory*, 237–88, particularly 241–45. See also Pasulka, *Heaven Can Wait*, 41.

65. Ombres, *Theology of Purgatory*, 33.

66. The term "suffrages" (*suffragia*) in a general sense means "voting; vote; right of voting; recommendation." Morwood, *Oxford Latin Desk Dictionary*, 183. The verb form "*suffragor*" also means to "express public support (for), canvass or vote for; lend support (to)." Morwood, *Oxford Latin Desk Dictionary*, 183.

67. Anderson, *Charity*, 176.

to act for themselves (i.e., gaining merit). Furthermore, souls in hell were also thought to receive consolations and alleviation of their punishments through prayers (e.g., Macarius the Great (d. 392), John Chrysostom (d. 407), and Mark of Ephesus (d. 1444)), not to mention that the saints were also believed to make intercessions on behalf of the living. It is conceded, however, that grave sins such as blaspheming against the Holy Spirit (e.g., Matthew 12:31) are not covered by this practice.[68]

In the Latin Church, suffrages further developed in the penitential system in reference to "sacrifices of masses, prayers, almsgiving and other acts of devotion."[69] In the thirteenth century, Thomas Aquinas, who paid a great deal of attention to the subject of suffrages, asserted that the act of the living, including the suffrages offered by the ones paying punishment of sins, can be of help for the dead. He claimed that the efficacy of suffrages depends on the recipient, just as a sacrament has its efficacy independently from those who administer.[70] In addition, the performer's actual deeds and intentions alike benefit the souls in purgatory by means of the ecclesiastical unity as the prayers benefit the recipients in such a way that the performers' intention is directed to the souls in purgatory.[71] Furthermore, when the prayer is offered as an aid, the act of prayer is relevant to the *aspect of satisfaction*, which does not apply for the performer due to the equality of justice, on the one hand, and the same act is pertinent to the *aspect of merit of charity* which benefits the performer and the recipients alike, on the other.[72] Souls in purgatory, however, have no such capability as to pray for the living, argued Aquinas. Being in the state of impeccability in purgatory, they suffer pains and are not in a state of offering prayers other than requiring them.[73]

---

68. Larchet, *Life After Death*, 205–39.

69. The Council of Florence (1438–1439) defines suffrages as such pious acts of the living as "sacrifices of masses, prayers, almsgiving and other acts of devotion." Tanner, *Decrees of Ecumenical Councils*, 2:527.

70. Aquinas, *Suppl.*, q71. a3. Aquinas articulates that suffrages of the living benefit the deceased in two ways: the bond of charity and the intention of the giver. Suffrages denote one's giving of assistance to those in need. This particular dynamic of giving and receiving in suffrages benefits the souls in purgatory, and further augments the communal unity between them in the bond of charity. Aquinas, *Suppl.*, q71. a8 and a2. See also Le Goff, *Birth of Purgatory*, 266–78, particularly, 274.

71. Aquinas, *Suppl.*, q71. a9.

72. Aquinas, *Suppl.*, q71. a4.

73. *ST* II–II. q83. a11.

Brief Overview of the History of Purgatory

The *magisterium* reaffirmed the vital values of suffrages with respect to the communal relationship. The Council of Florence (1438–1439) states in Session 6 and defines suffrages: "the suffrages of the living faithful avail them in giving relief from such pains, that is, sacrifices of masses, prayers, almsgiving and other acts of devotion which have been customarily performed by some of the faithful for others of the faithful in accordance with the church's ordinances."[74]

At the Council of Trent (1545–1563), where the subject of purgatory was treated in Session 25 (December 3–4, 1563), the "Decree on Purgatory" affirmed the efficacy of intercessions for the dead and the Eucharistic Sacrifice: "that there is a purgatory and that the souls detained there are helped by the acts of intercession of the faithful, and especially by the acceptable Sacrifice of the Altar."[75] In the First Vatican Council (1869–1870), the efficacy of suffrages was reaffirmed. In Session 2 (January 6, 1870) under the heading of "Profession of faith," it states: ". . . that the souls detained there are helped by the suffrages of the faithful."[76]

Emergence of the Formal Doctrine of Purgatory

By the end of the thirteenth century the notion of postmortem purgation already acquired the status of a dogma, and was perceived, as in the seventh century, as a *place* in the other world, which frequently appeared in sermons, wills, and obituaries.[77] From the thirteenth century onwards, the pontifical *magisterium* declared, confirmed, and reaffirmed the doctrine of purgatory by decrees.

The pontifical letter *Sub catholicae professione* was the first historic document that contains the name "purgatory" (*purgatorium*) for the purpose of dialogue with the Orthodox Church to resolve the damage incurred in the ecclesiastical relation by the Great Schism in 1054. On March 6, 1254, the year of the second centennial anniversary of the Great Schism, Innocent IV sent his legate Cardinal Eudes of Châteauroux with the letter

---

74. Tanner, *Decrees of Ecumenical Councils*, 527.
75. CCDD 1820:428.
76. Tanner, *Decrees of Ecumenical Councils*, 803.
77. Le Goff, *Birth of Purgatory*, 289–300, 326–28. Dante Alighieri's *Divina Commedia* also appeared in the fourteenth century. See Le Goff, *Birth of Purgatory*, 334–55.

to the Bishop of Tusculum, the legate of the Apostolic See.[78] The letter addresses the Latin position about postmortem purgation:

> because they [the Greeks] say that a certain and proper name was not indicated to them by their doctors for such a place of purgation; and because, according to the tradition and authority of the holy Fathers we call it "purgatory"; we wish that from henceforth it be called by this name among them. For indeed this temporary fire purifies sins, not however mortal or capital <sins> that were not previously remitted by penance, but small and minor <sins> that still weigh down after death even if during life they were forgiven.[79]

At the Council of Florence (1438–1439) the subject was readdressed in Session 6 (July 6, 1439) concerning specifically the rationale and function of the "purgatorial punishments" (*poenis purgatoriis*)."[80] At the Council of Trent (1545–1563) the existence of purgatory was reaffirmed in the most precise form. In Session 25 (December 3–4, 1563), the Council states:

> [t]he Catholic Church, instructed by the Holy Spirit and in accordance with Sacred Scripture and the ancient tradition of the Fathers, has taught in the holy councils and most recently in this ecumenical council that there is a purgatory . . . Therefore, this holy council commands the bishops to strive diligently that the sound doctrine of purgatory, handed down by the holy Fathers and sacred councils, be believed by the faithful and that it be adhered to, taught, and preached everywhere.[81]

The position of the Council of Trent was confirmed at the First Vatican Council (1869–1870). In Session 2 (January 6, 1870) for "Profession of Faith," the Council declares: ". . . purgatory exists . . ."[82] Analogously, the Second Vatican Council (1962–1965) reaffirms the statement as it addresses in chapter 7:[83] "Until the Lord shall come in his majesty, and all the

---

78. The editorial note in *CCDD* 276. See also Le Goff, *Birth of Purgatory*, 283–84.

79. *CCDD* 838:278.

80. "Likewise, <we define> that if those who are truly penitent die in the love of God before having satisfied by worthy fruits of repentance for their sins of commission and omission, their souls are cleansed after death by purgatorial punishment." *CCDD* 1304:336.

81. *CCDD* 1820:428–29.

82. Tanner, *Decrees of Ecumenical Councils*, 2:803.

83. The title of the chapter is "The eschatological character of the pilgrim church and its union with the heavenly church."

angels with him *[cf. Mt 25:31]*, and, death being destroyed, all things are subject to him *[cf. 1 Cor 15:26f]*, some of his disciples are exiles on earth, some having died are being purified, and others are in glory beholding 'clearly God himself triune and one, as he is.'"[84]

The best effort made at the Second Vatican Council was a mere reiteration of the decrees of the former councils.[85] Compared to the Council of Trent and the First Vatican Council, it can be argued that the attitude of the Second Vatican Council towards the doctrine of purgatory appears to be noticeably modified to the extent that the term "purgatory" (*purgatorium*) in a noun form—the core of Le Goff's argument—is veiled, and that the notion of purgatory is indistinctly addressed.[86] It should be acknowledged, on the other hand, that the Council advanced in developing the doctrine of purgatory by conceptualizing purgatory, not as a postmortem place, but as a *process* of postmortem *purification*.[87]

Practices of Indulgences

Indulgences

The concept and practices of indulgences developed gradually in the West, particularly during the High and Late Middle Ages. The term "indulgence" (*indulgentia*), which was borrowed from the Roman law,[88] was flexibly used as a synonym of remission, relaxation, and absolution,[89] and often appeared in a verb form (i.e., *indulgemus*).[90] In the mid to late eleventh century, the term began to be associated with a particular form of use (e.g., the crusade

---

84. *CCDD* 4169:901.

85. "This sacred council accepts with great devotion this venerable faith of our ancestors regarding this vital fellowship with our brethren who are in heavenly glory or who having died are still being purified; and it proposes again the decrees of the Second Council of Nicaea, the Council of Florence, and the Council of Trent." *CCDD* 4169:901; 4171:904.

86. "(They) are (being) purified," which is in the form of present, passive, indicative, and third person plural of *purificare* in the passive voice.

87. More contemporary position on purgatory in Roman Catholicism is treated in Appendix.

88. The term referred specifically to the Christian emperors' remission of the convicted criminals' penalties during the Easter season. Shaffern, *Penitents' Treasury*, 45.

89. Poschmann, *Penance*, 211.

90. Swanson, *Indulgences*, 9.

indulgence),[91] and from the thirteenth century onwards it became fixed specifically for an authoritative remission of penance.[92]

An indulgence, defined as "the remission before God of the temporal punishment due for sins already forgiven as far as their guilt is concerned,"[93] is not part of, but still closely related to, the sacrament of penance, and is "not of divine institution, but an ecclesiastical usage."[94] In the early penitentials and in public penance, sacrifices made for the Church did not remit penance, which was of later origin, but sin, following confession and repentance, was absolved through penance.[95] In the eleventh century indulgences as an authoritative remission of penance began to appear, and Palmer introduces three antecedents of this later practice.[96] First, under the notion of one body of Christ the sacrifices and sufferings of the martyrs were considered as intercessions for the reconciliation of the apostates.[97] After the period of martyrdom ended, the "principle of vicarious satisfaction" continued in the practice of the public penance.[98] Second, with tariff penance where each sin was taxed with specific penance, as described earlier, the value of vicarious satisfaction continued but in a different way that the living, by intercessions and almsgiving, which are the commutations of their penances, assisted the souls in purgatory who had died before the completion of their penances.[99] Third, the term "absolution" was used in intercessory petitions with reference to the dead (e.g., "What after death can help souls for their absolution (*ad absolutionem*)?" in Gregory the Great's *Dialogues*).[100] In addition, when absolution was granted for the sick, intercessory prayers also included a full remission of sins (i.e., including both punishment (*poena*) and sin (*culpa*)) in line with the power of the Office of the Keys (e.g., a letter of Hincmar, Bishop Rheims, to Hildebold,

---

91. Swanson, *Indulgences*, 10. See also Palmer, *Sacraments and Forgiveness*, 329–30.
92. Poschmann, *Penance*, 211; Swanson, *Indulgences*, 9–10.
93. *Enchiridion of Indulgences*, 21. See also *Catechism of the Catholic Church*, 1471.
94. Poschmann, *Penance*, 210–11.
95. Lea, *History of the Inquisition*, 1:41.
96. Palmer, *Sacraments and Forgiveness*, 321–29.
97. Eusebius, *Ecclesiastical History*, Chap 5. Bk 1. 177; Palmer, *Sacraments and Forgiveness*, 17–78.
98. Palmer, *Sacraments and Forgiveness*, 322.
99. Palmer, *Sacraments and Forgiveness*, 322–23.
100. *Dial* 4. 55. Palmer, *Sacraments and Forgiveness*, 324.

874).¹⁰¹ Furthermore, the letters of papal absolution contained a precondition of contribution to monastery churches (e.g., Stephan VIII in 941)¹⁰² and almsgiving to the poor as well as support for the brothers (e.g., Leo IX to King Edward in 1051).¹⁰³

The eleventh century is the turning point in this development with the crusade indulgences. John VIII's intercessory absolution in 878 granted for the soldiers who participated in the war was only preparatory, awaiting the emergence of a massive application of indulgences to the crusade.¹⁰⁴ For those who fought against the Moors, Alexander II granted in 1063 indulgences that required as a precondition confession and repentance, and at the Council of Clermont (1095), Urban II granted plenary remission for the participants of the war in defense of the Church.¹⁰⁵ From this time on, the promulgation of papal indulgences became a common practice,¹⁰⁶ and at the Fourth Lateran Council (1215), Innocent III extended the plenary remission of sin and punishment of the crusade indulgences to those who contributed to the cause.¹⁰⁷

Finally, with Pope Clement VI's notion of the "treasury of the church" on the basis of the teaching of Hugh of St. Cher (d. 1263),¹⁰⁸ which validated the application of indulgences to the souls in purgatory, the practice of indulgences acquired its most fully articulated theological basis.¹⁰⁹ Furthermore, Pope Sixtus IV's indulgences granted in favor of the Church of St. Peter at Xantines in France (1476) was the inaugural promulgation of the efficacy of indulgences for the souls in purgatory, not in the manner of absolution (*per modum absolutionis*), but in the manner of suffrage (*per modum suffragii*).¹¹⁰

---

101. Palmer, *Sacraments and Forgiveness*, 325–27.

102. The pontifical letter notes ". . . so far as apostolic power shall allow, we decree to be absolved (*absolutos esse decernimus*)." Palmer, *Sacraments and Forgiveness*, 328.

103. The term "indulgence" was employed in this letter with reference to pardon. Palmer, *Sacraments and Forgiveness*, 328–29.

104. Palmer, *Sacraments and Forgiveness*, 333–34.

105. Palmer, *Sacraments and Forgiveness*, 334.

106. Knowles, "From Gregory the Great," 240.

107. Palmer, *Sacraments and Forgiveness*, 337–38.

108. Palmer, *Sacraments and Forgiveness*, 340, 349–50.

109. Poschmann, *Penance*, 224.

110. Palmer, *Sacraments and Forgiveness*, 350–52.

Use of Indulgences

Concerns about the improper use of indulgences appeared long before the controversy between John Tetzel (d. 1519) and Martin Luther (d. 1546) in Germany. The subject of issuing indulgences had already been discussed at the Fourth Lateran Council (1215) where ecclesiastical guidelines and careful limits were addressed. On the occasion of dedicating a basilica, for instance, an indulgence cannot remain in force for more than a year, and on that of an anniversary of dedication, it cannot surpass forty days.[111] In this respect, the event of the plenary indulgences issued by Boniface VIII (d. 1303) for the Jubilee of 1300 was significant.[112] The Jubilee indulgences (February 22, 1300) promised the most complete (*plenissima*) forgiveness of all sins for all pilgrims to the Basilicas of St. Peter and St. Paul each centennial year. This historic affair superseded the level of the "Portiuncula" indulgences that Francis of Assisi (d. 1226) procured from Honorius III (d. 1227) for the complete remission of all post-baptismal sins, encompassing both sin and punishment, which was for those who visited the Basilica of Santa Maria de Portiuncula between the two vespers on August 1–2, 1223.[113]

Issues Concerning Indulgences

From the twelfth century onwards to the Reformation indulgences provided the source for controversies and disputes.[114] How indulgences were effective was "always contentious," Shaffern notes,[115] and part of the reason is that the theology of indulgences came after the practice more than a century and a half later,[116] and subsequently the former took the latter as "the object of critical judgement."[117] In a broad spectrum, issues about indulgences concerned a general principle and individual cases in practice. While the former is a theoretical debate (i.e., validity of the indulgences), the latter is a criticism of the misuse of indulgences.[118] In *Ethics*, Peter

---

111. *CCDD* 819:272–73.
112. Walls, *Purgatory*, 25. See also Le Goff, *Birth of Purgatory*, 330–31.
113. Lea, *History of the Inquisition*, 1:41–42.
114. Shaffern, *Penitents' Treasury*, 15.
115. Shaffern, *Penitents' Treasury*, 145–240.
116. Palmer, *Sacraments and Forgiveness*, 338.
117. Poschmann, *Penance*, 219.
118. Swanson, *Indulgences*, 279.

Brief Overview of the History of Purgatory

Abelard (d. 1142), for instance, criticized the increasingly covetous use of indulgences that made a great deal of a profitable traffic in salvation, which was then "one of sharp rejection"[119] and "a lonely voice"[120] that denounced the priests and bishops who out of greed relaxed penances.[121] In addition, criticism arose when indulgences were granted for the remission of both penalty and guilt.[122] Simon of Cremona (d. 1390), writer and preacher of the Order of St. Augustine in Italy, criticized the Franciscans who preached the remission of both guilt and punishment by means of indulgences.[123]

The crusade indulgences conveyed the same claim of the plenary remission,[124] but their unique circumstances generated other theological concerns. William of Auxerre (d. 1231), who highly recognized the functions of indulgences for the aid for the Holy Land,[125] posed a question about the efficaciousness of the crusade indulgences in a particular situation where soldiers die immediately after signing up for participation in the war, without being part of the actual expedition.[126] William asserted that "they [the soldiers] do not immediately go off to heaven, since the merits of the Church do not suffice for such."[127]

Furthermore, indulgences for the deceased kindled one of the most critical issues. Henry of Segusio (also called Hostiensis, d. 1271), cardinal and decretalist, for instance, denied the efficacy of indulgences for the dead, and asserted that in tradition the church had no jurisdiction over the deceased but only offered intercessions for them.[128] In reference to Sixtus IV on the indulgence for the dead (1476), Peter Martínez of Osma (d. 1480),

---

119. Poschmann, *Penance*, 219.

120. Shaffern, *Penitents' Treasury*, 147.

121. Palmer, *Sacraments and Forgiveness*, 187–89. Luscombe, *Peter Abelard's Ethics*, 109–13. See also Bysted, *Crusade Indulgence*, 96–97.

122. A technical term "*a pena et a culpa*" refers to this entire remission of sins. Shaffern, *Penitents' Treasury*, 147–59. In his commentary on the *Decretum*, Hugh of Pisa (d. 1210), an Italian canon lawyer, used the phrase "*a pena et a culpa*" not for indulgences, but for the effect of public penance. The phrase, however, came to be known as a "vulgar expression for plenary indulgences." Shaffern, *Penitents' Treasury*, 148, 158.

123. Shaffern, *Penitents' Treasury*, 147.

124. Shaffern, *Penitents' Treasury*, 148.

125. Bysted, *Crusade Indulgence*, 139.

126. Palmer, *Sacraments and Forgiveness*, 339–40.

127. Paulus, *Geschichte des Ablasses im Mittelalter*, 234n3, quoted in Palmer, *Sacraments and Forgiveness*, 340.

128. Shaffern, *Penitents' Treasury*, 166.

professor of Salamanca in Spain, castigated the notion of the pontifical right to grant indulgences for the souls in purgatory.[129] Moreover, Francis of Mayron (d. 1327), pupil of Duns Scotus and also known as Doctor Illuminatus, denied both papal jurisdiction over the souls in purgatory and the validity of indulgences for the dead.[130] In addition to Martin Luther who called into question the practices of indulgences (e.g., the *Disputation on the Power and Efficacy of Indulgences* of 1517), the University of Paris in 1518 condemned the preachers of indulgences as "false, ridiculous, scandalous and dangerous preachers."[131]

CONCLUSION

Reflection on the History of Purgatory

Purgatory defined as a place of postmortem purgation and consolidated with prayers for the dead is a pious belief introduced in the Western Christendom in Late Antiquity, articulated in post-Augustinian theology.[132] In fact, prayer for the dead, which appears to be associated with the notion of purgatory, neither implies nor proves the existence of purgatory.

In a broad sense, the notion of purgatory embedded in church history is not only subjective, to a large extent, but also diverse and even controversial. Since it is *not* a universal doctrine,[133] nor was it believed in such a way in Antiquity, it could have remained at most as a pious belief, not as a dogma, with its practice of remembering the deceased in prayer. Partially, it was the medieval scholastics that overemphasized and excessively developed it within the medieval penitential system. The early church fathers' thoughts and opinions, such as Augustine and Gregory the Great alike, for instance, were not only taken intensely into their theological considerations but became the major impulses to establishing the doctrine itself. The practice of suffrages in the West was one of the instances where

129. Palmer, *Sacraments and Forgiveness*, 353.

130. Shaffern, *Penitents' Treasury*, 168–69. See *CCDD* 1416–17 for Peter Osma's propositions condemned in *Licet ea quae de nostro mandato*, August 9, 1479.

131. Taylor, "God of Judgment, God of Love," 255, quoted in Salkeld, *Can Catholics and Evangelicals Agree?*, 48. Taylor notes that it was how Guillaume Petit, confessor of Francis I, described the indulgence preachers in Paris in 1518. Taylor, "God of Judgment, God of Love," 255n39.

132. Larchet, *Life After Death*, 176.

133. See the Eastern Church's objection addressed in Appendix.

the ecclesial communal relationship between the living and the dead was utilized with respect to the penitential satisfaction for the souls in purgatory. In the meantime, the practice of indulgences resulted in presenting the doctrine as even scandalous.

The relationship between the living and the dead or the notion of *ecclesial continuum* was not the main driving force of the notion of postmortem purgation to be developed later as a doctrine. A long-standing tradition of prayers for the dead in both East and West is the testimonial signature of this argument. Luther, for instance, despite the shift in his view of purgatory during the course of the Reformation, continued to hold the practice of individual prayers for the dead. Three documents support this position: first, in his sermon for the *Epiphany* (1522), Luther addressed that "I will not stop you if you desire to offer prayers for the dead."[134] Second, in the *Confession* (1528),[135] which is his "manifesto of faith" until his deathbed,[136] Luther affirms: "since no information is given in the Scripture, it is not a sin to pray for them once or twice as follow or freely in a similar way: 'Dear God, if this soul is in a condition accessible to mercy, be thou gracious to it.'"[137] Third, the *Apology of the Augsburg Confession* (*Apologia Confessionis Augustanae*, 1530; hereinafter *Apology*) drafted by Philip Melanchthon (d. 1560), who closely consulted with Luther when composing the document, whose content Luther subscribed, clarifies the Evangelical position in this regard and confirms that prayers for the dead are acceptable.[138] As far as Luther's stance is concerned on this subject, the practice of prayers for the dead in a strict sense is *not* fundamentally associated with the doctrine of purgatory, and thus ought to be differentiated from the doctrine itself.

---

134. AE 52:181; WA 10I 1:589.7–8.

135. AE 37:161–372; WA 26:261.1—509.28.

136. "I am determined to abide by it *until my death* and (so help me God!) in this faith to depart from this world and to appear before the judgment seat of our Lord Jesus Christ." AE 37:360; WA 26:499.21–23. Emphasis added.

137. AE 37:369; WA 26:508.2–3.

138. See both the first edition (May 1531) translated into English by Theodore G. Tappert, and the second edition (September 1531, also known as the "octabo edition") translated into English by Robert Kolb and Timothy J. Wengert. *BC¹* 26.94, 96; *BC²* 275.94, 276.96.

Luther's View of Purgatory

Relevance

How is this chapter relevant to the subject of Luther's view of purgatory? In other words, in what aspect is the review of the history of purgatory significant to the rest of this book? In a broad spectrum, it sheds light on "who Luther is" in a twofold way—Luther's self-identity, on the one hand, and Luther that we identify, on the other. Luther is a Catholic priest standing in the tradition of the Church Fathers (e.g., Augustine), and he is also a Reformer who articulates the subject of purgatory in his theological orientation. In the *Explanations* of 1518, for instance, Luther identifies himself as a *priest* who does not deviate from the mainline tradition as far as his theology is concerned, in general, and his view of purgatory, in particular. He defends his catholicity on the subject of purgatory by means of his allegiance of practicing prayers for the dead.

> I am positive that there is a purgatory, and it does not bother me much what the heretics babble, for St. Augustine, more than eleven hundred years ago . . . prayed for his mother and father and requested that intercession be made for them . . . Even if there had been no purgatory at the time of the apostles (as the disgusting Picard prides himself in), must, therefore, any credence be given a heretic who was born scarcely fifty years ago? And must it be contended that the faith of so many centuries has been false, especially since the Picard does nothing more than say, "I do not believe it," and by that means assumes that he has proved all his assertions and condemned all of ours, as though sticks and stones believe? But these matters pertain to his own work and time.[139]

Three particular reasons are plausible to consider. First, in the *Explanations* Luther attempts to demonstrate his catholicity in this regard so as to defend himself from any accusations on the subject of purgatory. Second, on this basis he argues that he believes in purgatory, and prays for the deceased just as Augustine did, and contends that he is not like such a heretic as Picardi in Bohemia.[140] And third, Luther is not hesitant to assert that Scripture does not speak about purgatory in the way that the opponents claim. Instead, he stresses that the subject of purgatory is suitable for academic discussions in universities, but not for public teaching in the church.[141]

139. AE 31:125–26; WA 1:555.36—556.5.
140. AE 31:125n19.
141. Luther's argument at the Leipzig Debate. WA 2:329.18-19.

Brief Overview of the History of Purgatory

Luther, a Catholic priest, is also a *Reformer* who attempts to reform the Church that stood under the influence of scholastic theology. Concerning the subject of purgatory, Luther in the *Explanations* (1518) discusses the subject of the punishments of purgatory within a twofold theological framework: the theology of justification and the theology of the cross, which will be discussed in detail in chapters 4 and 5 respectively. Suffice it to say succinctly here that Luther integrates the notion of purgatory into his theology of justification, and asserts that suffering and faith are inseparable insofar as the Christian life is concerned. In the same vein, Luther articulates the notion of purgatory in the theology of the cross in that he interprets the punishments of purgatory as the cross of suffering.

Thinking Forward in Relation to Luther's View of Purgatory

Had it not been for the misuse of indulgences, would Luther have called them into question and rejected them afterwards? This is a hypothetical question which raises another question: Had it not been for the scandalous and shocking discoveries about the papacy in early 1520 (i.e., the gospel condemned and burnt at the death of John Huss at the stake, and the forgery of the Roman imperial decree investigated and exposed in Lorenzo Valla's *Refutation*),[142] would Luther have denied the doctrine of purgatory? In theory, perhaps he would not. In 1521/22, when he redefined purgatory with reference to sufferings *in this life*, not as a postmortem place, he could have denied the formal doctrine and the notion of postmortem purgation all together. Instead, he assured his fellow Christians that it is not necessary to believe in purgatory and thus be free from apprehension if they denied purgatory. Nor did he force them to adhere to his position on this subject. By the time he published the *Recantation* (1530), the subject of indulgences for the souls in purgatory, as well as the doctrine of purgatory itself, had long been one of the alarming issues for him. Now, here is a major hypothetical question: In 1530, did Luther deny the notion of postmortem purgation as well as his personal pious belief in purgatory redefined as a foretaste of hell in this life *or* the doctrine of purgatory? If the latter was the case, *how could he retain both his belief in purgatory and the theology of justification by faith alone*? Provided that it was the case of the former, that is, the notion of postmortem purgation and his redefined definition of purgatory, then, would the last question lose the case? Not at all, since his

142. See "Discovery of the Antichrist" in chapter 3.

theology of justification had already substantially developed in 1518 when composing the *Explanations*. In either case, and even his denial in 1530 included all together, the last question—or the question in the main clause of that sentence—remains valid to be asked, and so to be answered.

3

Luther's View of Purgatory

"Let us never relax our grasp on the Hope and Pledge of our righteousness; I mean Jesus Christ, *who bore our sins in his own body on the tree; who did no sin, neither was guile found in his mouth, who steadfastly endured all things for our sakes*, that we might have life in Him. Let us imitate that patient endurance of His; and if we do have to suffer for His Name's sake, why then, let us give glory to Him. For that is the example He set us in His own person, and in which we have learnt to put our faith."

—POLYCARP OF SMYRNA

INTRODUCTION

LUTHER'S FORMAL REJECTION OF purgatory appears in his 1530 *Recantation*,[1] based on which it is generally assumed that until then Luther did not deny purgatory. In attempting to answer the major question as to *why it took so long for Luther to deny purgatory*, I claim that Luther's rejection of the doctrine of purgatory actually first appears in 1521/22, following his conviction of the papacy as the Antichrist. As a point of

1. AE 61:217–44; WA 30II:367.1—390.31.

departure, my research establishes the major premise that Luther's notion of purgatory needs to be differentiated from the formal doctrine of purgatory as it had been officially formulated by that time, and that the two main elements that constitute Luther's notion of purgatory consist of, first, a postmortem condition of torment and, secondly, existential suffering in this life, the distinction between which is a *sine qua non* in understanding his view of purgatory. It sets out the minor premise that Luther's differentiation between his notion of purgatory and the formal doctrine is apparent during his attacks on the latter in 1521/22, and that the terms and expressions employed in the attacks of 1521/22 offer striking parallels to those in his 1530 *Recantation*. It should also be noted as a point of reference that there are two significant turning points in Luther's view of purgatory: one in 1521/22 where he redefines purgatory with reference to sufferings in this life, and the other in 1525/26 when he dismisses the notion of postmortem torment. At the second turning point, Luther's notion of peaceful rest with respect to the intermediate state of the soul replaces the notion of a postmortem condition of torment.

The current chapter presents a chronological overview of Luther's account of purgatory prior to addressing his rejection of the doctrine. The former is divided into four periods to trace Luther's notion of purgatory (1517–1519; 1521–1522; 1523–1530; and post-1530) and the latter treats the point of Luther's rejection by comparing his terminology employed in his attacks on the doctrine between his writings in 1521/22 and his *Recantation* of 1530.

Subject of Purgatory

On October 31, 1517, when Luther sent a letter[2] to Archbishop Albrecht of Magdeburg[3] and Maintz, and afterwards when he circulated his *Ninety-five Theses* among his close friends,[4] the subject of purgatory was not the

---

2. Luther also sent his letter to Bishop Hieronymus Shultz of Brandenburg. Iserloh, *The Theses*, 61. See also, Leppin, *Martin Luther*, 36; Rupp, *Luther's Progress*, 53. Luther attached a copy of the *Ninety-five Theses* to his letter as an appendix. *From Conflict to Communion*, 25, 40; Wicks, *Man Yearning for Grace*, 239.

3. Albrecht von Brandenburg (d. 1545) became Archbishop of Magdeburg in 1513 at age twenty-three. Rupp, *Luther's Progress*, 51.

4. Rupp, *Luther's Progress*, 89–90. It was on November 11, 1517. See also von Loewenich, *Martin Luther*, 46–47. The *Ninety-five Theses* seemed not to have been posted to the door of All Saints' Church, known as Wittenberg Castle Church. Iserloh, *The*

agenda Luther intended to debate. As a doctor of the church, Luther adhered to traditional teaching about purgatory,[5] but did not consider it to be a major subject, nor did he regard it as an official doctrine of the Scripture in a strict sense. When copies of the *Ninety-five Theses* were circulated and subsequently purgatory came under the spotlight of controversy, Luther was then driven to criticize his opponents in public debate, as well as in his articles and sermons, particularly concerning their claim that purgatory is taught in the Scripture and proven by the Church with the biblical references they provide.

From Luther's perspective, the claim that purgatory is an article of faith was a more critical issue than the notion of purgatory itself. The doctrine of purgatory was inextricably associated with the power of the pope, and was based on the claim that the pope has authority over the departed souls suffering in purgatory and power to release them by means of the Office of Keys, as well as over the living, whom he can exempt from purgatory ahead of time.[6] With this, indulgences, pilgrimages, vigils, and the Masses for the dead were all intertwined in late medieval piety with respect to helping souls suffering torments in purgatory. At the center of late medieval religiosity stands purgatory unofficially as an indispensable theological presupposition.[7]

Indulgences in Late Medieval Religiosity

The growth of economy coincided with a profit driven commerce in the fourteenth and fifteenth centuries developed to be interwoven with ecclesiastical doctrines and practices in which the rich, by helping the poor, were

---

Theses, 76–97; see also Leppin, *Martin Luther*, 36. Concerning the purpose and nature of the *Ninety-five Theses*, scholars' views are divided into two camps: one is purely academic in nature, and the other is both academic and reformation. Lohse, for instance, stands for the former, and Oberman for the latter. See Lohse, *Martin Luther's Theology*, 102, and Oberman, *Reformation*, 148. See also Wengert, *Luther's Ninety-Five Theses*.

5. AE 31:125–26; WA 1:555.36—556.5. On Thesis Fifteen of the *Explanations* (1518). Köstlin comments that Luther's reinterpretation of the traditional teaching of purgatory appears in Thesis Eighteen where he rejects his opponents' biblical references to purgatory. Köstlin, *The Theology of Luther*, 1:275.

6. Wicks, *Cajetan Responds*, 22.

7. Concerning the role of purgatory in late medieval religiosity, see also MacCulloch, *Reformation*, 10–16. MacCulloch notes that purgatory was "one of the most successful and long-lasting theological ideas in the Western Church." MacCulloch, *Reformation*, 13.

convinced to be able to purchase spiritual benefits such as the remission of sins in this life and redemption of souls from purgatory,[8] and the sixteenth-century piety was a continuation of such "commercial religiosity."[9] By the early sixteenth century indulgences had already been long established[10] to be a source of revenue for both the clergy and the government rulers alike from ecclesiastical and public projects that procure such profits as military campaigns (e.g., crusade indulgences),[11] constructing church buildings (e.g., St. Peter's Basilica in Rome), hospitals, and bridges.[12] Frederick the Wise (d. 1525), Elector of Saxony, for instance, supported the construction of a bridge over the Elbe through the revenue from the indulgences in his territory.[13] Indulgences involved shareholders among ecclesiastical authorities and territorial rulers. A decision of the latter for approval of indulgences within their territories was frequently determined depending on their share in the incoming profit, and sometimes princes of neighboring territories in their mutual agreement did not authorize to let Roman indulgences be admitted into their territories (e.g., Duke George and Frederick the Wise in early 1517).[14] In the meantime, the purpose of indulgences was debased to a large degree in order to make profits, and yet indulgences were constantly interlocked with the teaching of assisting souls in purgatory.

Publications on Purgatory in 1521–1524

Between 1521 and 1524, the subject of purgatory was frequently discussed through publications widely circulated in German-speaking territories, as well as in sermons and public disputations, not necessarily all written

8. Carter Lindberg terms this development a "God-ordained investment" in which the merchant class played a key role. Lindberg, "There will be No Poor among You," 140–41. See also Hamm, *Early Luther*, 12–13.

9. Hamm uses the term "commercial religiosity" in his article "Martin Luther's Revolutionary Theology," 128, 131–32, in Lindberg, "There will be No Poor among You," 141.

10. Scott Hendrix notes four developments during the late Middle Ages, beginning from the eleventh century until the sixteenth century: first, plenary indulgences (e.g., Pope Urban II in 1095); second, the privileged authority and power of the pope in granting indulgences (e.g., Pope Clement VI in 1343); third, indulgences for the purpose of redeeming souls in purgatory; and fourth, the purchase of indulgences. Hendrix, *Luther and the Papacy*, 23–26.

11. Bysted, *Crusade Indulgence*.

12. Rittgers, "Penance and Indulgences," 89–90. See also Iserloh, *The Theses*, 13–17.

13. Schwarz, *True Faith*, 19.

14. Iserloh, *The Theses*, 13–17. See also Brecht, *Martin Luther*, 1:118.

by the Wittenberg theologians.[15] In addition to Luther's *Defense* (1521), which will be reviewed in a moment, Hulrych Zwingli defended publicly in Zurich his *Sixty-seven Articles* (January 1523) that outlined his theological position against papal doctrines[16] including the doctrine of purgatory (e.g., Theses between Fifty-seven and Sixty)[17] virtually identical to Luther's.

In 1523/24 a large number of pamphlets on purgatory were distributed in German-speaking territories. Woodbridge notes that Gerhard Westerburg (d. 1558), an Anabaptist who studied in Cologne and Bologna, as well as Andreas Rudolf Bodenstein von Karlstadt (d. 1541) who supported Luther only in the early phase of the Reformation, particularly during the indulgence controversy, published pamphlets on purgatory, which were widely distributed from Cologne to Strassburg, Augsburg, and Nürnberg (Nuremberg), a total of thirteen editions altogether, six of them written by Westerburg, and the other seven by Karlstadt. The quantity of the pamphlets in 1523 alone was remarkable: approximately 3,000 copies of Westerburg's pamphlets (e.g., 6–11 pages per pamphlet) were printed in Latin, and several thousand copies of Karlstadt's (e.g., 10–14 pages per pamphlet) were printed in German. As far as the content of both pamphlets are concerned, they are almost identical, and most of the scholars concur that Westerburg copied Karlstadts' except for a couple of minor theories (e.g., the collaboration theory where Karlstadt copied Westerburg's).[18] In his sermon *On the State of the Souls of the Christian Faithful* (1522) Karlstadt denied the intermediate state of the soul and claimed a "spiritual purgatory." Understanding the purifying fire in a figurative sense, Karlstadt stated, "So I would call the yearning and consuming desire for God (which comes from the living word of God) a Purgatory."[19]

---

15. In a broad context of the literature publication, particularly of pamphlets, the number increased about six times between 1518 and 1525 in Germany. Westhelle, "Communication and Transgression," 71.

16. Giselbrecht, "Hulrych Zwingli," 260–62.

17. Thesis Fifty-seven: the true divine Scriptures know nothing about purgatory after this life. Thesis Fifty-eight: the sentence of the dead is known to God only. Thesis Fifty-nine: and the less God has let us know concerning it, the less we should undertake to know about it. Thesis Sixty: that mankind earnestly calls to God to show mercy to the dead I do not condemn, but to determine a period of time therefore (seven years for a mortal sin), and to lie for the sake of gain, is not human, but devilish. Christian History Institute, *No.305: Zwingli's Sixty-seven Articles*.

18. Woodbridge, "Gerhard Westerburg," 104–17.

19. Koslofsky notes that the sermon was perhaps delivered on All Saints' Day in Wittenberg. Koslofsky, *The Reformation of the Dead*, 31–34.

Luther's View of Purgatory

It was Johan Wessel Gansfort (d. 1489, also written as Goesport) who influenced Karlstadt on the subject of purgatory.[20] Gansfort had studied in Cologne and Paris, and in his theological debates and correspondence treated several subjects including purgatory, but his collective writings that had survived among humanist friends and his followers were published only posthumously. His works were first published in 1520 in Zwolle where Gansfort was schooled in his youth, and then in Wittenberg and Basel. They were published again in 1522 entitled "Farrago" (i.e., miscellany), and soon afterwards the final collection volume was published in Zwolle[21] and included Luther's foreword[22] dated July 30, 1522. Luther notes:

> If this man had been read to me beforehand, it could have seemed to my enemies that Luther had drawn everything from Wessel—to such a degree does the spirit of each of us breathe together as one . . . But both my joy and my strength are increasing, and now I have no doubt that I have taught correctly, when this man, with such a consistent meaning and almost the very same words, at such a different time, under a different sky in a different land, and in a different situation, thus agrees with me in all particulars.[23]

The underlining theme in Gansfort's view of purgatory was postmortem *purification* as opposed to postmortem punishment, and the primary passage of the Scripture was 1 Corinthians 3:11–16 based on which he claimed that it is the spiritual fire that purifies the souls in purgatory.[24]

These publications demonstrate several points: first, they provide evidence that purgatory was not a marginal subject at the time of the Reformation;[25] second, such a phenomenon with a high number of

---

20. Koslofsky, *The Reformation of the Dead*, 32–33.

21. Koslofsky, *The Reformation of the Dead*, 27–28. *Farrago rerum theologicarum* (miscellany of theological matters). John Wessel Goesport. https://www.newadvent.org/cathen/15590a.htm.

22. *Christiano lectori Martinus Lutherus S.* WA 10II:316.1—317.31.

23. AE 59:9–11; WA 10II:317.13–18. *Martin Luther to the Christian Reader*, 1522.

24. Koslofsky, *The Reformation of the Dead*, 27–31. It is not frequent that Luther discussed about a purgatorial fire, partly because Luther did not agree with the opponents' exegetical practices to link the image of fire in the Scriptures to their teaching of purgatory. Luther in the *Explanations* (1518) speaks about the inner fire and the outer fire. By the former he refers to spiritual afflictions, but he does not clarify to which fire he refers by the latter. AE 31:130; WA 1:558.14–15.

25. According to the "Report of Anonymous" on the Marburg Colloquy (*Das Marburger Gespräch nach den Berichten von Hedio, Anonymus und Collinus*, WA 30III:110.1—144.5), Luther made preliminary remarks prior to the colloquy that discussions on the

publications on the subject of purgatory was not accidental when the indulgence controversy and its subsequent implications are taken into consideration; and third, it was probably this time that other reformers (e.g., Zurich, Basel, and Strassburg) began to accuse Luther for having incorrect understanding on the subject of purgatory.[26] It is noteworthy that as far as the subject of purgatory is concerned, Luther was different from other reformers, to a large extent. Robert Bellarmine (d. 1621), a Catholic controversialist in the late sixteenth century, notes in his *Purgatory* that Luther was "very different" among the protestant reformers, and at the Leipzig Debate discussed with Eck the subject of purgatory in "a Catholic sense."[27] Luther's stance on the subject, which shifted over time, deserves attention to trace its development in general and to answer why it took so long for him to finally deny purgatory.

CHRONOLOGICAL OVERVIEW

Luther's Use of the Term "Purgatory"[28]

Luther's use of the term "purgatory" is flexible. While Luther sometimes uses the full expression of "the doctrine of purgatory," frequently he also takes the single term "purgatory" in reference to the formal doctrine or to his idiosyncratic notion of purgatory as a postmortem place[29] and/or the condition of torment.[30] The term also refers to "cleansing" or "purifica-

---

Eucharist would be unproductive without concurring on "other important points" which include the subject of purgatory. AE 38:36; WA 30III:110.9–14, 111.10–21.

26. According to "The Report of Hedio," Luther openly stated that other reformers accused him of having misunderstanding on the subject of purgatory. AE 38:15; WA 30III:111.6.

27. Bellarmine, *Purgatory*, 8–9.

28. In general, the term "Fegefeür," "Fegefeur," or "Fegfewr" refers to purgatory. WA 30II:362–63 in *Ausgaben* and *Niederdeutsch*. It can also mean "hell-fire" (i.e., "eternal fire"). AE 22:96n68. On Matt. 25:41. Regarding an example of Luther's use of theological and technical terms, see "Purgatory where faith and love in Christ continually grow" in chapter 4. Also, on Luther's redefinition of purgatory in 1521/22, see "Analysis: Luther's reference to Tauler" in chapter 5.

29. E.g., the *Dictata*. AE 10:364; WA 55II:396.380–83. On Ps. 69:3. See also AE 67:360; WA 47:256.41–42. Sermon on Matt. 18:7.

30. E.g., Thesis Fifteen of the *Explanations* (1518), AE 31:125–30; WA 1:555.26—558.23.

tion" in reference to the persecution of the church,[31] as well as his notion of sufferings and afflictions in great intensity[32] (*tentatio* or *Anfechtungen*)[33] in this life. When Luther refutes the doctrine of purgatory as lies and deceit, for instance, he uses the term "purgatory," distinguishing it from the doctrine itself,[34] but referring it to the notion of postmortem suffering and *tentatio* in this life.[35] Luther also uses the term in a figurative sense. When he recollected his youth, for instance, he called the strict school rules and disciplines with torture and torments as "hell and purgatory."[36]

Luther's use of the term "purgatory," regardless, *always* connotes the single aspect of condition—*torment*. When discussing the subject of the postmortem punishments of purgatory, Luther describes it in view of dreadful fear of torment such as a foretaste of hell.[37] Also, when attacking the doctrine of purgatory in 1521/22, he redefines purgatory by referring it to the torment of suffering itself in this life, not dismissing the notion of postmortem torment entirely, which occurs later in 1525/26.[38]

Between 1517 and 1519

Post-circulation of the *Ninety-five Theses* (1517)

In response to Luther's *Ninety-five Theses*, Konrad Koch (d. 1531), also known as Wimpina, drafted theses, which Tetzel defended on January 20, 1518 at a chapter of the Saxon province of the Dominican order.[39] In

---

31. AE 10:283; WA 55II:312.78–93. AE 10:291–92; WA 55II:322.341–44.

32. Lohse, *Martin Luther*, 24.

33. Luther experienced *tentatio* or *Anfechtungen* throughout his life, the subject of which Luther profoundly treats in his later years. See Rupp, *Righteousness of God*, 105–6. See also "Luther's *Anfechtung*"in chapter 5 of this book.

34. E.g., Luther's sermon for the *Epiphany* (1522) AE 52:180–81; WA 10I 1:588.21—589.17. On Matt. 2:1–12.

35. E.g., *Sermon Annotations* (1534–1535). AE 67:305; WA 38:653.20–26.

36. AE 45:369; WA 15:46.6–7. See also Carlsmith, "Education in Early Sixteenth-Century Europe," 23.

37. AE 31:129; WA 1:558.1–3, 5–8.

38. AE 32:95; WA 7:451.11–18. The Thirty-seventh Article. The *Defense* (1521). Chapter 5 discusses Luther's notion of suffering and torment.

39. Hendrix, *Luther and the Papacy*, 23. See also Marshall, *1517*, 50.

mid-March 1518,[40] copies of Wimpina's theses circulated in Wittenberg[41] were burned in the market square.[42] About this time, Luther completed the *Explanations of the Ninety-five Theses*.[43] In April 1518, Tetzel published a treatise against Luther's *Sermon on Indulgences and Grace*[44] and defended the fifty anti-Luther theses in 1518 at the occasion of a doctoral degree awarded upon him in his battle against Luther.[45] Meantime, in February 1518 Pope Leo X composed a letter to Gabriele della Volta (d. 1537), Vicar General of the Augustinian Order, and gave him the direction to resolve the *causa Lutheri*[46] promptly.[47] In line with this direction, Luther presented in April 1518 his disputations[48] at a general chapter of the German Augustinians in Heidelberg. Two months later, Sylvester Mazzolini (d. 1523, known as Prierias) examined Luther's *Ninety-five Theses*, and accused Luther as a heretic for his denial of the efficacy of indulgence as well as for his view of the authority of the pope. It was Prierias' particular interest to make the subject of the papal authority *the* issue out of Luther's *Ninety-five Theses*, claiming that the authority of the pope stands over the Scripture.[49]

40. Brecht, *Martin Luther*, 1:207.

41. The name "Wittenberg" is a compound word of *weissen* (white) and *berg* (mountain) in German, which is also called *Leucorea* in Latin originated from *lukos oros* (λύκος ὄρος) for the same meaning. Schilling, *Martin Luther*, 95.

42. Marshall, *1517*, 50.

43. Saak, *Luther*, 284. On May 30, 1518, Luther sent Staupitz the *Explanations* with his cover letter. AE 48:65–70; WA 1:525–27.

44. *Eynn Sermon von dem Ablasz unnd grade*. WA 1:243–46. See also Aland, *Martin Luther's Ninety-five Theses*, 63–67.

45. Marshall, *1517*, 50.

46. This is a technical term used mainly from Cajetan's point of view. Beutel, "Luther's Life," 9. The term "*causa Lutheri*" was used from 1517 until 1520. Schilling, *Martin Luther*, 142.

47. Lull and Nelson, *Resilient Reformer*, 58. Della Volta, then, conveyed Leo X's direction to John Staupitz. AE 31:37.

48. *Disputatio Heidelbergae habita*. AE 31:39–70; WA 1:353–74.

49. Marshall, *1517*, 90.

Luther's View of Purgatory

Explanations of the Ninety-five Theses (1518)[50]

In the *Explanations*,[51] Luther makes an argument that the punishments of the souls in purgatory are not solely external but from within the conscience.[52] Indulgences, therefore, cannot resolve the condition of the souls in torments; instead, the infusion of grace is required so that they may grow in faith and love in Christ.[53] In addition, prayers should be offered for the souls in purgatory who suffer "not because of the fear of punishment, but because of their love for righteousness"[54] since it is God's will to help them.[55] Luther's concept of resignation to the will of God up to and including the punishment in purgatory, which cannot be done without the infusion of grace, resonates with his earlier *Lectures on Romans* where he contends that the grace of God is required for resignation to God's will.[56]

Concerning Luther's view of purgatory at this stage, several points are to be highlighted: first, Luther acknowledges that the notion of purgatory is drawn from the tradition,[57] not being as explicitly present in the Scripture as his opponents claim.[58] Second, with regard to the punishments of purgatory, Luther asserts that the punishments of hell and of purgatory are perceived as indistinguishable except for the duration,[59] and that Scripture speaks about those who suffer as tasting hell in this life; therefore, such punishments are also imposed on the souls in purgatory.[60] In this context, Luther does not reject the notion of purgatory as such but professes its existence: "I

---

50. *Resolutiones disputationum de indulgentiarum virtute.*

51. Lohse notes that the style of the composition follows a scholastic method, but the content of Luther's theses is "non-scholastic" with arguments based on the Scripture. Lohse, *Martin Luther*, 101.

52. AE 31:144; WA 1:566.29–30.

53. AE 31:131–32; WA 1:559.11–37. See also Thesis Eighteen: "Furthermore, it does not seem proved, either by reason or Scripture, that souls in purgatory are outside the state of merit, that is, unable to grow in love." AE 31:136–40; WA 1:562.1–564.31. See also AE 31:124; WA 1:555.4–5.

54. AE 31:145; WA 1:567.16–19.

55. AE 31:145; WA 1:567.19–21.

56. AE 25:381–82; WA 56:391.17–392.16. On Rom. 9:3.

57. AE 31:125–26; WA 1:555.29–40.

58. AE 31:138–39; WA 1:563.14–39. AE 31:140; WA 1:564.27–29.

59. AE 31:126; WA 1:556.8–11. See also WA 2:333.20–23.

60. AE 31:140; WA 1:564.16–17.

am positive that there is a purgatory."[61] Third, Luther only makes academic disputations in this regard based on the narratives of the Scripture with particular respect to the suffering of a foretaste of hell in this life,[62] claiming that his disputation on purgatory is "sufficiently rooted in the Scripture."[63] Fourth, Luther rejects the opponents' claim that their biblical references and their references to Augustine support the doctrine of purgatory.[64] Fifth, Luther does not seem to make a particular distinction between the doctrine of purgatory and his notion of a postmortem condition of torment so as to attack the former while maintaining the latter, which does not occur until 1521/22. Until then, both Luther and his opponents freely debate under the assumption that it is not an article of faith, and that they have freedom to do so in the setting of an academic disputation.[65] At least, that was how Luther understood the matter of debate on this subject.

Leipzig Debate (1519)[66]

In response to the recent development of the *causa Lutheri*, in August 1518 Emperor Maximilian composed a letter to Pope Leo X to advance the process of resolving the case, which subsequently engendered the Diet of Augsburg in October 1518. Thomas de Vio from Gaeta, known as Cardinal Cajetan, seemed different from Prierias and had sympathy with Luther's theses on indulgences.[67] Nonetheless, Cajetan thought it unavoidable to require Luther to recant on errors found in his *Sermo de poenitentia*[68] and his disputations (e.g., *Ninety-five Theses* and the *Explanations*).[69] In Novem-

---

61. AE 31:126; WA 1:555.36. Also AE 31:125–30; WA 1:555.26—558.23.

62. AE 31:145; WA 1:567.22–24. AE 31:128–30; WA 1:557.15—558.18. The notion of a foretaste of hell will be treated in chapter 5.

63. AE 31:143–45; WA 1:566.24–28.

64. AE 31:139; WA 1:563.29–35. Also AE 31:139–40; WA 1:564.5–6, 9–11, 14–16.

65. AE 31:145; WA 1:567.22–24.

66. *Disputatio Iohannis Eccii et Martini Lutheri Lipsiae habita*. WA 2:254–383.

67. In December 1517, Cajetan published his *Treatise on Indulgence* (*Tractatus de indulgentiis*) where he underlines three primary points: warning on excessive use of indulgences (chapter 8), indulgences concerning souls in purgatory only as petitions (chapter 5), and no efficacy of indulgences in delivering souls from purgatory (chapter 11). Wicks, *Cajetan Responds*, 13.

68. WA 1:317.1—324.29. The English translation of the *Sermo de poenitentia* is forthcoming in volume 70/71 of AE.

69. Cajetan highlighted two points: first, for Luther the Office of the Keys is the root

ber 1518, Pope Leo X issued the bull *Cum postquam*, which promulgated the efficacy of indulgences and which explicitly condemned Luther as a heretic on this matter.[70] While Emperor Maximilian's death on January 12, 1519 seemed to cause a delay in the case of Luther, critiques against Luther continued in general, and the Leipzig Debate (June–July 1519) was a public occasion.[71]

Prior to the debate with Johann Eck (d. 1543) in Leipzig, Luther published the *Instruction on Several Articles*,[72] probably at the end of February 1519,[73] to dispel any misconceptions on several subjects[74] including purgatory.[75] Luther affirms his belief in the existence of purgatory, as well as the condition of souls suffering unspeakable torments in purgatory. As far as the nature of torment is concerned, on the other hand, it is unknown, Luther admits. Nor would there be any one who knows sufficiently whether pains are for satisfaction or for improvement since, implied in his statement, Scripture is silent about it. There seem two things about which Luther is certain, however: first, there is no other instruction than to help the souls in purgatory (e.g., prayer); and second, God alone knows what is required for them in torments.[76]

Two months prior to the debate in Leipzig, Luther responds in May 1519 to Eck's Thirteen Theses,[77] the *Disputation and Defense of Brother Martin Luther against the Accusations of Dr. Johann Eck*.[78] In Thesis Four Luther relates the punishment of purgatory with the notion of "carrying

---

of indulgence, not the merits of Christ and the saints (e.g., Thesis Fifty-eight); second, Luther's claim that the Sacrament is properly received through faith alone (*fides sacramenti*) (e.g., Thesis Seven and the *Sermo de poenitentia*). Wicks, *Cajetan Responds*, 19–23. See also Olivier, *Trial of Luther*, 51; Marshall, *1517*, 51–52; Rex, *Making of Martin Luther*, 96.

70. Von Loewenich, *Martin Luther*, 137.
71. Marshall, *1517*, 51–52; Rex, *Making of Martin Luther*, 96.
72. *Unterricht auff etlich Artickell*. WA 2:69.1—73.21.
73. WA 2:66.19.
74. WA 2:69.17—73.21
75. Rupp, *Luther's Progress*, 61.
76. WA 2:70.15-22.
77. Editor's Introduction notes that it was originally Eleven Thesis, but Eck added the twelfth in attacking Luther's Thesis 22 of the *Explanations*. A thirteenth thesis was also added on the freedom of the will which Eck had already disputed with Karlstadt. AE 31:310.
78. *Disputatio et excusatio F. Martini Luther adversus criminationes D. Iohannis Eccii*. AE 31: 310; WA 2:158–61.

the cross,"⁷⁹ and Thesis Six is a brief recapitulation of the theme that "God is not a cruel God"⁸⁰ towards a dying person, which was also discussed in the *Explanations* (Thesis Seventeen). In Theses Eight and Nine, Luther alludes to the notion of the "theologians of the cross" and distinguishes it from the "would-be theologians" (that is, the inexperienced) the experienced theologians who know about pains of hell in this life,⁸¹ thereby Luther reaffirms his Theses Fifteen, Seventeen, and Eighteen of the *Explanations*. Luther's response to Eck's Thirteen Theses becomes the baseline of his debate in Leipzig.⁸²

In Leipzig, following the debate on the power of the chief bishop of Rome that ended in the afternoon on July 8, 1519,⁸³ Luther's debate with Eck continues on the subject of purgatory.⁸⁴ From the outset, Luther rejects the opponent's biblical reference to purgatory,⁸⁵ and asserts that other than heaven and hell the Scripture says nothing about purgatory,⁸⁶ and that the canonicity of the Books of Maccabees is not recognized.⁸⁷ During the debate, Luther reaffirms his view of purgatory previously discussed in the *Explanations*. Luther's arguments with Eck seemed not as robust and persuasive as presented in the *Explanations*. Luther seemed to take a cautious approach in his articulations on the subject, perhaps partly because he was well aware of how shrewd and skillful Eck was in the setting of an academic debate,⁸⁸ and partly, but more importantly, because he was conscious of the fact that Scripture is silent on the subject. In this premise, Luther's position

79. AE 31:317; WA 2:161.3.

80. AE 31:317; WA 2:161.10–12.

81. AE 31:318; WA 2:161.17–22. See also AE 31:130; WA 1:558.14–18.

82. AE 31:310.

83. *De potestate, immo de primata Romani pontificis*. WA 2:255.1—322.15. According to the title on the page: *Incipit disputatio Excellentium theologorum Iohannis Eckii et Martini Luttheri Augustiniani. Que cepta fuit Quarta die Iulii M.D.xix. hora septima*, the debate began on July 4, 1519 at seven o'clock. WA 2:254.1.

84. "*Hora secunda*" in WA 2:319.1 indicates the debate on the power of the pope, which began July 4, 1519 at seven o'clock, ends on July 8, 1519. WA 2:313.1; 322:19, followed by the subject of purgatory. WA 2:322.19—344.24.

85. WA 2:324.18–19.

86. WA 2:323.15–16.

87. WA 2:324.11–12. Recognizing the same book for edification, on the other hand, Luther affirms that it is not a sin to pray for the dead (2 Macc. 12:45). WA 2:340:33.

88. Brecht, *Martin Luther*, 1:311–16. See also Marshall, *1517*, 51–52; Rex, *Making of Martin Luther*, 108–28. See also Roper, *Martin Luther*, 112–32, particularly 112–13, 121, 124, and 126.

on purgatory is resolute and consistent: first, it is only God who knows the condition of souls in purgatory;[89] second, his theses represent only his academic disputations with examples drawn from the Scriptures[90] and not from the opinions that the Scriptures teach purgatory explicitly,[91] on the basis that the church enunciates unanimously that the punishments of hell and of purgatory are parallel except for the duration;[92] third, the fathers with their opinions on postmortem purgation did not make purgatory an article of faith;[93] and fourth, therefore, the subject of purgatory is to be discussed in universities, but not taught in the church.[94]

During the Leipzig Debate, Luther did not fully extrapolate the postmortem state on the basis of the notion of peaceful rest expressed in the Scripture. Concerning Revelation 14:13, Luther interprets the passage in a figurative sense,[95] similar to the distinction made earlier in his *Lectures on Romans*, and criticizes Eck for abolishing the aspect of the punishments of purgatory for the sake of the peaceful condition of souls.[96] For the final reply to Eck in writing, Luther notes that those who are at rest in the grave rest in Christ, for when the soul is separated from the body, there is no more labor as far as the body is concerned.[97] In this debate Luther takes the imagery of peaceful rest expressed in the Scripture and applies it to the

---

89. WA 2:333.4.

90. WA 2:341.8-9.

91. WA 2:324.17-19.

92. WA 2:333.20-23.

93. WA 2:330.37-40. Here Luther begins to argue that purgatory should not be taught as an article of faith, which appears more explicitly in his sermon for the *Epiphany* (1521; AE 52:180-81; WA 10I 1:588.24—589.1, 3, on Matt. 2:1-12.) as well as sermons on Christmas Day (1522; AE 75:238n17; WA 10I 1:111.14-16, on Titus 3:4-8), and in the *Defense* (AE 32:95-97; WA 7:451.19—452.31). See also Köstlin, *The Theology of Luther*, 1:324, 361.

94. WA 2:329.18-19. Consistent in claiming that the subject of purgatory is not an article of faith, Luther's reasoning follows: first, Scripture speaks only about heaven and hell (WA 2:323.15-16); second, the church unanimously holds the punishments of hell and of purgatory to be identical except for the duration (WA 2:333.20-23. See also AE 31:126; WA 1:556.8-11); therefore, the condition of souls in purgatory is dread and trembling (i.e., guilt) for which reason they require the increase of grace (WA 2:332.38—333.2).

95. Luther notes that the body in the grave is at rest in peace (i.e., a scriptural image of bodily death), but the departed soul in purgatory suffers torment.

96. WA 2:333.38—334.2. In reply, Eck charges Luther's assertion on "rest in peace" as a new glossary. WA 2:338.8-12.

97. WA 2:342.14-23. See also WA 2:333.38-39.

state of the body in the grave. For Luther at this stage, the biblical image of *rest in Christ* is not fully transmuted to the peaceful state of soul until he discards the notion of postmortem torment. Until then, souls in purgatory are perceived to suffer dread and fear and are in need of help (i.e., prayers offered for them) to continue to grow in faith in and love for Christ, and finally obtain rest in peace.

Between 1521 and 1522

Five documents are significant for review regarding this period: the *Defense* (March 1521), Luther's *Letter to Nicholas von Amsdorf* (January 13, 1522), two sermons on *the Christmas Day* (Titus 2:11–15; 3:4–8, early 1522), and a sermon for the *Epiphany* (Matthew 2:1–12, early 1522). During this period of the Reformation, Luther does not deny the notion of postmortem purgation entirely, but he begins to lay a significant landmark towards denial and comes to his rejection of the doctrine of purgatory by early 1522. Furthermore, Luther differentiates his personal notion of purgatory precisely from the formal doctrine of purgatory. While Luther's view in these five documents is more or less consistent and repetitive, the nature and purpose of each document deserves attention since they provide significant features of development in Luther's view of purgatory in early 1520s.

Defense and Explanation of All the Articles (1521)[98]

In the composition of the bull *Exsurge Domine* there were in total three committees involved, and one of the first two committees submitted non-abrasive recommendations in condemning strictly Luther's theological errors, not about the *persona* of Luther. The arrival of Eck in Rome in May 1520, at which the third committee was formed, swiftly modified the atmosphere and proceeded to finalize the bull of forty-one articles, condemning Luther with sixty-days to recant,[99] including a warning of condemnation against those holding or defending Luther's theses.[100] Luther receives the bull on October 10, 1520, and in response he writes articles, one of which

---

98. *Grund und Ursach aller Artikel*, March 1521.
99. Hendrix, *Luther and the Papacy*, 107–8. See also Brecht, *Martin Luther*, 1:389–90.
100. *Papal Encyclicals Online*, "Exsurge Domine."

is the *Defense* (1521).[101] On December 10, 1520 at 9:00 A.M. Luther conducts the ceremony of burning of the bull and other books including the Decretals at the East Gate of Wittenberg, anticipating the next bull to be promulgated for his excommunication (i.e., *Decet Romanum Pontificem*, January 3, 1521).[102] At this point, Luther crossed "the point of no return."[103]

In this *Defense*, Luther treats the subject of purgatory in two articles—four and thirty-seven. In the fourth article Luther attempts to define purgatory as "great fear" that bars the entry to heaven, and in the thirty-seventh article he contends that the opponents' biblical references to purgatory cannot be proved. A particular attention is due to the fourth article where Luther revisits his previous theses in the *Explanations*.[104] At the point of departure, Luther underlines the premise that nothing "deficient" can enter heaven, as if referring to Revelation 21:27, and claims that where there is imperfect love for God, which is nothing but "deficiency and sinful" with *fear* accompanying, there is essentially lack of love for and trust in God.[105] "Such fear and terror," claims Luther, "is the result of nothing but a bad conscience."[106] Admitting that there is no particular way to prove or disprove it, Luther turns to the notion of spiritual afflictions in this life—*tentatio* in great intensity, and claims that the "pains of hell" with which purgatory is identified are "fear, terror, the desire to flee, and despair" about

---

101. Luther also wrote three articles at the end of 1520: *Adversus execrabilem Antichristi bullam* (November 1520), *Wider die Bulle des Endchrists* (November 1520), *Assertio omnium articulorum M. Lutheri per bullam Leonis X. novissimam damnatorum* (December 1520). AE 32:5.

102. Hendrix, *Luther and the Papacy*, 117. See also Brecht, *Martin Luther*, 1:427; Rex, *Making of Martin Luther*, 155–56. Other books that Luther burned include *Summa angelica de casibus conscientiae* (1476) of Angelus de Clavasio (Angelo Carletti di Chivasso, d. 1495), which presents late medieval penitential theology that treats suffering in view of fasting or prayer as a contributing element or satisfaction for salvation. It was Johannes von Freiburg (d. 1314) who published *Summa confessorum* as early as 1287/8 on the sacrament of penance and suffering, which was then popular and influential in the later Middle Ages. See Rittgers, *Reformation of Suffering*, 27–28.

103. Leppin, *Martin Luther*, 50.

104. The notion of purgatorial punishments in Theses Fifteen, Sixteen, and Seventeen.

105. Luther's latter claim is based on 1 John 4:18: "There is no fear in love, but perfect love casts out fear. For fear has to do with punishment, and whoever fears has not been perfected in love." See also Thesis Fourteen of the *Explanations*. AE 31:123; WA 1:554.27–28, the *Explanations*; AE 31:123–25; WA 1:554.27—555.25, the *Defense*.

106. AE 32:32; WA 7:350.9–10.

which the Scripture speaks profoundly,[107] but about which "the bull and its masters know nothing."[108]

It is definitive for Luther that purgatory is not an article of faith, nor is it a command of God.[109] Luther states decidedly in the Thirty-seventh article: "The existence of purgatory I have never denied. I still hold that it exists, as I have written and admitted many times, though I have found no way of proving it incontrovertibly from Scripture or reason."[110] Luther stresses that it is a theological subject for continual discussion and debate freely in the light of Christian freedom. To believe or not to believe is entirely up to individuals. Thus, "no one is bound to believe more than what is based on the Scripture, and those who do not believe in purgatory are not to be called heretics."[111] What Luther repudiates is the opponents' *certainty* in claiming that Scripture teaches purgatory, and that their biblical references prove it.[112] Luther underscores the rationale of his disputation: "There is only one thing that I have criticized, namely, *the way in which my opponents refer to purgatory passages in Scripture* which are so inapplicable that it is shameful."[113] Suppose that the authority of the Books of Maccabees is equal to the level of other books of the Scripture; nonetheless, Luther further disputes, a single passage alone is insufficient to substantiate purgatory as an article of faith.[114]

Luther's *Letter to Nicholas von Amsdorf* (1522)[115]

When writing his letter to von Amsdorf, Luther as Knight George (*Junker Jörg*) was in exile to the Wartburg Castle, his "Patmos Island,"[116] in the Thuringian Forest.[117] Being isolated for over ten months, Luther learned

---

107. Pss. 2:5; 6:2–7; Prov. 28:1; Deut. 28:65.
108. AE 32:31–32; WA 7:349.13—350.13.
109. AE 32:96; WA 7:452.11–13.
110. AE 32:95; WA 7:451.11–14.
111. AE 32:96; WA 7:452.1–2.
112. E.g., 2 Macc. 12:43; 1 Cor. 3:15; Ps. 6:12; Matt. 12:32; Mark 3:29.
113. AE 32:95; WA 7:451.19–20. Emphasis added.
114. AE 32:96–97; WA 7:452.14–30.
115. *Luther an Amsdorf*, January 13, 1522. AE 48:360–62; WA Br 2:422.1—423.67. No. 449.
116. Lohse, *Martin Luther*, 50.
117. Luther also called the Wartburg Castle "the mountain" and "the land of the

from von Amsdorf's letter about Andreas Karlstadt's wedding, as well as the radical reformers' visit from Zwickau, also known as the Zwickau prophets. In his reply to von Amsdorf, Luther addresses two theological topics: a postmortem peaceful condition and purgatory, the subjects for which von Amsdort asked for Luther's opinions.[118]

Concurring with von Amsdorf who rejects the notion of purgatory as a "definite place,"[119] Luther attempts to define purgatory, not necessarily associated with its location or place, but strictly from the perspective of existential *tentatio* that some people experienced in this life including Christ, Moses, Abraham, David, Jacob, Job, and Hezekiah, and claims that the departed souls' tormenting punishment itself is to be purgatory.[120] In other words, whether this type of torment as tasting hell takes place here in this life or hereafter, emotionally or physically,[121] such a *tentatio* of torments itself *is* purgatory, which resonates and needs to be construed with Luther's statement in the *Defense* about a year earlier.[122] Luther's underlining emphasis is laid precisely on his pastoral approach to the subject in this letter with care and assurance: "Even if you deny purgatory, you are no heretic, since you do not deny that the punishment [of purgatory] can be felt physically and emotionally, but you only deny that purgatory is a definite place and that it has been proven that such punishment is felt emotionally. This I deny too."[123] In this statement,[124] Luther confirms that the notion of a definite or certain postmortem *place* is not his concern or interest in this regard, nor is proven—although it cannot be denied—that the punishment of purgatory is felt emotionally. What matters most for Luther is the notion of a tormenting *condition* in this life and hereafter—the pains of hell—which constitutes purgatory.

---

birds." Schilling, *Martin Luther*, 203, 212.

118. Editor Gottfried G. Krodel notes that the copy of von Amsdorf's letter is unavailable. AE 48:362n20. Thus, reconstruction may be required to be made on the basis of the elements which Luther addresses in his replying letter to von Amsdorf.

119. AE 48:360-61; WA Br 2:422.1-17.

120. AE 48:362; WA Br 2:422.31—423.2. See also AE 48:362n17.

121. The Latin phrase "*extra corpus . . . in corpore*" ("emotionally or physically") may also be said "internally or externally." See also AE 48:362 and 362n19.

122. AE 32:95; WA 7: 451.15, 17.

123. AE 48:362; WA Br 2:422.38—41.

124. AE 48:360-62; WA Br 2:422.1—423.67.

Luther's View of Purgatory

Sermons on Christmas Day (1522)[125]

Luther's Postil, which was composed during his "exile" between June 1521 and mid-February 1522, has the purpose of making homiletical resources available for clergy.[126] Luther's Christmas sermons written based on St. Paul's Epistle to Titus in the *Wartburg Postil*[127] deserves attention as it demonstrates Luther's continuing development regarding purgatory.

On Titus 2:11–15, Luther affirms the Scripture's reticence about purgatory, and contends that it is thus "dangerous" to establish an article of faith about which God has made no mention. "*Not that I now deny purgatory*," reiterates Luther, "rather, it is dangerous to preach it even if it were true by itself since God's Word and the Scripture say nothing about it."[128] Just as he stated in the *Defense* (1521), Luther again differentiates in this sermon his personal belief in purgatory from the doctrine itself.[129] In addition, the statement "Not that I now deny purgatory" resonates with his previous remark, "I still hold that it [purgatory] exists."[130] In another Christmas Day sermon on Titus 3:4–7, Luther further notes, "I wish purgatory had not been *invented*, or had never entered the pulpit, because it does such dreadful harm to Christian truth and true faith."[131] Unmistakable is Luther's use of the term "invention" in his sermon. Luther is fully aware of how harmful the *doctrine* of purgatory is since it has deeply permeated into the lives of Christians through indulgences, Masses for the dead, and most of all, the power of the pope over the souls in purgatory.

---

125. *Weihnachtspostille. Die Epistell czu der Meß ynn der Christnacht.* Titus 2:11–15, WA 10I 1:18.4—58.3; *Zu der frue Christmeß Epistell Pauli.* Titus 3:4-7, WA 10I 1:95.8—128.7.

126. AE 52:ix–x.

127. The word "*postillae*" is a compound word of "*post*" and "*illa*," meaning "after these [words]" in a literal sense, which introduces a "section-by-section exposition of a biblical text." AE 75:xiii.

128. AE 75:198; WA 10I 1:40.15–17. Emphasis added.

129. AE 32:95; WA 7:451.8–18. AE 32:95; WA 7:451.17–18.

130. AE 32:95; WA 7:451.11–12.

131. According to the editor, this particular statement is found in the editions of 1522, 1528, and 1532, but not in the 1540 edition of the *Winter Postil.* AE 75:238n17; WA 10I 1:111.14–16.

Luther's View of Purgatory

The Gospel for the Festival of the Epiphany (1522)[132]

In his sermon for the *Epiphany*, concerning the rumor of Samuel's apparition from the dead, Luther exhorts that it be treated as a trickery and deceit.[133] To the question as to whether purgatory should also be denied in such a manner, Luther advises pastorally:

> If you do not believe in a purgatory, you are not therefore a heretic. The Scriptures know nothing about it. It is better that you disbelieve what is not taught in the Scriptures, than that you reject what is found in the Scriptures ... They [the pope and the papists] have made an article of faith of purgatory because it has brought them the world's riches ... God has given no command concerning purgatory ... Accept God as more reliable and truthful ... more so since their [the pope and the papists'] doctrines are lies and deceit which do little to inspire faith in purgatory. I will not stop you if you desire to offer prayers for the dead. In my opinion purgatory is not our common lot as they teach; I think very few souls get there. Nevertheless, as I said, there is no danger at all for your soul if you do not believe in purgatory. You are not obliged to believe more than what is taught in the Scriptures ... [Concerning the words of the church fathers in this regard,] [o]ur faith must have a foundation which is God's word and not sand or moss, which are the delusions and works of men.[134]

In this statement, Luther stresses several fundamental points on which his denial of the doctrine is established unequivocally: first, the doctrine of purgatory cannot bind anyone in a captivity of dogma, for Scripture says nothing about purgatory as the doctrine defines and teaches; second, it is not an article of faith; third, it was a man-made teaching only for the purpose of gaining profits; and fourth, it is lies and deceit since God has given no command concerning purgatory. Luther's reference to the silence of the Scripture and his rejection of purgatory as an article of faith resonates with his debates with Eck in Leipzig, but his claim in this sermon that a post-mortem torment is *not* a "common lot" but only for few souls displays a certain refinement of his view. Furthermore, if Luther's letter to von Amsdorf (January 13, 1522) is taken into account in conjunction with this sermon,

---

132. *Evangelium am Tage der heiligen drei Könige*. AE 52:159–286; WA 10I 1:555.16–728.24. On Matt. 2:1–12.

133. Regarding evil spirits at the time of the Reformation, see Evener, "Wittenberg's Wandering Spirits," 531–55.

134. AE 52:180–81; WA 10I 1:588.21–589.17.

it is conceivable to argue that Luther's statement of this sermon alludes to the notion of the postmortem state of peaceful rest *as a common lot* as far as those who depart in faith are concerned. Luther, however, at this stage does not explicitly explore or articulate it.[135]

It is worth noting that *continuity* remains in Luther's view of purgatory. Luther has been consistent in claiming that Scripture is silent about purgatory as taught in the Roman Church. Also, Luther already criticized his opponents for having made their teaching of purgatory an article of faith. Amid such continuity emerges *discontinuity* in which he differentiates the notion of a postmortem purgatory from the official doctrine, repudiating the latter as lies and deceit. During the Leipzig Debate, Luther did not seem to articulate as boisterously and explicitly as now in making such bold statements. Threatened with condemnation under the bull *Exsurge Domine* (June 15, 1520), which Luther received on October 10, 1520, and officially condemned by the bull *Decet Romanum Pontificem* (January 3, 1521), it is an audacious undertaking for him to claim that denying purgatory makes no one a heretic. In the past, Luther addressed concerns about indulgences practiced mainly for the purpose of profits, but until now he did not raise the same concern about the doctrine of purgatory. These critical points in this sermon will reappear in his later criticism of the doctrine of purgatory in the *Recantation* of 1530.

Between 1523 and 1530

From 1521/22 until late June 1530 Luther composes no major articles or treatises about purgatory other than occasional references to the subject. In this period, Luther continues to remind Christians with pastoral advice that it is unnecessary to believe in purgatory since Scripture is silent about it. In this particular duration occurs the *second turning point* when Luther dismisses the notion of postmortem torment and fully acknowledges instead the postmortem state of rest in peace.

---

135. Luther's notion of the postmortem peaceful rest will be reviewed later in this chapter. See "Postmortem Peaceful State of the Soul."

The Adoration of the Sacrament (1523)[136]

In the treatise of *Adoration*, addressing to the Waldensians in Bohemia and Moravia, Luther affirms his stance underlined in his sermon for the *Epiphany* (1522), to a certain extent, and his emphasis is laid more on God's absolute power in hidden will (*Deus absconditus*) as far as the postmortem tormenting condition is concerned. Luther notes that, first, God commands no one to believe in purgatory; second, even if there is a purgatory made for some people, it is strictly God's choice and privilege, and thus no one knows about it except for them; third, it is a matter of the judgment of God alone, which is hidden from all humankind; and fourth, thus it is unnecessary to believe or know about it. While seemingly still holding the notion of postmortem torment, Luther leans towards acknowledgment of God's absolute power in hidden will. In this treatise, Luther's salient point is decisive: it is *unnecessary* to believe in purgatory.[137]

Personal Prayer Book (1524) and *A Meditation on Christ's Passion* (1525)[138]

The following two booklets—*Personal Prayer Book* and *Meditation*—deserve attention, not because of their content, but because of the critical omissions with respect to the subject of purgatory in their later editions. Since 1517, Luther published devotional booklets[139] to make evangelical devotional materials available for pastoral concerns. In line with this effort, Luther published the *Personal Prayer Book* in 1522 with several editions afterwards.[140] In the fifth petition of the Lord's Prayer (1522), Luther includes the following prayer: "Help all who are in peril of death and despair, particularly those whom we name [in our prayer before you]. *Have mercy*

---

136. *Meynen lieben herrn und freunden, den Brudern genant Valdenses ynn Behemen und Mehren Gna und frid ynn Christo*, published April 1523. AE 36:275–305; WA 11:431.1—456.25.

137. AE 36:299; WA 11:451.25-31.

138. *Betbüchlein*, 1524; *Ein Sermon von der Betrachtung des heiligen Leidens Christi*, 1525.

139. E.g., *Seven Penitential Psalms, Sermon on Contemplating the Holy Suffering of Christ* (1519), and *Short Form of the Ten Commandments, the Creed, and the Lord's Prayer* (1520).

140. There were about nine editions published in 1522, four in 1523, two in 1525, and each edition per year until 1530. AE 43:6–7.

upon all poor souls in purgatory, especially those we name [in our prayer]. Be forgiving of every guilt toward them and us all, comfort them, and take them under your mercy."[141] A certain omission is noticeable in the 1524 edition concerning the particular petition for all souls in purgatory.[142]

A similar pattern is captured in Luther's *Meditation* (1525), a pastoral treatise on the subject of Christ's Passion.[143] Early in mid-March of 1519 Luther planned to write the treatise[144] when he was reviewing the curriculum of Wittenberg University, writing a treatise on the Lord's Prayer, and preparing the publication of his lectures on Galatians,[145] in addition to his preparations for the Leipzig Debate. Luther sent George Spalatin a copy of the *Meditation* on April 5, 2019[146] wherein he addresses the subject of Christ's passion with his pastoral concerns for those who seem reluctantly indifferent and insensible to the passion of Christ:

> He who is so hardhearted and callous as not to be terrified by Christ's passion and led to a knowledge of self, has reason to fear. For it is inevitable, whether in this life or in hell, that you will have to become conformable to Christ's image and suffering. At the very least, you will sink into this terror in the hour of death *and in purgatory* and will tremble and quake and feel all that Christ suffered on the cross.[147]

In this treatise, the phrase "and in purgatory," which also appears in the edition of 1520, is omitted in the 1525 edition.[148] These two omissions in these booklets are not printing errors but purposefully prearranged to guard Christians pastorally from the doctrine of purgatory that had gravely affected the lives and thoughts of Christians.

---

141. AE 43:36; WA 10II:404.12–14. Emphasis added.

142. AE 43:36n28.

143. AE 42:XIV–XV.

144. Luther's letter to George Spalatin on Invocavit Sunday on March 13, 1519. AE 48:114; WA Br 1:359.26–27.

145. AE 27:x.

146. AE 42:5.

147. AE 42:10–11; WA 2:138.33–38. Emphasis added.

148. AE 76:428n26.

Notes on Ecclesiastes (1526)[149]

In his *Ecclesiastes*, Luther criticizes Jerome's interpretation of 9:5–6[150] where he relates the text to purgatory. In contrast, Luther reads the passage precisely against the notion of a postmortem purgatory, claiming that the passage promotes the state of souls resting in peace instead: "Solomon seems to feel that the dead are asleep in such a way that they know nothing whatever. And I do not believe that there is a more powerful passage in Scripture to show that *the dead are asleep* and do not know anything about our affairs—this in opposition to the invocation of saints and the *fiction of purgatory*."[151] Here occurs *the second turning point* in a continuing development of Luther's notion of purgatory in which he extrapolates the state of souls in line with the notion of sleep in replacement of that of a postmortem torment. Analogous with his former letter to von Amsdorf (January 13, 1522), Luther in this commentary treats the two notions—postmortem peace (i.e., rest in sleep) and postmortem torment (i.e., purgatory)—in a concise way, placing them in direct opposition to each other. Luther's term "fiction" employed in the *Ecclesiastes* in reference to purgatory also resonates with his sermon for the *Epiphany* (1522) where Luther criticizes: "their doctrines are lies and deceit."[152]

Luther's modified view of the postmortem state of rest in peace will be revisited in a moment. Suffice it to say here that as far as Luther's perception of purgatory as a condition of torment (i.e., such sufferings as tasting hell) is concerned, there is no change. The only significant change in this respect is a shift of his perception in terms of *when* one experiences purgatory: not hereafter, but *here* in this life. Since there is no postmortem purgatory; that is, since there is no postmortem torment, there is instead the postmortem state of peaceful rest, a notion which Luther finds in Scripture. Since early 1522, Luther already went along, to a certain extent, with the notion of peaceful rest concerning the state of the departed souls, and tends to interpret the postmortem state accordingly. It has not been so definitive until

---

149. *Annotationes in Ecclesiasten*, delivered in 1526. AE 15:1–187; WA 20:7–203.

150. "5 For the living know that they will die, but *the dead know nothing, and they have no more reward*, for the memory of them is forgotten. 6 Their love and their hate and their envy have already perished, and forever they have no more share in all that is done under the sun." Emphasis added.

151. AE 15:147; WA 20:160.26–29. Emphases added. See also Woodbridge, "Gerhard Westerburg," 102.

152. AE 52:181; WA 10I 1:589.6–7.

now for Luther that he accepts the expression of sleep from the Scripture and affirms it confidently, a notion which he used to apply symbolically at most, not to the state of souls in purgatory, but to the body in the grave.

Confession Concerning Christ's Supper (1528)[153]

In 1528, publishing the *Confession* Luther highlights a threefold purpose: first, to give alarm to all Christians about his opponents of their failure in replying to his arguments for the Real Presence; second, to give a thorough analysis on the biblical passages on the Sacrament of the Altar; and third, to make public an unalterable, personal manifesto of faith with regard to those subjects so that no one can claim otherwise or alter his theological stance afterwards.[154] Concerning the condition of the dead, Luther affirms that since no information is available in the Scripture, it is not a sin to pray for them once or twice as follow, or freely in a similar way: "Dear God, if this soul is in a condition accessible to mercy, be thou gracious to it."[155] As far as vigils and the annual celebration of the Masses for the dead are concerned, however, Luther criticizes them as the "devil's annual fair."[156]

On the subject of purgatory Luther underscores the following points: first, as far as purgatory as a postmortem place or torment is concerned, it is unnecessary to believe it, for it is "certainly fabricated by goblins";[157] second, God may allow the departed souls to be tormented, however, since there is nothing impossible to God,[158] which Luther mentioned earlier in the *Adoration* (1523); third, nonetheless, nothing is written or spoken about purgatory in the Scripture, thus God wishes no one to believe it. In this inalterable manifesto of faith, Luther still holds his personal notion of purgatory drawn from his experiences of *tentatio* and his interpretation of suffering as the cross and a foretaste of hell. He states: "I know of a purgatory, however, in another way, but it would not be proper to teach anything

---

153. *Vom Abendmal Christi, Bekendnis.* AE 37:161–372; WA 26:261.1—509.28.

154. AE 37:163; WA 26:262.19–25. ". . . I desire with this treatise to confess my faith before God and all the world, point by point. I am determined to abide by it *until my death* and (so help me God!) in this faith to depart from this world and to appear before the judgment seat of our Lord Jesus Christ." AE 37:360; WA 26:499.19–23. Emphasis added.

155. AE 37:369; WA 26:508.2–3.

156. AE 37:369; WA 26:508.5–6.

157. AE 37:369; WA 26:508.7.

158. AE 37:369; WA 26:508.8–9.

about it in the church, nor on the other hand, to deal with it by means of endowments or vigils."[159] Unequivocal is the statement of Luther that purgatory is not an article of faith. Nor is his view of purgatory associated with the doctrine or its practice. It is not even about the tormented condition of the departed souls, but about the existential sufferings or *tentatio* that Christians experience here in this life.[160]

A Recantation of the Doctrine of Purgatory (1530)[161]

Luther's indicative imperative to revoke the doctrine of purgatory in 1530 can be traced both in a wide and in an immediate context. As for a wide context, close to the end of 1524, Pope Clement VII publicly announced year 1525 as Holy Year of Jubilee, and promulgated two bulls—major and minor: *Inter Sollicitudines* (December 17, 1524) and *Pastoris aeterni* (December 19, 1524).[162] Having taken the two bulls as an attack on evangelical faith, Luther translated the two bulls into German and published them with a preface and glosses in 1525.[163] In the marginal glosses Luther states: "Purgatory was once a nice fable for the Romanists' purse. But all the secrets of their method have been spilled. People recognize the rogues, however sweetly they talk."[164] As an immediate context, in his letter to Melanchthon on July 3, 1530,[165] Luther indicated that he had reread Melanchthon's *Apology*[166] and was pleased except for one part. While it is unclear exactly what part Luther was referring to in that letter, Luther's letter to Justus Jonas on July 21, 1530[167] seems to contain a clue. According to both Hans von Schubert and Otto Clemen, as noted in the Excursus, Luther was referring to Melanchthon's "stepping softly" on critical issues such as the doctrine of purgatory, the veneration of

---

159. AE 37:369; WA 26:508.11–12.

160. AE 37:369; WA 26:508.6–12.

161. *Widerruf vom Fegefeuer.* AE 61:217–44; WA 30II:367.1—390.31.

162. AE 59:103, Editor's note on Luther's *Preface and Glosses to Two Bulls of Pope Clement VII on the Jubilee Indulgence*, 1525.

163. AE 59:104–10; WA 18:255–69.

164. AE 59:12; WA 18:262.9–17.

165. AE 49:342–44; WA Br 5:435.1—436.19. No. 1621. The name "Melanchthon" is the translation of his German name *Schwarerd* ("black earth") into Greek. Erick W. Gritsch, "Luther as Bible Translator," 63.

166. Luther received it on June 26, 1530.

167. WA Br 5:495.1—496.31. No. 1657.

the saints, and the pope as Antichrist.[168] Soon after receiving Melancthon's *Apology* (June 29, 1530),[169] Luther began to write a booklet—*Recantation*—on the doctrine of purgatory as early as on June 30, 1530.[170]

The *Recantation* consists of three parts: a preface type of introduction entitled "Martin Luther to all who come after us," and the main body entitled "On the Sophists' Lies and Abominations Concerning Purgatory," which is divided into six chapters, followed by a concluding remark without a particular formality or a subtitle.

In the preface Luther notes that he feels compelled once again to address his opponents' teaching about purgatory because they have neither regretted nor repented, Luther criticizes, of their lies and abominations associated with their doctrine. In this treatise, Luther intends to exhibit publicly on what unbiblical basis his opponents have accused and condemned him as a heretic, as well as on what basis purgatory has been taught publicly.[171]

In the first chapter, Luther tackles 2 Maccabees 12:43–45,[172] the "cornerstone and best basis" of the opponents' teaching, argues Luther, on which the doctrine of purgatory was primarily established.[173] In the second chapter, Luther treats his opponents' four lies based on Psalm 66:12.[174] In the third chapter, Luther denounces their interpretation of Revelation 14:13 whereby vigils and Masses for the dead are required to assist the souls in purgatory.[175] Here Luther reiterates the scriptural expression of the postmortem state of the soul in peaceful rest in place of purgatorial torment, claiming that those who die in the Lord are blessed and rest in peace.[176]

---

168. AE 49:345, Excursus in reference to WA Br 5:496.6. No. 1657. See also Brecht, *Martin Luther*, 2:395.

169. AE 49:343n6.

170. AE 49:347.

171. AE 61:220–21; WA 30II:367.9-13, 368.6-7.

172. "43He also took up a collection, man by man, to the amount of two thousand drachmas of silver, and sent it to Jerusalem to provide for a sin offering. In doing this he acted very well and honorably, taking account of the resurrection. 44For if he were not expecting that those who had fallen would rise again, it would have been superfluous and foolish to pray for the dead. 45But if he was looking to the splendid reward that is laid up for those who fall asleep in godliness, it was a holy and pious thought. Therefore he made atonement for the dead, so that they might be delivered from their sin." NRSVCE.

173. AE 61:221; WA 30II:368.11-12.

174. "[Y]ou let men ride over our heads; we went through fire and through water; yet you have brought us out to a place of abundance."

175. AE 61:228; WA 30II:375.24-29.

176. AE 61:229; WA 30II:376.10-11, 16-17, 28-30.

Luther's View of Purgatory

In the fourth chapter, Luther contends that his opponents' interpretation of 1 Corinthians 3:15[177] in reference to purgatory is a shameful lie and deceit. The passage does not mention interceding for the souls in purgatory, argues Luther, nor did the fathers interpret the text with the intention of establishing purgatory as an article of faith.[178] In the fifth chapter, Luther disputes that there has been no "richer lie" to the world than the doctrine of purgatory,[179] for people are condemned as heretics who simply do not follow the Roman doctrine of purgatory.[180] In the sixth chapter, Luther deplores that the Scripture is falsely interpreted with reference to purgatory,[181] and that Psalms are exploited in such a way.[182]

In the closing remark, Luther reproaches this exploitation of Psalms for the purpose of profits, as well as their judgment and condemnation against those who do not comply with their teaching of purgatory,[183] for which still no regret or repentance has yet been made.[184] Concerning the purpose of composing the booklet, Luther aims to encourage and strengthen his contemporary evangelical Christians to abide with the Scripture, and also give warning to the next generations of the evangelical faith.[185] Finally, Luther highlights for what reason he is condemned to be a heretic, not only because he does not consent to the doctrine of purgatory, but also because he does not serve Mammon as his opponents do.[186] Therefore, "[P]overty is my error and heresy," deplores Luther.[187]

---

177. "If anyone's work is burned up, he will suffer loss, though he himself will be saved, but only as through fire."

178. AE 61:233, 238; WA 30II:379.9–11, 383.27–32.

179. AE 61:239; WA 30II:385.12–14.

180. AE 61:240; WA 30II:386.14–17.

181. AE 61:240; WA 30II:386.23–25.

182. Nine Psalms: 5; 6; 7; 23; 25; 27; 40; 41; 42. Six Psalms of Praise: Pss. 51; 62; 63; 130; Is. 38:10–20; Pss. 148–50. AE 61:240–41; WA 30II:386.23—387.5–14.

183. AE 61:243; WA 30II:389.21–26.

184. AE 61:244; WA 30II:389.30–31.

185. AE 61:244; WA 30II:390.4–12.

186. AE 61:244; WA 30II:390.26–29.

187. AE 61:244; WA 30II:390.29–30.

Post-1530

Sermons on the Gospel of St. John (1531–1532)[188]

Upon returning from the Diet of Augsburg, Luther temporarily filled in on the pulpit responsibility during the absence of Johannes Bugenhagen (d. 1558, also known as Pommeranus) who was away in Lübeck in northern German territory for the purpose of teaching the Evangelical faith and theology. Luther preached Saturdays from November 5, 1530 to March 9, 1532, which Johannes Aurifaber (d. 1575) recorded.[189]

On John 6:58,[190] delivered on Saturday April 15, 1531,[191] Luther addresses two ways of perceiving Christ who abides in a believer: *notional* versus *true*. If Christ's abiding in a Christian is perceived notionally, then the effectiveness of Christ's salvation and holiness is denied in this life, and consequently the invention of purgatory is required.[192] If Christ's abiding is truly received through eating and drinking of the true body and blood of Christ, however, Christ's life, holiness, righteousness, forgiveness of and satisfaction for sin follow in a true sense. This is the context in which Luther addresses the doctrine of purgatory,[193] criticizing it in the framework of Law and Gospel, particularly in line with a mystical union of "Joyous Exchange" (*Frölich Wechsel*). He notes:

> The words read: "Christ abides in me." If you have sin, He has righteousness. If you have an abscessed or wounded conscience, He is the Healer, and almighty Physician who can cure you indeed. If you are sick and at death's door, He will restore you to health and life. *Even if you are thrown into purgatory—if this were possible—it*

---

188. *Wochenpredigten über Joh. 6–8*.

189. AE 23:ix–x.

190. "This is the bread that came down from heaven, not like the bread the fathers ate, and died. Whoever feeds on this bread will live forever."

191. AE 23:155n118.

192. "However, their most perversion is that they have made a public market of the Mass, selling their Sacrifice for the benefit both of the living and of the dead in their imagining purgatory." AE 13:314, WA 41:181.32–35. *Commentary on Psalm. 110* (*Der CX. Psalm, Gepredigt und ausgelegt durch D. Mart. Luth.*), preached on May 8, 1535. "No one in the world sees what a great foolishness it is that the pope takes money from the people and wants to help souls escape purgatory." AE 67:220; WA 47:512.36–38. Sermon on Matt. 23:29–30 (*Predigt D. M. Luthers uber das 23. Cap: Matthei. Dominica 14. Post Trinitatis, quae erat 7. Septembris*), preached between 1537 and 1540.

193. AE 23:369; WA 46:63.25–26. On Jn. 16:13.

will not harm you . . . Thus Christ abides in us and daily cures all our infirmities. Therewith this sermon is concluded, and this is its Christian interpretation. May God help us to grasp it. Amen.[194]

Luther's statement on purgatory[195] resonates with his previous statement in the *Confession* (1528) with regard to the notion that all things are possible to God who may let the departed souls be tormented in purgatory *only if* he wills.[196] Luther's pastoral concern is also embedded in this statement to assure his fellow Christians about the forgiveness and satisfaction of their sins and thus their salvation solely through Christ who abides in them through the Sacrament of the Altar. Compared to his previous statements, Luther's articulation about purgatory in this sermon is distinctive to the extent that it highlights the effectiveness of the Gospel that assures forgiveness and salvation obtained in this life.

Sermon Annotations on St. Matthew (1534/35)[197]

On Matthew 16:28, Luther addresses the state and condition of the departed souls, and while admitting no particular knowledge is available with respect to the nature of peace in Christ after death, Luther affirms the postmortem peaceful state of the soul in Christ. Analogous with the three types of dying souls in Thesis Seventeen of the *Explanations*,[198] Luther asserts that those who die without fear do not taste death and remain at rest in peace until the Day of Judgment. As far as those who die with fear are concerned, they taste death but do not suffer postmortem torment. With the notion of "rest from their labor" in Revelation 14:13, from which Luther affirmed in the *Recantation* (1530) the notion of peaceful rest of the soul, he repudiates the doctrine that endorses postmortem torments in purgatory. Concerning

---

194. AE 23:154–55; WA 33:242.1–11, 17–22. Emphasis added.

195. By purgatory in this context, Luther refers to the notion of a postmortem condition, not the doctrine.

196. AE 37:369; WA 26:508.8–9, in *Confession* (1528). See also AE 36:299; WA 11:451.25–31, in *Adoration* (1523).

197. *Annotationes in aliquot capita Matthaei* (1534/35, published in 1538) was composed for the purpose of a "private use" for Hieronymus Weller (1499–1572) who as a doctoral student was appointed to be a student preacher for Wednesdays (1534–1535) but struggled with writing sermons. AE 67:xxx–xxxiv, xlv.

198. AE 31:131–32; WA 1:559.11–67.

purgatory, Luther turns instead to the notion of *tentatio*, agonizing afflictions in great intensity, which he finds in the Scripture:

> The Papists and those who hung up contradictions boast that I have professed purgatory. And I still profess it. But I profess the one that we often encounter in the psalms, where the saints praise God because they have been freed from the lowest hell, from the darkness and the shadow of death, from the hand of hell, from the perils of hell, from the bands and gates of death and the life [Ps. 116:3; 2 Sam. 22:6; Ps. 9:13; 86:13; Isa. 9:2; Matt. 4:16; Luke 1:79; Ps. 49:15]. But [this purgatory was not] by means of their sacrifices or by the works of the little sacrificing priests—those most wicked, completely impure, utterly godless men who have nefariously sold their Masses for money and scoffed at God and men with their "worked works."[199]

As for his comment on the opponents' boast above, Luther seems to refer to Johann Fabri (d. 1541) who published the *Antilogiarum Martini Lutheri Babylonia* printed in Augsburg on September 5, 1530.[200] The treatise comprises fifty-two chapters wherein chapter thirty-nine presents the subject of purgatory in a form of a dialogue between Luther and his interlocutor. In the seventh dialogue Luther says, "I firmly believe and dare to say that there is a purgatory since it is addressed in the Scriptures."[201] Returning to the *Sermon Annotations*, Luther clarifies what purgatory he still holds:

> Finally, this purgatory [that I still profess] is not a made-up purgatory (as theirs is), asserted on the basis of human opinions (even if they are the fathers'), but something real which is all too serious a matter for those who, with the prophets and all the saints in the school of Christ, learn this harsh lesson: 'He brings down to hell and brings back; He kills and He makes alive' [1 Sam. 2:6]. But I have said enough elsewhere about the Papists' false purgatory.[202]

Luther addresses the subject as if he were in a debate with his opponents, presenting his notion of purgatory as "something real" (*res ipsa*)

---

199. AE 67:305; WA 38:653.20–26.

200. The treatise was composed to be submitted to Charles V in view of the Diet of Augsburg. AE 67:305n143.

201. "Credo fortiter et ausim dicere purgatorium esse, cum de eo in scripturis mentio fiat." This is my translation. Fabri, *Antilogiarvm*, Bk 39. *Dial* 7.

202. AE 67:306; WA 38:653.7–14, 27–33.

and dismissing his opponents' claim as "a made-up purgatory" (*fictum purgatorium*).[203] This is not the first time Luther speaks about his notion of purgatory—suffering itself or *tentatio* in this life—as a *true* purgatory.[204] However, he has never articulated it in such a way in which he depicts his notion of suffering as a "real purgatory" which one experiences in the school of Christ. This type of purgatory augments faith that trusts in Christ.

Smalcald Articles (1537)[205]

Following Pope Paul III's bull *Ad dominici gregis curam*[206] that convokes a general council to be convened at Mantua, which does not occur until 1545 at Trent (1545–1563), Johann Frederick (d. 1554, known as Magnanimous), the successor of Frederick the Wise, assigns Luther on December 11, 1536 to draft Luther's "last will and testament."[207] At the Smalcald League in February 1537 Luther's articles are initially presented, but the League decides to adopt the *Augsburg Confession* (*Confessio Ausgustana*, 1530) and its *Apology* instead. In 1538 Luther attaches a preface to the articles where he notes the intention and purpose of his articles,[208] in a similar tone to that presented in his *Confession* (1528).[209] Concerning purgatory, together with the masses that are exploited for purchasing and selling for the dead, it should be considered as an "apparition of the devil," contends Luther, because it is "against the chief article that Christ alone (and not human works) is to help souls." In the article, Luther affirms again that God has neither

---

203. "The true church knows nothing of purgatory or the invocation of the saints." AE 67:360; WA 47:256.41–42. Sermon on Matt. 18:7, preached between 1537 and 1540. Concerning the doctrine of purgatory as a "man-made" purgatory, Luther already mentioned it in his sermon for *Epiphany* (1522). AE 52:180–81; WA 10I 1:588.21—589.17.

204. On Ps. 51, Luther also notes that David experienced "true purgatory" under the intensity of the sorrows of sin and the wrath of God. AE 12:387; WA 40II:436.23–25. Luther lectured on Ps. 51 between June 10 and August 1532, and on 51:45 between March 5 and November 4, 1532, published in 1538 by Veit Dietrich. AE 12:VIII.

205. *Articuli Smalcaldici*, 1536, published 1537.

206. It was published on June 2, 1536.

207. Luther, Smalcald Articles, in *BC*² 295.

208. "I wanted to do this so that those who live and remain after me will have my testimony and confession to present, in addition to the confession that I have already published. I have held fast to this confession until now and, by God's grace, I will continue to hold to it." Luther, Smalcald Articles, in *BC*² 298.3, in *The Preface of Doctor Martin Luther*.

209. AE 37:360; WA 26:499.16–23.

commanded nor instructed anyone concerning purgatory; therefore, "it may be best to abandon it, even if it were neither error nor idolatry."[210]

Postmortem Torment versus Assurance of the Gospel

Since 1530, when reprimanding the doctrine of purgatory as the "real blasphemy against the keys given by Christ,"[211] Luther emphasizes the damage it has caused against the gospel of and trust in Christ. In a similar tone, yet more strongly, Luther expresses his frustrations: "For with this [the blasphemous fraud of purgatory] they [the pope and the papists] also completely extinguished that one and only comfort and trust in Christ . . ."[212] Apparent is Luther's charge against the pope's cruelty for not providing the promise of salvation for afflicted consciences, but drawing them to purgatory instead.[213] Concerning true rest and consolation, Luther's remark is succinct: it is found in absolution. "I absolve you from your sins in the name of Christ, who died for you and rose again, and said: 'Because I live, you will live also' (John 14:19). This is solid and firm consolation. In it alone the godly can find rest."[214] In contrast to the teaching on postmortem torment, Luther employs the christocentric, gospel-oriented emphasis[215] by which he assures salvation by faith alone.[216]

---

210. Luther, Smalcald Articles, in BC^2 303.12–304.15, in the "Second Article."

211. AE 67:176; WA 38:548.8, on Matt. 16:19. The *Sermon Annotations*, 1534–1535.

212. AE 47:42, WA 30III:309.27–28. *Dr. Martin Luther's Warning to His Dear German People* (1531). In the *Sermon on the Mount*, Luther also says: "Whenever I have looked at the papacy, I myself have been amazed at how the devil has managed to use the abominations of the pope to throw the dear Gospel into a manure pile and a puddle, how he has buried it so deeply under the perversion of Masses, purgatory, and innumerable other things that it seemed impossible to me for the truth ever to come out from under all this." AE 21:165; WA 32:436.12–18. On Matt. 6:16–18. *Commentary on the Sermon on the Mount* (1532).

213. AE 8:189; WA 44:717.11–13. On Gen. 48:21.

214. AE 8:189; WA 44:717.18–19.

215. On Saturday after All Saints' Day on November 3, 1537, Luther addresses, "Whoever does not have Christ, will not be saved—whether it be Moses, pope, cardinal, Mass, purgatory, vigils, and requiem—all this nothing but death, death, yes, the devil himself. For God has placed His grace solely in the only Son. If we are without Him, we can fast ourselves to death, confess, observe vigils; but for all that we will never have a good and cheerful conscience." AE 22:158; WA 46:673.20–25. See also AE 22:158n126.

216. AE 4:315; WA 43:362.13–15. On Gen. 25:7–10.

LUTHER'S DENIAL OF THE DOCTRINE OF PURGATORY

We turn to address the first major question "Why did it take so long for Luther to deny purgatory?" In answering the question, it is fundamental to distinguish between the formal doctrine of purgatory and Luther's notion of purgatory. Without this distinction, a claim can be made mistakenly that Luther still believed in purgatory in 1528 (e.g., the *Confession* of 1528), but that two years later with the publication of the *Recantation* (1530) he denied purgatory—both the doctrine and his notion—entirely. Luther had no reason to deny purgatory in such a fashion, however. On the contrary, early in 1516/17, Luther questioned the interpretation of the teachers of the Latin Church concerning the biblical references that they provide for purgatory.[217] In 1518/19, he then objected to their claim with their scriptural references, and soon afterward in 1521/22 he criticized the doctrine of purgatory. Between 1521 and 1522 appeared the first turning point in Luther's notion of purgatory where he redefined purgatory primarily with existential afflictions, still maintaining postmortem torment but only for few souls. Simultaneously correlated in that shift was Luther's inclination to assent, to a certain extent, to the notion of peaceful rest of souls. With this finding, we will now trace key information about Luther's attacks on the doctrine of purgatory to answer the question on the table. In brief, Luther's rejection of the doctrine of purgatory occurred arguably in 1521/22.

Timeline of Denial: in 1530?

In *The Reformation of the Dead*,[218] Koslofsky claims that Luther, still admitting in 1528 a lack of biblical reference for purgatory, was "unwilling to deny postmortem purgation outright," but "in 1530 he decisively denied

---

217. In his early lectures on Galatians (1516/17, printed in 1519), Luther had doubts about the scriptural references for purgatory. Luther interpreted them with respect to labors in this life. AE 27:401; WA 2:611.33–35.

218. In this book Koslofsky claims that "the Reformation helped separate the living from the dead both *spiritually* and physically, and that this parallel separation was fundamental to the development of the Reformation." Koslofsky, *The Reformation of the Dead*, 19. Emphasis added. By "spiritually" with respect to the separation of the living from the dead, Koslofsky refers to the denial of purgatory as well as prayers for the dead, and by "physically" he refers to the "removal of the dead [e.g., burial] from the world of the living." Koslofsky, *The Reformation of the Dead*, 40.

Purgatory and espoused soul-sleeping in his *Repeal of Purgatory.*"[219] Koslofsky also claims that since 1520 Luther's notion of purgatory "slowly shifted" whereas his denunciation of prayers for the dead occurred soon after his broke with the Roman Church (e.g., *On the Misuse of the Mass*, 1521).[220] Koslofsky raises a similar question to the first major question in this book, "Why, then, was he [Luther] so slow to reject the idea of postmortem purification, even though he saw no scriptural evidence for it?" Koslofsky provides a threefold reason: first, Luther was closely engaged in the concept of German mysticism that emphasized the progression of purgation in the journey of a soul in faith to God;[221] second, Luther was expanding his existential notion of purgatory to refer to afflictions and sorrows in this life, which corresponds with the mystical concept of progression; and third, Luther's rejection of postmortem purification occurred "in a polemic against the Roman doctrine of Purgatory."[222]

According to Koslofsky, the underlining reasons for the delay in Luther's denial of postmortem purification until 1530 involved a polemical dispute against the doctrine of purgatory, in addition to his notion of mystic progression of purification drawn from German mysticism. In response to his claim, I pose two questions: first, in what respect was Luther's notion of postmortem purification interrelated with the doctrine of purgatory itself, and how did the former have to do with his denial of the latter in 1530? If Luther's notion of postmortem condition had *already* been differentiated from and no longer interrelated with the doctrine of purgatory even *before* 1530, Koslofsky's claim becomes questionable. Second, should Luther's

---

219. Koslofsky, *The Reformation of the Dead*, 37. It is the same treatise of Luther, *A Recantation* of 1530. Concerning Koslofsky's comment on Luther's unwillingness to deny postmortem purgation "outright," Brecht also notes that "the concept of purgatory was not entirely called into question." Brecht, *Martin Luther*, 2:321.

220. Koslofsky, *The Reformation of the Dead*, 34. Koslofsky asserts that Luther's suggestive prayer: "Dear God, if this soul is in the state so that it still can be helped, I pray that you would be merciful to it" was far different from the intercession for the dead in the Roman Church tradition and practice; it was rather a "model agnostic prayer for the dead." Koslofsky, *The Reformation of the Dead*, 35. Luther's suggestive prayer in AE 37:369; WA 26:508.2–3.

221. E.g., the "three stages" in *Theologia Deutsch: via purgativa, via illuminativa*, and *via unitiva*. RD 36–37. See Luther's *Preface to the Complete Edition of a German Theology* (*Vorrede zu der vollständeigen Ausgabe der "deutschen Theologie." 1518*). AE 31:75–76; WA 1:378.1—379.14.

222. Koslofsky, *The Reformation of the Dead*, 37.

statement in the *Confession* of 1528[223] be considered as his *unwillingness* to deny the notion of postmortem purification as Koslofsky suggests,[224] or as Luther's notion of God's absolute power in hidden will? Did Luther, who was unwilling to deny the notion of postmortem purification in 1528, come to a decisive moment for denial with the publication of the *Recantation* in 1530?[225] If Luther maintains even after 1530 the notion of God's absolute power in hidden will with a particular reference to a postmortem tormenting condition, it signifies that his statement of 1528 does not necessarily refer to his unwillingness to deny the notion of postmortem purification, as Koslofsky construes, and consequently, Koslofsky's claim on this part also becomes questionable. The following sections address these two questions.

Premise: Two Elements

First Turning Point

The premise of this chapter, as noted earlier, is to distinguish Luther's personal notion of purgatory from the formal doctrine itself. This premise needs clarification. There are two elements that constitute Luther's notion of purgatory: first, a postmortem condition of torment; and second, existential afflictions of *tentatio* in this life. When Luther discussed the subject of purgatory in 1518, for instance, claiming that he still held purgatory, he did so in the presupposition that his profession of purgatory was in line with the traditional view of church fathers with strong detestation of those who denied purgatory (e.g., the Picardi of Bohemia).[226] During the Leipzig Debate in 1519, for another instance, Luther and Eck freely debated on the subject in an academic setting mainly concerning the postmortem state and condition in purgatory,[227] but neither Luther nor Eck encountered an issue of a denial of purgatory. At one point, Luther even charged Eck for abolishing the notion of purgatorial torment for the sake of keeping the peaceful

---

223. AE 37:369, WA 26:508.7–9. In *Confession* (1528).

224. Koslofsky, *The Reformation of the Dead*, 36.

225. Koslofsky claims that "Luther arrived independently at a position similar to that of Gansfort. They each stressed that Purgatory was a place of purification, rather than of satisfaction..." but "... by 1530 he [Luther] denied the existence of Purgatory altogether." Koslofsky, *The Reformation of the Dead*, 34.

226. AE 31:125–26; WA 1:555.36—556.5. On Thesis Fifteen of the *Explanations* (1518).

227. Brecht, *Martin Luther*, 1:322.

state and condition of the departed souls.²²⁸ For Luther at this stage the first element (i.e., a postmortem condition of torment) plays the central role in understanding purgatory while the second element (i.e., existential afflictions) is a point of reference to the postmortem condition.

Soon afterwards, Luther abandons this line of thought, and begins to attack the magisterially defined doctrine of purgatory, particularly in the *Defense* (1521), his letter to von Amsdorf (January 13, 1522), and the *Sermons on Christmas Day* (1522) as well as a sermon for *the Epiphany* (1522). Meantime, a significant shift occurs in Luther's view of purgatory where he redefines it from the perspective of the existential *tentatio* in this life, on the one hand,²²⁹ and maintains the condition of postmortem torment as a marginal notion, on the other,²³⁰ arguing that no one is bound to believe what Scripture has not commanded to be believed (i.e., purgatory).²³¹ This shift in redefining purgatory implies three significances: first, Luther's redefinition of purgatory is dovetailed with his *differentiation* between the notion of a postmortem condition and the doctrine of purgatory; second, the first element—the notion of postmortem torment—surrenders its central role and moves to the margin in retention of possibility of postmortem torments but only for few souls; third, the second element—existential afflictions—takes charge of Luther's key notion of purgatory, and now plays the major role, which is the *first* turning point in Luther's view of the subject. Here one finds the answer to the first question above that in 1521/22 Luther's notion of postmortem condition was *already* differentiated from the formal doctrine of purgatory.

Second Turning Point

The *second* turning point occurs when Luther dismisses the notion of postmortem torments and affirms the notion of the peaceful state of the departed souls, which appears in 1525/26, particularly in his *Notes on Ecclesiastes* (1526). Luther states: "I do not believe that there is more powerful passage in Scripture to show that the dead are asleep and do not know anything about our affairs—this in opposition to the invocation of saints

---

228. WA 2:333.38–334.2.
229. AE 32:31–32; WA 7:349.13—350.13. Also, AE 32:95; WA 7:451.8–18.
230. AE 52:181; WA 10I 1:589.8–9.
231. AE 32:95–97; WA 7:451.19—452.31.

and the *fiction of purgatory*."²³² Woodbridge claims that Luther's rejection of the doctrine of purgatory occurs in this lecture of 1526.²³³ One may argue, on the other hand, that this statement of 1526 should not be considered as Luther's denial of the postmortem purgatorial condition or doctrine since Luther does not deny postmortem purification outright until his *Recantation* of 1530, and in the *Confession* (1528) Luther still notes: "I maintain it is not necessary to believe in it [purgatory]; *although all things are possible to God, and he could very well allow souls to be tormented after their departure from the body.*"²³⁴ Concerning Luther's statement in the *Confession*, the key question is whether the statement indicates Luther's *willingness* to maintain the notion of postmortem torment, or his *acknowledgment* of the divine realm in which all things are possible to God including the possibility of the departed souls' being tormented. Should the former be the case, Luther would not—or should not—make the statement once he denied postmortem purgation with the publication of the *Recantation*. Thus, in answering the second question, it is necessary to have a quick review of Luther's statements after the *Recantation* to confirm whether he maintains it after 1530.

As reviewed earlier, in his *Sermon on John* delivered in 1531, Luther addresses the subject quite in a similar fashion: "Even if you are thrown into purgatory—*if this were possible*—it will not harm you."²³⁵ In both cases—*Confession* of 1528 and *Sermon on John*, 1531—Luther makes the identical statements and discusses his *acknowledgement* of the divine will which is hidden and thus unknowable. In fact, Luther never disregards or discards it. Earlier in the *Bondage of the Will*,²³⁶ for instance, Luther discusses God's hidden and secret will while proposing to set the boundary of discussion within the subject of God's preached and revealed will.²³⁷ By this, Luther does not dismiss the subject of God's hidden will. He acknowledges it without question, but intends to treat it under a separate category about which no theological discussions can be made on the basis of Scripture since the subject remains unknown. Luther's statements of God's absolute power in

---

232. AE 15:147; WA 20:160.27–29. Emphasis added.

233. Woodbridge, "Gerhard Westerburg," 102.

234. AE 37:369; WA 26:508.8–9. Emphasis added.

235. AE 23:154; WA 33:242.9–11. Emphasis added.

236. *De servo arbitrio*, 1525.

237. AE 33:138–44; WA 18:684.26—688.26. See also Paulson, *Luther's Outlaw God*, particularly "Luther's Theologoumenon: Preached/Unpreached," 2:29–62.

hidden will in 1528 and 1531 should not be thus taken to claim that Luther was still maintaining, or unwilling to deny, his notion of postmortem purgation.

Returning to the two questions raised concerning Koslofsky's claim, it is demonstrated that Luther's attacks on the doctrine of purgatory began in 1521/22, and that his notion of a postmortem condition continued until 1525/26. By the early 1520s Luther's notion of purgatory as a postmortem condition was *already* differentiated from the formal doctrine, and much earlier than 1530 the former had no intrinsic relation with the denial of the latter. Furthermore, even after his denial of the doctrine Luther maintained the notion of the departed souls to be tormented but in the domain of God's hidden will. Therefore, Luther's 1528 statement should be understood in reference to his *acknowledgement* of God's omnipotence in hidden will. In company with all this, it is also proved that before 1528 Luther already dismissed the notion of postmortem purgation in torment.

Parallel between 1521/22 and 1530

Luther's Attacks on the Doctrine of Purgatory

Until the early 1520s Luther debated the subject of purgatory freely in line with the ecclesiastical tradition, criticizing not the notion of purgatory itself but only his opponents' claim that it is a scriptural teaching and thus an article of faith. Luther's new approach to the subject emerges in 1521/22 during which he attacks the doctrine of purgatory as lies and deceit. The critical terms and expressions that Luther employs in 1521/22, for instance, are strikingly parallel with those in the *Recantation* of 1530. This is a distinctive milestone that signifies Luther's rejection of the doctrine of purgatory in 1521/22, which is then reaffirmed in 1530.

Point One: "Lies and Deceit"

In the *Defense* (1521) Luther asserts that "[t]he pope and his partisans . . . fabricate many wild articles of faith and thus make it possible to silence and suppress the true articles of the Scripture."[238] In his sermon for the *Epiphany* (1522) Luther objects to the doctrine of purgatory and says, "their doctrines are lies and deceit which do little to inspire faith in

238. AE 32:96; WA 7:452.1–2.

purgatory... Our faith must have a foundation which is God's word and not sand or moss, which are the delusions and works of men."[239]

An identical tone of criticism appears later in 1530. In the first chapter of the *Recantation*, Luther charges his opponents' teaching of purgatory as "a cursed blasphemy and a lie," for in the Book of Maccabees (e.g., 2 Maccabees 12:43-45) is given no command to believe in purgatory. Furthermore, Judas himself did not believe in the existence of purgatory, nor did such a purgatory exist in his time, which is "the finest lie," argues Luther.[240] Also in the second chapter, Psalm 66:12 speaks only about the sufferings of the saints, contends Luther, and the offerings are burnt offerings, which is not applicable concerning the souls in purgatory. Furthermore, there was no purgatory at the time of the Psalmist.[241] In the fourth chapter, Luther asserts that 1 Corinthians 3:15 has no reference to purgatory and reprimands the opponents' interpretation of the text as a shameful lie.[242]

Point Two: "Not an Article of Faith"

In the *Recantation* Luther repeats throughout the treatise that purgatory has been made an article of faith with no scriptural basis. In the second chapter, Luther criticizes the opponents for claiming purgatory unjustifiably with the image of water in Psalm 66:12, as well as for making purgatory an article of faith only to condemn and persecute those who deny it.[243] Likewise, in the first chapter Luther charges the opponents' interpretation of the Book of Maccabees with establishing purgatory as an article of faith.[244] Luther's attacks, which appear in early 1520s, are indisputably parallel.[245] In the sermon for the *Epiphany* (1522), for instance, Luther asserts, "They [the pope and the papists] have made an article of faith of purgatory because it has brought them the world's riches ... [but] God has given

---

239. AE 52:180-81; WA 10I 1:589.6-7, 16-17. On Matt. 2:1-12.

240. "*Eine verfluchte lesterung und luegen*" and "*die allerfeineste [luegen]*," respectively. AE 61:222-23; WA 30II:371.3-7, 13-17.

241. AE 61:227; WA 30II:373.9—374.1-10.

242. AE 61:232-33; WA 30II:378.22-27, 379.2-6, 21-34.

243. AE 61:226-27; WA 30II: 373.3-5, 374.17-20, 375.1-5.

244. AE 61:222; WA 30II:369.2-6, 19-20.

245. Luther's contention of an article of faith begins in the Leipzig Debate. See "The Leipzig Debate" (1519) in this chapter. See Köstlin, *The Theology of Luther*, 1:324, 361.

no command concerning purgatory."[246] In his sermon on *Christmas Day* (1522) Luther deplores the fact that purgatory has been made an article of faith and preached publicly.[247]

Point Three: "Not Believing in Purgatory, You Are Not a Heretic"

The third point concerns the papal condemnation against those who deny the doctrine of purgatory. In the fifth chapter of the *Recantation*, Luther confutes that there has been no "richer lie" than the doctrine of purgatory, and yet anyone who rejects the doctrine of purgatory is condemned as a heretic.[248] Likewise, in the *Defense* (1521) Luther states that no one is bound to believe more than is taught in the Scripture, and that those who do not believe in purgatory are not to be called heretics.[249] Also, in his sermon for the *Epiphany* (1522) Luther affirms, "If you do not believe in a purgatory, you are not therefore a heretic."[250] In addition, in his letter to von Amsdorf, Luther assures his colleague on this subject in the same manner and says, "Even if you deny purgatory, you are no heretic."[251]

As briefly reviewed, it is not a coincidence that Luther's terms which criticize the doctrine of purgatory in the early 1520s are strikingly parallel to those of the *Recantation*. In essence, Luther's denunciation in 1521/22 signifies his rejection of the doctrine of purgatory based on his exegetical analysis and theological discretion which reflect his Reformation theology. Referring to purgatory, Luther enunciates, "You are not obliged to believe more than what is taught in the Scriptures."[252] That is to say, faith—and conscience or one's entire being before God[253]—is bound to Scripture alone, as he declared publicly at the Diet of Worms (1521): "Unless I am convicted by Scripture and plain reason—I do not accept the authority of popes and councils, for they have contradicted each other—my conscience

---

246. AE 52:180–81; WA 10I 1:588.24—589.1, 3. On Matt. 2:1–12.

247. AE 75:238n17; WA 10I 1:111.14–16, on Titus 3:4–7 (1522).

248. AE 61:239; WA 30II:385.12–14, 24–30.

249. AE 32:96; WA 7:452.1–2.

250. AE 52:180; WA 10I 1:588.21–22.

251. AE 48:362; WA Br 2:422.38. January 13, 1522. No. 449.

252. AE 52:181; WA 10I 1:589.11. In the sermon for the *Epiphany*. On Matt. 2:1–12, 1522.

253. See Roper, *Martin Luther*, 172–73 on Luther's use of the term "conscience."

is captive to the Word of God. I cannot and I will not recant anything, for to go against conscience is neither right nor safe . . ."[254]

In Luther's rejection of the doctrine of purgatory, however, there was more than his theological and exegetical analysis and judgment, for early in the *Explanations* (1518) Luther had already pointed out that Scripture is silent about purgatory in the way that the opponents claim with their biblical references to the subject. Likewise, during the Leipzig Debate (1519) he also reprimanded the opponents' biblical reference to claim that purgatory is an article of faith of the Scripture. It is, therefore, reasonable to infer that there must have been a critical circumstance or occasion that inspired Luther to shift his stance concerning the subject of purgatory *prior to* his attacks on and denial of the doctrine of purgatory in 1521/22. In this context, we raise a question as to how to comprehend Luther's stance in 1521/22, and what happened prior to 1521/22.

Discovery of the Antichrist

The duration of Luther's exile at Wartburg (May 1521–March 1522) was for him a time of "despondency and depression."[255] It may perhaps be considered as his existential *tentatio* since his exile was the culmination of a series of trials where Luther, a doctor of the church, was condemned, excommunicated, and outlawed,[256] and began to live in such "tumultuous years."[257] Whether or not Luther himself considered his exile as a foretaste of hell in this life, his primary reason to attack the doctrine of purgatory was fundamentally associated with certain discoveries[258] prior to his receipt of the bull *Exsurge Domine* on October 10, 1520.

On February 14, 1520, about four months after the coronation of Charles V (d. 1558),[259] Luther discovered from a copy of John Huss' *On*

---

254. Bainton, *Here I Stand*, 180.

255. Wicks, *Luther*, 115.

256. In this book, Olivier traces Luther's trials particularly for four years between 1518 and 1521. Olivier, *Trial of Luther*, ix.

257. AE 42:XIII.

258. Saak highlights Luther's two significant discoveries in early 1520. Saak, *Luther and Reformation*, 340–45. The baseline of this sub-section is constructed on these two discoveries.

259. He was King of Spain as Charles I and archduke of Austria as Charles I (d. 1556). *Encyclopaedia Britannica*, s.v. "Charles V, Holy Roman Emperor."

the Church,²⁶⁰ which he received on October 3, 1519, that the gospel had already been condemned and burned in Bohemia a century earlier.²⁶¹ In his letter to Spalatin Luther notes:

> I have taught and held all the teachings of John Huss, but thus far did not know it . . . In short we are all Hussites and did not know it. Even Paul and Augustine are in reality Hussites. See the monstrous things into which we fall, I ask you, even without the Bohemian leader and teacher. I am so shocked that I do not know what to think when I see such terrible judgments of God over mankind, namely that the most evident evangelical truth was burned in public and was already considered condemned more than one hundred years ago. Yet one is not allowed to avow this. Woe to this earth.²⁶²

Just as the gospel had already been declared heresy, condemned, and burned at the stake, it may possibly be so again, this time in the case of Luther himself, of which Prierias (Sylvester Mazzolini, d. 1527) already reminded him, and so did Johann Eck during the Leipzig Debate, but Luther denied it.²⁶³

Following this initial discovery comes another shockwave for Luther, this time with the discovery of Lorenzo Valla's *Refutation*.²⁶⁴ Luther notes to Spalatin:

---

260. Huss's identifying the pope as the Antichrist was based, not on teaching a doctrine against the Scripture, but on the pope himself living contrary to Christ. Huss notes, "As for antichrist occupying the papal chair, it is evident that a pope living contrary to Christ, like any other perverted person, is called by common consent antichrist." Huss, *Church*, 128. Nonetheless, Huss made it clear that the head of the church is Christ, not the pope, and claimed, "No pope is the most exalted person of the catholic church but Christ himself; therefore no pope is the head of the catholic church besides Christ." Huss, *Church*, 133. Huss not only denied the power of the pope over souls in purgatory but also doubted the existence of postmortem purgatory. Reeves, *Unquenchable Flame*, 29–30. It is unknown, however, whether Huss directly influenced on Luther's attack on the doctrine of purgatory in 1521/22.

261. AE 48:153n15.

262. AE 48:153; WA Br 2:22–30. No 254. Letter to George Spalatin, February 14, 1519. See also Hendrix, *Luther and the Papacy*, 97–98.

263. Saak, *Luther and Reformation*, 302. See Luther's letter to Spalatin on August 28, 1518, AE 48:73–74; WA Br 1:190.6–23. Also, regarding Prierias's criticism against and involvement in Luther's development, see Lindberg, "Prierias," 45–64.

264. The *Refutation* (*De falso credita et ementita Constantini donatione declamatio*) published in 1440 discovers that the *Donation of Constantine* was written, not in the fourth-century Latin, but in the eighth-century Latin. Reeves, *Unquenchable Flame*, 33.

> ... from the print house of Dominicus Schleupner, Lorenzo Valla's refutation of the Donation of Constantine, published by Hutten. Good God! You would be amazed how in God's judgment not only such impure, *such crass and naked lies* of such massive Roman darkness or Roman iniquity have lasted through the ages, but also how they have prevailed and been handed down in Canon Law, one following after the other, lest some sort of the most horrible beast imaginable be kept from infecting the articles of faith. I am so overwhelmingly horrified in the very depths of my being that I can scarcely no longer doubt that *the pope is that very Antichrist* which, as commonly known, the world has expected, since it all fits, how he lives, what he does, what he says, and what he proclaims.[265]

Luther's suspicions about the pope's being the Antichrist, in fact, began in 1518 when he was dealing with Prierias, Eck, and Cajetan, discussing the issues of indulgences and the authority and power of the pope. Luther wrote a letter to Wenzel Link (Wenzeslaus Linck, d. 1547) on December 18, 1518,[266] and stressed that the papacy is under the authority of the Scripture and merely a "human category."[267] Three months later, while preparing the Leipzig Debate, Luther sends a letter to Spalatin:

> I am studying the papal decretals for my disputation. And, confidentially, I do not know whether the pope is the Antichrist himself or whether he is his apostle, so miserably is Christ (that is, the truth) corrupted and crucified by the pope in the decretals. I am extremely distressed that under the semblance of laws and the Christian name, the people of Christ should be so deluded ... I don't even mention the other works which are so very similar to those of the Antichrist and of which the Roman Curia has an overabundance. Daily greater and greater help and support by virtue of the authority of Holy Scripture wells up in me."[268]

In this letter, as Kittelson rightly comments, Luther does not claim in a definite sense that the pope is the Antichrist,[269] but with a series of dis-

---

265. Luther's Letter to George Spalatin on February 24, 1520. No 257. WA Br 2:48.20—49.29, quoted in Saak, *Luther and Reformation*, 341. Emphases added. See also Hendrix, *Luther and the Papacy*, 98.

266. WA Br 1:270.1—271.43, quoted in Rex, *Making of Luther*, 105; Whitford, *Luther*, 97; Leppin, *Martin Luther*, 40.

267. Wriedt, "Luther's Theology," 98.

268. AE 48:114; WA Br 1:359.28–32, 360:34–36. Letter to G. Spalatin, March 13, 1519; see also Rex, *Making of Luther*, 105.

269. Kittelson, "Luther and Modern Church History," 262.

coveries Luther is now personally convinced[270] that the papacy itself *is* the Antichrist. Saak describes the case:

> The papacy, the pope as pope, not the pope as individual, or even as bishop of Rome, was not sitting on St Peter's throne; that was the medieval Pope as Antichrist critique; the pope as pope, the papacy, was sitting on his own throne and that throne was the throne of the Antichrist. The entire papal Church was the structure of the Church of Antichrist that which had been seen as the very mouthpiece of Christ, to whom Christ had given his power, was a diabolical lie. That was Brother Martin's horror.[271]

Soon after the discoveries, Luther begins to write against the papacy,[272] the Antichrist, under whose lies the gospel was condemned and burned. Pope Leo X's bulls *Exsurge Domine* (June 15, 1520) and subsequently *Decet Romanum Pontificem* (January 3, 1521) only confirm Luther's conviction about the pope as Antichrist.[273] Luther's discoveries followed by several confirming occasions make permanent changes to his perspective on and approach to the doctrine of purgatory.

---

270. Scholars' views on this subject differ. Lohse, for example, argues that Luther began to suspect the pope to be the Antichrist at the end of 1518 and was convinced about it between 1518 and 1519 (e.g., Luther's Letter to Wenzel Link on December 18, 1518. WA Br. 1:121.11–14). Lohse, *Martin Luther*, 47, 178. Rupp, however, comments that Luther's thought about the pope as Antichrist began during his debates with Eck in Leipzig in 1519, and it was confirmed with the bull *Exsurge Domine* (1520). Rupp, *Luther's Progress*, 82. Wriedt also note that in August 1518 Luther "felt confirmed in his suspicion, until then only cautiously voiced." Wriedt, "Luther's Theology," 97. On the other hand, Hendrix claims that Luther's suspicion about the pope as Antichrist began in 1519 and that he was convinced in February 1520. Hendrix, *Luther and the Papacy*, 97–98.

271. Saak, *Luther and Reformation*, 344. See also Whitford, "The Papal Antichrist."

272. *On the Papacy at Rome* (*Von dem Bapstum zu Rome widder den hochberumpten Romanisten zu Leiptzck*, 1520) AE 39:55–104; WA 6:285–324; *A Treatise on the New Testament. That is, the Holy Mass* (*Eyn sermon von dem newen Testament, das ist von der heyligen Messe*, July 1520) AE 35:79–111; WA 6:353–78; *On Open Letter to the Christian Nobility* (*An den Christlichen Adel deutscher Ration von des Christlichen standes besserung*, June 1520) AE 44:123–217; WA 6:404–69; *The Babylonian Captivity of the Church* (*De Captivitate Babylonica Ecclesiae*, October 1520) AE 36:11–126; WA 6:497–573; and *The Freedom of a Christian* (*De Libertate Christiana*, November 1520) AE 31:333–77; WA 7:49–73.

273. Daniel, "Luther on Church," 339.

Postmortem Peaceful State of the Soul[274]

Luther's notion of the postmortem state of the soul in peaceful rest deserves attention for two reasons: first, it is dovetailed with his notion of purgatory as a postmortem condition;[275] second, it plays a key role in tracing his dismissal of the postmortem notion of torment. The question why it took so long for Luther to deny purgatory (i.e., postmortem condition of torment) can be thus answered partially by tracing Luther's notion of the postmortem peaceful state of the soul.

Luther addressed the subject on several occasions but primarily in the context of opposing and attacking the doctrine of purgatory and the notion of postmortem torment (e.g., *Recantation* and *Lectures on Genesis*) where he contrasts the state of souls in peaceful sleep and in torment.[276] Luther had no intention of addressing the subject as a dogma, nor did he set the tone in such a manner.[277] Admitting lack of knowledge and information from the Scripture of the intermediate state of the soul,[278] Luther, sparing his breath, accepted the expressions of the Scripture and articulated the peaceful state of the soul accordingly.[279] Meantime, Luther's notion on this

---

274. In the early church the fathers employed the concept of "sleep" or "dormition" and developed in the East (e.g., Syriac and Nestorian). Larchet comments concerning the concept of sleep in reference to a postmortem condition, "The Fathers certainly speak at times of sleep in connection with death, and the Orthodox Church, in treating of the Mother of God and the saints, prefers to speak of 'dormition' rather than 'death.' But here we are dealing with a symbolic expression that wishes to signify that the awakening of the resurrection will ensue, or that the soul is in a state of repose but is not, as it would be if entirely dead, completely inactive; it is only inactive with respect to this world, but in fact displays another form of activity in the hereafter." Larchet, *Life After Death*, 165.

275. Luther's notion of the intermediate state of the soul, or often described as soul sleep, differs from a conventional view to the degree that while the latter claims no consciousness or awareness during the state of soul sleep, in Luther's view a soul in sleep is awake and aware of surroundings. Understanding death as separation between the body and the soul, Luther articulates the analogy of sleep in extrapolating the notion of peaceful rest expressed in the Scripture and applies it to the state of the departed souls. See also O'Reggio, "A Re-examination," 154–70.

276. Since mid-1520s, Luther's position on the state of the soul is consistent that souls remain at rest in peace until the Day of Judgment. Luther, on the other hand, acknowledges God's absolute power in hidden will (e.g., *Confession* of 1528). AE 4:308–18; WA 43:357.6—364.18. *Lectures on Genesis* (1538–1542). See also AE 7:291–305, particularly 293–94; WA 44:516.6—526.6, particularly 517.13–30. *Lectures on Genesis* (1543–1545).

277. Köstlin, *The Theology of Luther*, 2:578.

278. AE 4:313; WA 43:360.18–23. Also, AE 7:294; WA 44:518.8–14.

279. Köstlin, *The Theology of Luther*, 2:577–78.

subject displays development, to a certain extent, as Köstlin comments: "The views which he himself adopts concerning the condition of departed souls are but slightly developed."[280] Luther's notion of the postmortem state of the *soul in sleep* signifies the state of the *soul living* as opposed to the soul in torment.[281] Furthermore, employing the analogy of sleep, Luther underscores a critical difference between sleep in this life and sleep hereafter, for in the latter the soul is awake and conscious, to the extent that it is unaware that it is in sleep.[282]

Luther's notion of the intermediate state of souls may appear to be inconsistent,[283] for on another occasion he speaks about unconsciousness or unawareness. When he defines the condition of sleep as "a kind of migration," "translated to another kind of life," for instance, Luther addresses the state of unconsciousness.[284] It needs clarification, however, for when Luther's analogy of sleep refers to the aspect of *migration* or *transition* from a previous condition to another, it describes unconsciousness insofar as souls are unaware of the former condition or physical surroundings while in sleep. When Luther addresses the analogy in the context of the *difference* between the sleep of this life and that of the future life, on the other hand, Luther highlights the state of consciousness of the latter to the extent that the soul is awake and conscious, and experiences "visions and the discourses of the angels and of God."[285] Therefore, Luther's use of the analogy of sleep only appears to be inconsistent, but is not, as he speaks in two different contexts.

In his letter to von Amsdorf (1522), Luther discusses the analogy of sleep as a postmortem state and condition, but does not fully accept it, partly because of some exceptional cases in the Scripture (e.g., St Paul's ecstasy and Elijah's and Moses' ascension), and also partly because of uncertainty of the state and condition of the departed souls.[286] Luther's notion of sleep

---

280. Köstlin, *The Theology of Luther*, 2:573.

281. AE 4:312; WA 43:359.31–38.

282. AE 4:313; WA 43:360.24–41.

283. Roper notes that the intermediate state seemed not a major subject for Luther. Roper, *Martin Luther*, 346–48.

284. AE 7:295; WA 44:518.14–25.

285. AE 4:313; WA 43:360.28.

286. AE 48:360–61; WA Br 2:422.4–17. "Who knows how God deals with the departed souls? Can't [God] just as well make them sleep on and off (or for as long as he wishes [them to sleep]), just as he overcomes with sleep those who live in the flesh?" AE 48:361; WA Br 2:422.12–14. No. 449. On January 13, 1522.

as the postmortem state appears in his *Fastenpostille* (1525) and in his *Notes on Ecclesiastes* (1526).[287] In the former he notes:

> A Christian neither tastes nor sees death. That is, he does not feel it and is not terrified by it, but goes into it *calmly and peacefully as though he were going to sleep* and were not really dying. A godless man, however, feels death and is eternally terrified by it. The word of God makes this difference. The Christian has this word and holds fast to it in death . . . *For just as a man who falls asleep and sleeps soundly until morning does not know what has happened to him when he wakes up, so we shall suddenly rise on the Last Day; and we shall know neither what death has been like or how we have come through it.*[288]

In this sermon Luther does not recall the three types of dying souls as presented in Thesis Seventeen of the *Explanations* (1518), but speaks about two types—a Christian as a whole and a godless person, describing the death of the former as that which does not taste death.[289] Two salient points of Luther's description are noteworthy: first, compared to the death of the godless in fear and terror, a Christian does not taste death; second, Christians rely on the Word of God in which they fall asleep until the Day of Judgment.

Concerning the notion of "tasting death," in his *Sermon Annotations* based on St. Matthew 16:28, Luther further differentiates between the notion of tasting death and that of *not* tasting death. By the former, he refers to dying in anguish and fear,[290] and by the latter, dying in Christ[291] and so resting in peace. With regard to the whereabouts of the departed souls, in his *Lectures on Genesis* Luther plainly avers, "It is the Word of God or

---

287. Woodbridge claims that Luther's full adoption of the peaceful state of the soul appears in 1526. Woodbridge, "Gerhard Westerburg," 101.

288. WA 17II: 234.36—235.2, 235.17-20, quoted in Althaus, *Theology of Martin Luther*, 409, 414. Emphases added.

289. Althaus explicates this text within the framework of Luther's notion of righteous and a sinner at once (*simul iustus et peccator*), as well as of the distinction of Law and Gospel, in which he interprets Luther's two opposite aspects of Christian death: terror and sleep. The first type is the death of a Christian as a sinner, and the latter that of a Christian as a righteous. Althaus places the text of *Fastenpostille* (1525) under the category of the latter. Althaus, *Theology of Martin Luther*, 408-9.

290. E.g., the type of dying without faith as in Thesis Seventeen of the *Explanations*. AE 31:131. WA 1:559.11-14.

291. This is equivalent to the type of dying with complete faith as in Thesis Seventeen of the *Explanations*. AE 31:131-32. WA 1:559.15-24.

the promises in which we fall asleep."²⁹² With this statement Luther does not articulate the notion of sleep in depth but rather accepts the scriptural expression of death, highlighting the peaceful aspect of rest in the Word of Christ. Luther's intention is not only to distinguish death in faith (i.e., not tasting death but peaceful rest as falling asleep) and death in unbelief (i.e., tasting death in fear and anguish), but also to nullify the notion of imaginary purgatory (i.e., postmortem state of torment) or any claim associated with it. Purgatory is thus the "greatest falsehood," contends Luther, established on the basis of "ungodliness and unbelief."²⁹³ Rejecting the doctrine of purgatory, or even denying the notion of postmortem torment, does not mean for Luther there is no intermediate state. On the contrary, those who die in the Word and the promise of God have no tribulations or afflictions hereafter but enjoy peace in the bosom of Christ.²⁹⁴ Luther's inclination to the notion of the postmortem peaceful state of souls already appeared in early 1522 when he attacked the doctrine of purgatory and redefined purgatory—the state of torment—in an existential sense. It has not been affirmative, however, until 1525/26.

Timeline of Denial

Already in 1518

The claim that Luther maintains in the *Explanations* (1518) his use of the term "purgatory" without necessarily professing it since his doubts about purgatory already began to appear in 1518²⁹⁵ overlooks Luther's affirmation in the same document where he holds the notion of the postmortem "fire and place" of purgatory and the postmortem punishments of purgatory. In addition, Luther intentionally distanced himself from those who denied purgatory such as the Picardi in Bohemia.²⁹⁶ Furthermore, when Luther de-

---

292. AE 4:314; WA 43:361.13. On Gen. 25:7-10.

293. AE 4:315; WA 43:362.13-14. On Gen. 25:7-10. Luther lectured chapter 25 sometime after June 1540. AE 4:x.

294. AE 4:315; WA 43:362.6-22. On Gen. 25:7-10.

295. Ji-Hoon Hong made the comment based on Lohse, *Martin Luther's Theology*, 105n43, which was sent to author via e-mail message on my paper "The Historical Development of the Doctrine of Purgatory and the Source of Luther's Definition of Purgatory" presented *in absentia* to Korea Luther Study Society / Koreanische Luther-Gesellschaft in Seoul, Korea on February 10, 2012.

296. AE 31:125-26; WA 1: 555.36—556.5., Thesis Fifteen of the *Explanations* (1518).

bated with Eck in Leipzig (1519), he affirmed as presented in the *Ninety-five Theses* that souls in purgatory suffer, and that while they—or not all of them—are uncertain of their salvation, the grace of God increases in purgatory.[297] In addition, in the *Defense* (1521) Luther reaffirmed his Theses on purgatory[298] and claimed that he never denied purgatory.[299]

Not until 1530

The claim that Luther's denial of the doctrine of purgatory, as well as of his notion of postmortem purification, did not occur until the publication of the *Recantation* (1530) fails to recognize *the* significant development in Luther's view of purgatory between 1521 and 1526. Such terms as "lie," "fabricate," and "abomination" and other similar terms with which Luther would reject the doctrine of purgatory in the *Recantation* already appear in his writings in 1521/22. This is the paradigm shift in 1521/22 or *the first turning point* in Luther's view of purgatory, which is anticipated, to a certain extent, if we take into consideration that the doctrine of purgatory developed closely with the power and authority of the papacy. When Luther's suspicion of the papacy as Antichrist turned into full conviction, Luther treated the doctrine of purgatory as lies and deceit, which occurred just after 1520, not in 1530.

Between 1521/22 and 1525/26

In discussing the timeline of denial, it is essential to make a distinction, as noted earlier, between the doctrine of purgatory and Luther's notion of purgatory as postmortem state of torment. With respect to the former, the point of denial can be as early as 1521/22. A broader context supports this view, and the omission of phrases involving the term "purgatory" in the *Personal Prayer Book* (1524) and in *A Meditation* (1525 edition) buttresses it. From these two omissions it can be inferred that following the criticism and rejection of the *doctrine* of purgatory approximately in 1521/22, as

---

Luther affirmed his position during the Leipzig Debate. WA 2:324.14–15.
297. WA 2:332.38—333.2.
298. E.g., Fourth and Thirty-seven Theses.
299. AE 32:95; WA 7:451.11–12.

well as the liturgical reconstruction in 1523,[300] Luther began to eliminate terms and expressions in reference to purgatory for the purpose of pastoral guidance, which in a broad context also supports the timeline of denial proposed in this book.

Luther's suspicion about the papacy began to appear in 1518, and his doubts about purgatory might have already begun to appear in 1518.[301] Luther's coincident doubts, should the latter be considered in such a way, emerged during controversies that irrupted after the copies of the *Ninety-five Theses* were circulated. Nonetheless, this is only the stage of doubts, if it were his doubts, *not as a denial*, for Luther still firmly believed in the existence of purgatory as a postmortem condition of torment. It does not make sense to suppose that Luther, while denying purgatory, or having already denied it, continued to debate about purgatory as if he still professes the existence of purgatory, for instance, in the Leipzig Debate of 1519[302] and the *Defense* of 1521.

Should the date of denial be traced with respect to Luther's notion of postmortem torment, not the doctrine, it can be arguably as early as

---

300. Also, Luther's efforts to remove the Mass in the territory of Electoral Saxony in general and in Wittenberg in particular began in March 1523 until December 1524. Editor's Introduction to *The Abomination of the Secret Mass* (*Vom Greuel der Stillmesse*, 1525). AE 26:309.

301. With respect to the comment that Luther's doubts about purgatory began to appear in 1518, Lohse refers to the fifth paragraph of Thesis Seventeen in the *Explanations*. Lohse, *Martin Luther's Theology*, 105n43. Luther's statement, however, does not seem to indicate his doubts about purgatory. In Thesis Seventeen, following the claim that as the term "purgatory" implies a cleansing, and that purgatory is not merely a "workshop of punishment" (*poenarum officina*), Luther contends that his opponents' notion of "cleansing" as payment of punishment (e.g., satisfaction) creates ambiguity, and consequently "both meanings" of cleansing—one, cleansing of faults, and the other, cleansing as punishment—"become doubtful and uncertain," and the former meaning of cleansing, which Luther proposes, is distorted and completely dispersed. By the expression of "become doubtful and uncertain," Luther refers to the ambiguity and distortion caused by the opponents' claim. Furthermore, Luther's statement should be understood in a broad context which supports his Thesis Seventeen as a whole (Thesis Seventeen: "It seems as though for the souls in purgatory fear should necessarily decrease and love increase") since he plainly states in the beginning of this paragraph, "Nevertheless, I speak in favor of this thesis [Thesis Seventeen] for a fifth reason." Luther's goal of supporting this thesis is accomplished, and can only be so, primarily by demonstrating the opponents' ambiguity of their claim on cleansing, not by presenting his doubts about purgatory. AE 31:135; WA 1:561.28–38. Fundamentally, Luther's theses are his academic disputations that employ rhetorical and logical claims to make his thesis persuasive.

302. Levy, "Leipzig Disputation," 137.

1525/26 (e.g., *Fastenpostille* in 1525 or *Notes on Ecclesiasts* in 1526) when Luther fully acknowledges the postmortem peaceful state of souls, banishing the notion of torment. Therefore, the timeline of denial can be discussed in a twofold sense: in a narrow sense, it refers to Luther's attacks on the doctrine of purgatory (e.g., 1521/22), and in a wide sense it refers to his dismissal of the notion of postmortem torment (e.g., 1525/26). Supposing both aspects are to be taken into account, it can be then said that Luther's rejection of purgatory—both the *doctrine* and his *notion* of postmortem torment—occurs between 1521/22 and 1525/26.

Significant is Luther's assertion that denying purgatory does not harm anyone, nor does it make one a heretic, which appears frequently in 1521/22. It signifies the demonstration of Luther's pastoral care for the Christians captivated under the doctrine of purgatory. Here, Luther—just as his name itself implies[303]—was indeed a *liberator*[304] providing pastoral care and guidance to the weak conscience with respect to their concerns about their departed loved ones, as well as their belief in purgatory.

CONCLUSION

This chapter has attempted to answer the question why it took so long for Luther explicitly to deny purgatory. With the distinctions of Luther's notion of purgatory and the formal doctrine itself, as well as the two major elements that constitute Luther's notion of purgatory (i.e., the postmortem condition of torment and existential *tentatio*), on the one hand, together with the key terms that validate Luther's parallel attacks on the doctrine of purgatory between 1521/22 and 1530, on the other hand, I have demonstrated that Luther's rejection of the doctrine occurred as early as 1521/22. If we count from the composition of the *Ninety-five Theses*, it took about *four to five* years for Luther to deny it, but from the discovery of the Antichrist it took just over *a year or two*. Luther's denial of the doctrine of purgatory is certainly pertinent to his claim that Scripture is silent on the subject, but fundamentally it ensued from his conviction that the *doctrine* itself was intrinsically

---

303. Luther's original name was Luder, which means "dirt" or "garbage" in High German. His new name "Luther" from *eleuthérios* (ἐλευθέριος) means the "liberated." Wriedt, "Luther's Theology," 86n2. In his letters between 1516 and 1519, Luther's signature block occasionally includes his new name *Eleutherius* in a Latinized form. WA Br 1:83.58—303.84. Schilling notes that changing one's family name was a common practice among the humanists for a scholarly pseudonym. Schilling, *Martin Luther*, 139.

304. See Hamm, *Early Luther*, 166–67, 177–78.

associated with the power and authority of the papacy, and from his discovery that the papacy, which burned the gospel at the stake with Huss's death, is the Antichrist. Luther argued that "[t]he papacy and the whole hierarchy are all but built upon it [purgatory],"[305] and enormous was the cascading, detrimental harm of the doctrine of purgatory on the church.[306]

By the time Luther denied the doctrine of purgatory, he could have dismissed the term and notion of purgatory wholesale. He maintained the term instead by redefining it as the condition of torment in an existential sense. For Luther the term "purgatory" *always* refers to the condition of *torment*, never that of peaceful rest. It is, therefore, not a coincidence that Luther *redefines* purgatory as suffering in this life when he rejects the doctrine with respect to the postmortem state of torment. Furthermore, by the time Luther redefines purgatory as suffering in this life, he tends to accept—not fully until 1525/26—the notion of the postmortem peaceful state of souls. In other words, it can be argued that in 1525/26 Luther's use of the term "purgatory" and his notion of the postmortem state are settled in such a way that as far as the former is concerned, it only refers to an existential suffering, and as far as the latter is concerned, it is nothing but peaceful rest. Luther's statements of 1528 and 1531 concerning "all things are possible to God" in which the departed souls may be tormented[307] are, therefore, only his acknowledgement of God's hidden will. Luther would lose nothing if he denied the second element—existential *tentatio*—of purgatory altogether. Taking into consideration the purpose and intention of the *Great Confession* (1528) as a lifetime confession,[308] however, it can be also assumed that Luther continued to hold the notion of existential *tentatio* until his deathbed, not necessarily with the term "purgatory," but only its content,[309] which will be treated in a moment.

Having treated the question of *why* it took so long for Luther to deny purgatory, we are now to pursue the next question: *How* Luther could hold both purgatory and justification by faith alone simultaneously until 1521/22. The following chapter will attempt to answer the question, followed by the final question in the subsequent chapter: "Why is it significant to examine Luther's view of purgatory despite his denial of purgatory, after

305. AE 32:97; WA 7:451.19—452.31. On the *Defense*, 1521.
306. AE 75:238n17; WA 10I 1:111.14–16. A sermon on Titus 3:4–7, 1522.
307. AE 37:369; WA 26:508.8–9; AE 23:154; WA 33:242.9–11.
308. AE 37:163; WA 26:262.19–25. See also AE 37:360; WA 26:499.21–23.
309. AE 37:369; WA 26:508.11–12.

all?" In other words, "What was Luther's intention and purpose in treating the subject of the punishments of purgatory in the *Explanations*, and how did he maneuver it?"

4

Luther's Perception

Simul Purgatorium et Iustificatio Sola Fide[1]

> "Whoever holds fast in confident desperation to the promises of the complete removal of the guilt of sin will await more eagerly the beginning of the new era, which will bring with it the complete overcoming of the power of sin, than the one who dreams of a present life of victory and of complete sanctification."
>
> —Adolf Köberle

INTRODUCTION

IN THE WAKE OF his conviction that the papacy itself is the Antichrist,[2] Luther began to attack the current formal doctrine of purgatory as lies and deceit. As far as Luther's view of purgatory is concerned, noticeable are two turning points which occurred between Luther's reception of the bull *Exsurge Domine* of 1520 and his composition of the *Recantation* of 1530 on the occasion of the presentation of Melanchthon's *Apology*. Up until 1521/22, Luther viewed the punishments of purgatory mainly as a post-mortem condition of torment associated with the notion of near despair,

---

1. "Purgatory and Justification by Faith Alone Simultaneously."
2. Saak, *Luther and Reformation*, 344.

without denying entirely the aspect of punishments that occurred before death. Describing the notion of postmortem fear through the painful afflictions and *tentatio*, Luther asserted that some people experienced the pains of hell in this life. While both postmortem torment and existential afflictions constitute Luther's view of the punishments of purgatory, for instance in the *Explanations* (1518), the former plays the primary and the latter a marginal role, particularly until his attacks on the doctrine of purgatory. During the attacks (1521/22), however, Luther redefines purgatory mainly as existential *tentatio*, which is the *first* turning point, and keeps the aspect of postmortem torment only as a marginal notion potentially for few souls. In 1525/26 occurs the *second* turning point where he explicitly dismisses the notion of postmortem torment and accepts the postmortem peaceful state of the soul.

With this brief recapitulation of Luther's view of purgatory and its development, a question arises as to how Luther could hold both purgatory and his theology of justification simultaneously, particularly until 1521/22. The early stage in the development of Luther's theology of justification appears in his *Dictata*, and by the time he drafts the *Explanations* of 1518 the notion of purgatory was already integrated into his theology of justification. In this context, this chapter claims that in the *Explanations* Luther integrates the notion of suffering as the cross of souls in purgatory into his theology of justification in view of the soul's continual growth in faith and love in Christ.

Examining the way in which Luther accommodates the notion of purgatory in the framework of his theology of justification, we first undertake a brief review of "Luther's Reformation Breakthrough." In agreement with Oswald Bayer's assertion that Luther does not make such distinction between justification and sanctification as if the latter follows the former as "two separate acts," but that Luther speaks about justification when discussing the subject of sanctification,[3] this chapter examines Luther's theology of justification in chronological order, and establishes a major premise as a point of departure that Luther's theology of justification embraces both the instantaneous effect and the continual effect of the external righteousness of God, the former corresponding to the notion of forgiveness, the latter to the removal of sin. Subsequently, with particular attention to

---

3. Oswald comments that Luther's understanding of sanctification is the work of the Holy Spirit, not as "a matter of personal and individual development and orientation." See Bayer, *Living By Faith*, 58–68, particularly 58–59. See also Bayer, *Promissio: Geschichte der reformatorischen*.

four significances of the continual effect (i.e., first, it anticipates the final destination; second, it involves growing in faith and love in Christ; third, it references Luther's notion of the imperfect righteousness of faith; and, fourth, it is inextricably interwoven with the notion of a journey of faith under the cross), I propose as a minor premise that until 1521/22 Luther perceived the postmortem purgatorial condition in line with the notion of a continual effect of the external righteousness of God. In this respect, Luther considered afflictions in purgatory as bearing the cross with respect to the soul's continual growth in faith and love in Christ prior to its entry into the eternal destination.

In examining Luther's theology of justification, the primary sources include the selected works of Luther composed between 1513 and 1536. Regarding Luther's perception of purgatory in the framework of justification, we concentrate on the *Explanations* of 1518.

LUTHER'S REFORMATION BREAKTHROUGH

The subject of Luther's Reformation breakthrough or discovery is still debated by scholars. Reviewing each individual's stance and comparing their arguments in detail are beyond the scope of the current task. Prior to discussing Luther's theology of justification, however, a brief sketch of Luther's Reformation breakthrough suffices to lay out a point of reference. In a nutshell, initial discussions in Luther scholarship treat the Reformation breakthrough as a special *event* occurring in a specific timeline, but the corresponding discussions consider the subject as a *process* instead of a one-time special event. Recent proposals, however, tend to distinguish between Luther's theological discoveries and his Reformation breakthrough, and treat the latter as a special event particularly associated with the breakup with the Church in Rome. Such diverse views on the timing of Luther's Reformation breakthrough and discoveries can be grouped into three: first, dating the breakthrough during or before Luther's *Lectures on Romans*; second, sometime after the composition of the *Ninety-five Theses*; and third, a series of gradual discoveries from early lectures on.

Supporters of Luther's early discovery base their proposals on Luther's hermeneutical rediscovery in the early lectures,[4] and among them are Rupp

---

4. Lohse, *Martin Luther's Theology*, 86.

(i.e., before the *Lectures on Romans*),⁵ von Loewenich (i.e., the *Dictata*)⁶ and Wriedt (i.e., the *Dictata*)⁷ and H. Bornkamm (i.e., the *Lectures on Romans*).⁸ Some among the first group concur that Luther's breakthrough seemed associated with his hermeneutical discovery, but propose that it was closely tied with the indulgence controversy.⁹ Outstanding among them are Bayer (i.e., the "hermeneutical discovery" occurred particularly during the reflection on the sacrament of penance in 1518),¹⁰ Brecht¹¹ and Schilling (i.e., the *Sermon on Palm Sunday*, May 28, 1518 while the initial breakthrough occurred between 1517 and 1520 in a broad sense)¹² as well as Aland (i.e., between February 15, 1518 and March 28, 1518),¹³ and Wicks (e.g., the *Sermo de Poenitentia*, 1518).¹⁴

Differentiated from the two proposals above, to a certain extent, the third group claims a series of discoveries instead, and either takes or avoids the methodology based on Luther's letter to Staupitz in 1518 and his recollection in 1545, in general, but refuses the approach of finding Luther's discovery as a single event, in particular.¹⁵ Oberman considers the subject as "a series of breakthroughs" between 1513 and 1519,¹⁶ proposing that Luther's autobiographical fragment refers to sometime between 1518 and 1519.¹⁷ In a similar vein, Beutel comments that Luther's Reformation discovery is "a complex development process" throughout several years between 1514/15 and 1518.¹⁸ Also, Kolb proposes to treat the subject as a process towards Luther's "evangelical maturation" rather than "a dramatic breakthrough."¹⁹

---

5. Rupp, *Luther's Progress*, 4.
6. Von Loewenich, *Martin Luther*, 81.
7. Wriedt, "Luther's Theology," 91.
8. Von Loewenich, *Martin Luther*, 81.
9. Lohse, *Martin Luther's Theology*, 86.
10. Bayer, "Luther as Interpreter," 76.
11. Brecht, *Martin Luther*, 1:229.
12. Schilling, *Martin Luther*, 122, 329.
13. Von Loewenich, *Martin Luther*, 81.
14. Wicks, *Man Yearning for Grace*, 257.
15. Leppin, *Martin Luther*, 35, 40, 50.
16. Oberman, *Luther*, 164–66. The *Dictata*, for instance, was Luther's theological breakthrough. Oberman, *Reformation*, 95.
17. Saak, *Luther and Reformation*, 102.
18. Beutel, "Luther's Life," 7.
19. Kolb, *Martin Luther*, 42.

Lohse finds Luther's discovery occurred during the *Dictata*;[20] however, as far as the development of Luther's theological insight is concerned, it continued up to 1520, and concerning the subject of the righteousness of God, it still continued even in the 1530s.[21]

Hamm, as a proponent of the gradual progress view, also prefers to describe Luther's discoveries as "a gradual transition" rather than gradual "process" or "development" to avoid any connotation that involves a "teleological aspect" in Luther's discoveries. Furthermore, by the term "gradual" Hamm does not refer to "a gradual shift of emphasis" but "the character of sudden leaps" or "turning points."[22] Leppin takes the view of Luther's gradual discoveries with the term "transformation," underlining *continuity* in its development,[23] on the one hand, and rejecting a particular methodology of reading Luther's early accounts in seeking his Reformation breakthrough based on the autobiographical fragment in 1545, on the other.[24] Leppin argues that Luther's departure from the Church in Rome was not associated with the doctrine of justification but with the issue of the papal authority.[25] In this respect, Luther's Reformation is closely connected with his burning the bull *Exsurge Domine* on December 10, 1520, not necessarily with the *Ninety-five Theses*.[26]

Not everyone can be identified within the proposed three groups addressed above. Saak, for instance, argues that Luther's Reformation breakthrough, which is not necessarily associated with Luther's theological discoveries, did not occur until February 1520.[27] Saak argues that until

20. Lohse, *Martin Luther*, 30.
21. Lohse, *Martin Luther's Theology*, 86, 94.
22. Hamm notes "[T]hey [changes] appear each time as something qualitatively and surprisingly new." Hamm, *Early Luther*, 109.
23. Leppin, "Luther's Transformation," 116.
24. Saak, *Luther and the Reformation*, 104–5, 111. Also, Leppin comments on Luther's autobiographical fragment that it appears as a similar conversion account as St. Paul's and Augustine's. Leppin, *Martin Luther*, 35. In this regard, Wicks proposes to draw attention to Luther's early writings rather than to the autobiographical fragment. Wicks, *Man Yearning for Grace*, 12.
25. Leppin, *Martin Luther*, 40.
26. Leppin, *Martin Luther*, 50.
27. Luther's doubts about the papacy to be the Antichrist came to be realization with two discoveries in early 1520, as mentioned earlier: the gospel burned at the stake with John Huss's death (July 6, 1415) on February 14, 1520, and his reading of Lorenzo Valla's *The Donation of Constantine* (1444) on 24 February 24, 1520. Saak, *Luther and the Reformation*, 341.

1520 Luther was not a Reformer in the commonly understood sense of later Protestantism but only a successor of the late medieval Augustinian reform movement, and asserts that just as the Augustinian reform movement failed, so did Luther's. Until the breakup with the Church in Rome in 1520 Luther remained "the papist Luther," and thus any theological discoveries prior to 1520 can only be framed as "a confessional dilemma." It is a dilemma, according to Saak, for Luther cannot be fully "evangelical" without having both his theological discoveries *and* his attack on and thus separation from the Church in Rome.[28]

For the purpose of this chapter, I underline the following combined views: first, Luther's theological discoveries which occurred during his early lectures continued in a gradual process of transition or development towards maturity (e.g., Oberman, Kolk, and Hamm); second, while Luther's breakup with the Church in Rome occurred as a result of his discoveries in February 1520 (e.g., Leppin and Saak),[29] followed by the burning of the bull *Exsurge Domine*, Luther's critical discernment and judgment in criticizing and attacking the papacy and its doctrines from 1520 onwards cannot be isolated from his theological insight which developed throughout a series of discoveries beforehand.[30] That is to say, the former should be considered as the implication of the latter. On this premise, I propose that Luther undertakes a theological reorientation throughout a series of discoveries, and that he perceives and discusses purgatory in line with his developing theology of justification.

LUTHER ON JUSTIFICATION AND TWO KINDS OF EFFECTS OF THE ALIAN RIGHTEOUSNESS OF GOD

This section lays a foundation in finding Luther's line of thought between his notion of purgatory and his theology of justification. The subject of the latter has long been discussed in Luther scholarship, and three claims are noticeable: first, the forensic view (i.e., being declared righteous); second,

---

28. Saak, *Luther and Reformation*, 100.

29. See "Discovery of Antichrist" in chapter 3 for scholars' diverse views on this subject.

30. Wriedt, "Luther's Theology," 91. Luther's doubts about the pope as the Antichrist, for instance, began as early as late in 1518, which was confirmed in early 1520. Also, Rupp who proposes Luther's discovery occurred in *Dictata*, comments that Luther's reaction of burning the bull on December 10, 1520 is "the true inauguration of the Reformation." Rupp, *Luther's Progress*, 90.

the progressive view (i.e., being made righteous); third, the union or divinization view of the Finnish School. The forensic view based on the concept of God's imputation rejects the progressive view as well as the union view, and the Finnish School refuses the forensic view. One of the reasons to dispute the forensic view of justification finds its basis on the claim that it was Melanchthon, not Luther, who proposed it, and that the forensic view requires a systematic distinction between justification and sanctification.[31] On the other hand, a rationale in objecting to the progressive view in general is that it is a continuation of a medieval tradition which Luther rejected later.[32] Also, apparent is the reason to oppose the personal union view of the Finnish School that Luther's justification by faith alone is not an ontological term but a relational term.[33]

Undertaking a critical analysis of the three different proposals in detail is beyond the scope of this research, nor is it the purpose of this section. In reference to both the *instantaneous* effect and the *continual* effect of the external (or alien) righteousness of God, this section discusses several themes essential to the subject—the righteousness of God, the notion of *motu* and *simul*, and the analogies of healing, leaven, and a journey. Subsequently, I assert that the significances of the latter effect provide a theological context

---

31. E.g., McGrath and Strehle. See Clark, "*Iustitia*," 279–80. See also Flogaus, "Luther versus Melanchthon?" 6–46. On Luther's theology of justification, see also Schwarz, *Martin Luther: Lehrer der christlichen Religion*.

32. Clark, for instance, claims that during 1513 and 1521 Luther's view of justification gradually developed to reject the progressive view of justification in favor of the forensic view. Clark, "*Iustitia*," 287–88. The argument of Stayer, which is Clark's reference to his claim, is that Luther's autobiographical fragment of 1545 in the Latin edition indicates that after the controversy with the papacy Luther left his early theology. Stayer, *Martin Luther, German Saviour*, 12, quoted in Clark, "*Iustitia*," 287–88. Luther's statement, however, may not be taken as definitive that Luther discarded all his theology up to early 1520, but as a gradual progression in the sense that since 1520 Luther began to articulate his theology by rejecting the theological elements associated with the power and authority of the pope. Luther's view of purgatory, for instance, exhibits Luther's gradual process of removing the papal theological elements (e.g., any expressions associated with the term "purgatory" are omitted in the later editions of the *Personal Prayer Book* (1524) and the *Meditation* (1525)). In this regard, Luther's view of purgatory demonstrates a gradual change with respect to continuity and discontinuity before and after 1521/22 (i.e., the first turning point in Luther's view of purgatory) in a narrow sense and 1525/26 (i.e., the second turning point in Luther's view of purgatory) in a wide sense.

33. Hamm, *Early Luther*, 99; also see 99n56. Kolb also comments that for Luther justification is not merely a forensic interpretation but a reality that God's word effectively creates. Kolb, *Martin Luther*, 5. Analogously, Kolb argues that Luther's notion of a mystical union is not an "ontological absorption." Kolb, *Martin Luther*, 79.

where Luther articulates the punishments of purgatory in the framework of his theology of justification.

Until 1512

During his early years between 1505 and 1512 occurs Luther's initial discovery associated with his experiences of acute spiritual afflictions to the point of "near despair" (*Anfechtungen* or *prope desperatio*).[34] In the cloister, the theology of *habitus* or quality taught him that a sinner has natural knowledge and ability to love God, and that God in the covenant (*pactum*) with himself is committed to help "those who do their best."[35] As far as the theological training in the cloister is concerned, Luther seemed not allowed to read the Scriptures except during his personal spare time.[36] Instead, he studied mainly nominalist theology (e.g., Occam-Biel school)[37] in a late medieval piety which emphasized the intensive *awareness of sin*, on the one hand, and the greater efforts of reaching *perfect obedience*, on the other.[38] Luther's struggles with uncertainty as to whether God would accept or abandon him eternally increased his spiritual anxiety and caused great spiritual angst.[39] Encountering the moment of "near despair," Luther seemed to have felt "stretched out with Christ," being already at "the threshold of condemnation and at the entrance of hell."[40] Amid his spiritual agony,

---

34. AE 31:128–30; WA 1:557.33—558.18. AE 31:27; WA 1:234.5–6, and 8. Luther also describes it as "very near the horror of despair" (*proximus desperationis horrori*). AE 31:27; WA 1:234.6. Hamm terms it "radical *Anfechtung*." Hamm, *Early Luther*, 55–58.

35. "*Facere quod in se est*" is the technical phrase for "to do what is in them" in Latin. Oberman, *Harvest of Medieval Theology*, 132–34, 175–76. The full sentence of this medieval theology of justification is "facienti quod in se est deus non denegat gratiam (God will not deny his grace to the one who is doing what is in him)." *From Conflict to Communion*, 43.102.

36. Brecht, *Martin Luther*, 1:86. Luther seemed to have read the *Epistle to Romans* in 1509/10. Lohse, *Martin Luther's Theology*, 54.

37. Luther studied nominalist theology from Jodocus Trutvetter (d.1519) and Bartholomäus Arnoldi of Usingen (d. 1535) and learned from Trutvetter that the Holy Scripture is the only book that deserves trust. Dieter comments, however, that nominalism, the counterpart of which is realism, cannot be identified simply as the school of *via moderna*. Dieter, "Luther as Late Medieval Theologian," 32, 34.

38. Hamm, *Early Luther*, 34–41.

39. Brecht, *Martin Luther*, 1:79–80.

40. AE 31:130; WA 1:558.19–23. Luther's description in Thesis Fifteen of the *Explanations* (1518).

Luther found no hope in himself, but discovered his *Anfechtung* relevant to "a new theological and Christological meaning: *Anfechtung* (or *tentatio*) as cross and as grace."[41] Luther discovered this grace, not within himself as *habitus* or a qualitative disposition, which Luther later attacks,[42] but outside of him, namely, "in Christ."

Through *Anfechtung* perceived as participation in the sufferings of Christ on the cross, of which Staupitz advised him, "Look upon the wounds of Christ and his blood shed for you,"[43] Luther began to have a new perspective on spiritual afflictions, not as God's wrath of judgment, but as God's mercy to have one united with Christ in his passion, and perceived in this respect God's "nearness"[44] or the "transcendence" of God.[45] It is the beginning of Luther's theological discovery that leads to his discovery of justification by faith alone in the righteousness of God.[46]

Between 1513 and 1517

First Lectures on the Psalms (1513/15)[47]

In the *Dictata*, the righteousness of God in a broad sense corresponds to self-accusation (*accusatio sui*).[48] Luther's notion of self-accusation excludes a moral sense of a human work and refers exclusively to the work of the Holy Spirit wherein one accuses oneself in acknowledgment of sin and stands in spiritual humility in repentance before God.[49] Luther already understands the two corresponding themes of the notion of "outside of us" (*extra nos*) and the term he later called "passive righteousness" to a certain extent.[50]

---

41. According to Hamm, this was Luther's initial theological discovery. Hamm, *Early Luther*, 42, 44.

42. Lohse, *Martin Luther's Theology*, 47.

43. Köstlin, *The Theology of Luther*, 1:68–69.

44. Hamm, *Early Luther*, 51–55.

45. The concept of God's transcendence is from Augustine. Wicks, *Man Yearning for Grace*, 17.

46. Hamm notes that it is "the beginning of the Reformation reorientation." Hamm, *Early Luther*, 42.

47. *Dictata super Psalterium*.

48. Köstlin, *The Theology of Luther*, 1:98.

49. Rupp, *Righteousness of God*, 148.

50. On Ps. 4:4 Luther interprets the expression "be angry" in a philological sense that in Hebrew it denotes: "cause yourselves to become angry, or receive the admonition

Luther also affirms that God's mercy is his righteousness, which he receives and by which he is made righteous.[51] In this respect, self-accusation in humility is God's alien operation (*opus alienum Dei*) wherein one is led to seek God's mercy; that is, God's righteousness.[52]

Justification *in motu*

Luther's view of self-accusation in justification in the *Dictata* cannot be fully grasped without acknowledging that he discusses the subject within the context of continual progress. The Christian life is never standing still but always in motion (*in motu*). By the notion of a continual progress in motion, Luther refers to *Anfechtung* or *tentatio* of spiritual tribulations, in particular. As far as Christian life is concerned, faith, hope, and love increase when one is in affliction or *Anfechtung*.[53] In reference to Revelation 22:11 "Let him who is righteous still be justified,"[54] Luther asserts that "the state of the righteous" in this life is never static, but "always to run back to the beginning and always to start anew."[55] "Because God justifies the one who is now wretched," contends Luther, the righteous "hunger and thirst for righteousness more and more and for that reason are always justified, always seeking 'to receive mercy,' always acknowledging the righteousness

---

which is being given you so that you may be provoked to anger." In the same vein, Luther interprets the term "know" as "permit yourselves to become people who know." On Ps. 2:10 "O king, understand" means, according to Luther, "you shall be given understanding" or "He is the one who wants to teach you and give you understanding, and it is for you not to resist but to receive and permit yourselves to be thus formed and taught and have understanding given to you." AE 10:65; WA 55II:76.21–32.

51. AE 10:47; WA 55II:53.1–7. "For unless He Himself has mercy, I am not righteous . . . But if I have received it, then I have been made righteous." AE 10:47; WA 55II:53.16–17. "His mercy is my righteousness." AE 10:47; WA 55II:53.15.

52. "But now the whole righteousness of God is this: To humble oneself into the depth. Such a one comes to the highest, because he first went down to the lowest depth. Here he properly refers to Christ, who is the power of God and the righteousness of God through the greatest and deepest humility. Therefore He is now in the highest through supreme glory." AE 10:402; WA 55II:432.209–14.

53. AE 10:51; WA 55II:62.1–2.

54. AE 10:53; WA 55II:64.8. Revelation 22:11.

55. AE 10:53; WA 55II:64.13–14.

received earlier"[56] to the extent to which the Christian life is "always in motion and at the beginning" simultaneously.[57]

The Notion of *Simul*

Luther's notion of the state of the righteous in a continual motion is pertinent to the concept of *simul* (e.g., *simul iustus et peccator*).[58] The concept of *simul* appears both in the field of philosophy and that of theology. Aristotle, for instance, proposed the concept of a continual motion that implies imperfection, and in the case of Augustine, the present moment is always in motion within the context of a lifelong journey to a homeland. Adopting the concept of motion or process, Luther integrates it into his developing theology of justification.[59] With the concept of "in part" (*partim*) Luther perceives that the present state of the righteous is always *imperfect*, "always in part acquired and in part to be acquired, always in the midst of opposites, and standing at the same time at the starting point and at the goal."[60] In this line of thought, Luther describes the concept of *simul*: standing at the point of departure and at the point of destination simultaneously, on the one hand, and having "eternal rest" "in part in the conscience" and having "troubles in part in the flesh," on the other.[61] For Luther, a Christian who receives God's righteousness (i.e., God's mercy) is yet to be always made righteous in the respect that "every righteousness for the present moment is sin with regard to that which must be added in the next moment."[62]

In the *Dictata*, Luther identifies self-accusation as the beginning of righteousness, the state of which implies a continual motion in lifelong self-accusation—always running back to the starting point where sins are

---

56. AE 10:53; WA 55II:64.20–23.

57. AE 10:53; WA 55II:64.15.

58. This technical phrase—*simul iustus et peccator*—in Luther's theology denotes that we are sinners and righteous simultaneously. AE 10:53; WA 55II:64.15.

59. Carey, "Luther and the Legacy of Augustine," 41. Medieval mysticism also captures the notion of *simul*, and Luther often refers it to Bernard of Clairvaux. Closer to Luther's earlier study, the concept of *simul* appears in Biel's theology concerning the uncertain state of a *viator* tossed simultaneously between hope and fear. Oberman, *Harvest of Medieval Theology*, 182–83.

60. AE 11:494; WA 55II:971.2293–95.

61. AE 11:494–95; WA 55II:971.2294–99.

62. AE 11:496; WA 55II:973.2350–51.

found, so as to acknowledge sins, repent of them, and continue to be justified until reaching the final destination.

Lectures on Romans (1515/16)[63]

Righteousness of God

Noticeable in the *Lectures on Romans* is Luther's further advancement with regard to the notion of the righteousness of God.[64] Luther's passive view of righteousness continues to develop with his emphasis on faith that trusts in the word of Christ. As in the *Dictata*, Luther still treats justification with respect to self-accusation in humility as part of God's alien operation for salvation. Self-accusation even to the point of near despair,[65] however, does not lose hope in trusting God's salutary work, the particular notion of which is expressed with the term "trusting despair."[66] "He makes us such [righteous]," states Luther, "when we believe His Word is such, that is, righteous and true."[67] Luther's statement highlights his view of justification as a relational term to the extent to which the external righteousness of Christ,[68] which justifies a self-accusing person, never becomes the penitent person's own quality.[69]

Luther repudiates the scholastic notion of being righteous in a qualitative sense, and perceives it instead with respect to "through faith" in particular emphasis on the *external* righteousness of God in Christ; that is, *extra nos*. In this context, Luther employs the concept of joyous exchange

---

63. *Römervorlesung*.

64. Lohse, *Martin Luther*, 148.

65. AE 25:258; WA 56:270.6–7.

66. Hamm, *Early Luther*, 97–100. The term "confident doubt" denotes the same concept, which Luther obtained from his "near to grace" (*gratiae propinqua*) experience—*Anfechtung*. Hamm, *Early Luther*, 32, 56.

67. AE 25:211; WA 56:227.5–6.

68. Luther addresses the notion of *extra nos* on Rom. 4:7: "Therefore, I was correct when I said that all our good is outside of us, and this good is Christ, as the apostle says (1 Cor. 1:30): 'God made Him our wisdom, our righteousness, and sanctification, and redemption.' And none of these things are in us except through faith and hope in Him." AE 25:267; WA 56:279.22–24.

69. Hamm, *Early Luther*, 99. Ever since his theological discovery, Luther kept this theological position throughout his life. Regarding Luther's later writing, see Saak, *Luther and Reformation*, 189.

(*Fröhlicher Wechsel* or *commercium admirabile*),⁷⁰ and argues that only those who believe in Christ and are thus in union with him receive Christ's righteousness.⁷¹ The notion of exchange appears throughout his works. In the early *Lectures on Galatians* (1516/17), for instance, Luther underscores that the sins of the one who trusts in Christ are transferred to Christ in this joyous union, and simultaneously Christ's righteousness becomes a Christian's own.⁷² In this exchange, the law is fulfilled; sins are destroyed; and a sinner is reckoned righteous simultaneously.⁷³ Luther clarifies what his theology of justification signifies. No longer are the sins of the Christians theirs in this exchange, nor are they considered sinners in Christ, not in the sense that all sins are already removed from them, but that there is no condemnation against them. Sins still remain in them, but their sins are not imputed for condemnation.⁷⁴

Analogy of Healing

Luther's articulation of justification is well illustrated in the analogy of healing, particularly with respect to faith in the promise of Christ.⁷⁵ The analogy of healing is a classic allusion appearing in the patristic and medieval theologies as well as in scholastic theology.⁷⁶ In his use of the analogy of healing integrated with justification, Luther differentiates *forgiveness* from the *removal* of sin to the extent that the former corresponds to the instantaneous effect of justifying grace, and the latter is a continual effect.⁷⁷

---

70. Glossary, *OHMLT* 644.

71. At the time of composing this lecture, Luther was already aware of the notion of joyous exchange. It is found in his letter to George Spalatin on April 8, 1516. Hamm, *Early Luther*, 101n61. From his early lectures on Galatians (1516/17, published 1519) the notion appears frequently in the *Explanations* (1518), the sermon on *Two Kinds of Righteousness* (1519), and the *Freedom of A Christian* (1520).

72. AE 27:241; WA 2:504.6–12. On Gal. 2:21.

73. "Take note, therefore, of a new righteousness and a new definition of righteousness ... Here it is stated that righteousness is faith in Jesus Christ or the virtue by which one believes in Jesus Christ." AE 27:240–41; WA 2:503.34–37. Luther's notion of God's reckoning of righteousness also appears in the *Dictata*. AE 10:146; WA 55II:177.47–50. See also Rittgers, *Reformation of Suffering*, 90–91.

74. AE 27:227; WA 2:495.8–9.

75. AE 25:39, 40; WA 56:46.15. Rupp, *Righteousness of God*, 169.

76. Lohse, *Martin Luther's Theology*, 76. See also Griffith, "Medical Imagery," 107–12.

77. AE 25:260; WA 56:271.31—272.7.

Luther's View of Purgatory

Prior to his initial discovery of *Anfechtung*, Luther considered the forgiveness of sin equivalent to the complete removal of sin. Only after the discovery Luther found it essential to distinguish between the two. In other words, while one receives true forgiveness *here and now* in the promise of forgiveness, the complete removal of sin still awaits in hope in its continual progress. Here comes Luther's theological logic: the promise is effective at present, and it is thus considered valid and true until the promise is fulfilled. It is valid since a penitent, or a self-accuser, receives forgiveness in certainty through faith. As regards the removal of sin, however, it has begun, is in progress at present, and anticipates its completion.[78]

Associated with the analogy of healing are several themes including imputation, a righteous person and a sinner simultaneously, the notion of "in part" (*partim*) and "entirely" (*totus*), and the concept of "in motion" (*in motu*) that elucidate Luther's theology of justification:

> Now, is he perfectly righteous? No, for he is at the same time both a sinner and a righteous man: a sinner in fact, but a righteous man by the sure imputation and promise of God that He *will continue* to deliver him from sin *until* He has completely cured him. And thus he is entirely healthy in hope, but in fact he is still a sinner; but he has the *beginning of righteousness*, so that he continues more and more always to seek it, yet he realizes that he is always unrighteous.[79]

Luther explicates the concept of imputation that God does not reckon sins but covers them.[80] At this early stage, however, Luther's notion of imputation is still framed in a conditional premise: "For inasmuch as the saints are

---

78. ". . . Either I have never understood, or else the scholastic theologians have not spoken sufficiently clearly about sin and grace . . . [I]n my foolishness I could not understand in which way I should regard myself a sinner like other men and thus prefer myself to no one, even though I was contrite and made confession; for I then felt that all my sins had been taken away and entirely removed, even inwardly . . . Yet God has promised that they are forgiven to those who confess them. Thus I was at war with myself, not knowing that it was a true forgiveness indeed, but that this is nevertheless not a taking away of sin except in hope, that is, that the taking away is to be done, and that by the gift of grace, which begins to take sin away, so that it is not imputed as sin." AE 25:260–61; WA 56:273.3—274.14.

79. AE 25:260; WA 56:272.16–21. Emphases added.

80. AE 25:259–60; WA 56:271.25–27. Also, the term "imputation" is used in a positive sense. "[T]he righteousness of God even without works is imputed to those who believe." AE 25:263; WA 56:276.20–21. Also, On Rom. 12:1, "But be transformed," Luther interprets it with respect to progress in newness of life. AE 25:433; WA 56:441.13–16.

always aware of their sin and seek righteousness from God in accord with His mercy, for this very reason they are always also regarded as righteous by God."[81] Luther seems to set this precondition in the theological framework of God's alien work and God's proper work.[82] The emphasis is laid primarily on the former which leads a sinner in *Anfechtung* to repentance, and subsequently on the latter whereby God justifies a sinner by his imputation. In this respect, Luther's theological articulation makes a pivotal statement, "They [the saints] are actually sinners, but they are righteous by the imputation of a merciful God."[83]

The analogy of healing also illuminates the concept of *simul*. The patient is sick at present, on the one hand, and is well according to the prognosis of the doctor, on the other. The doctor's treatment for healing has already begun, and the patient trusts the doctor's words of prognosis. That is to say, the penitent person is a sinner and righteous at once; a sinner in fact but righteous based on the promise of forgiveness.[84] Luther's paradoxical statement reaffirms the dialectic state of the righteous in justification: "[T]hus he is *entirely* healthy in hope, but in fact he is *still* a sinner."[85]

Partim and *Totus*

Luther's use of the terms "in part" (*partim*) and "entirely" (*totus*) explicates the notion of *simul* from two different angles. The former implies the aspect

---

81. AE 25:258; WA 56:269.25-27. "Therefore if we are always repentant, we are always sinners, *and yet thereby we are righteous and we are justified*; we are in part sinners and in part righteous, that is, we are nothing but penitents." AE 25:434; WA 56:442.20-22. Emphasis added. Luther's notion of "in part" will be discussed in a moment.

82. Earlier in the *Dictata*, Luther already discusses two kinds of God's saving work toward a human being where one experiences God's unexpected and strange work (*opus alienum dei*) of judgment followed by God's proper work (*opus proprium dei*). Rupp, *Righteousness of God*, 146. God's alien work of judgment involves a human being's self-accusation in humility and penitence in self-condemnation in order to have the accused person to be justified and righteous in God's proper work. AE 10:406; WA 55II:435.43-60. Ps. 72:1. Odo of Cluny (d. 942) made a distinction between the work of God (*opus dei*) and that of others (*opus alienum*) including that of the devil, and God uses the work of others for his purpose. Luther seemed to have employed the distinction to articulate his notion of God's "foreign" work in reference to suffering under God's wrath. Viladesau, *Triumph of the Cross*, 114.

83. AE 25:258; WA 56:269.29.

84. AE 25:260; WA 56:272.16-19.

85. AE 25:260; WA 56:272.19-20. Emphases added.

of incompleteness or imperfection in a journey,[86] while the latter indicates wholeness drawn from a theological concept of the communication of attributes (*communicatio idiomatum*) in reference to a whole person (i.e., Christ's one Person and two natures).[87] Unambiguous is Luther's articulation in using both terms in that while each term diverges in perspective, they converge on the notion of a continual progress in motion often expressed in the dialectic of "in hope" and "in fact."

In the illustration of healing, for instance, Luther frames the state of the righteous in the distinction between "in hope" (*in spe*) and "in fact" (*in re*). A penitent Christian, who is entirely healthy in hope, is still a sinner in reality, not as "in part" but "entirely"; thus, "a sinner and righteous at once." In this respect, the dialectic of "in hope" and "in fact" underscores the process of healing which has already begun and anticipates its completion; therefore, a penitent sinner is in the "beginning of righteousness."[88] This progress should not be considered as a process of a qualitative possession, however;[89] it is a continuing operation of God wherein one is "always seeking and striving to be made righteous, even to the hour of death."[90] "This entire life is a time of willing to be righteous, but never achieving it," asserts Luther, "for this happens only in the future life."[91] Acknowledgment of this incomplete progress neither disappoints nor makes him despair even at the moment of a spiritual affliction in *Anfechtung*.[92] Believers are aware in certainty of God's will and intention to leave them in a spiritual battle so that they in fear of God might continue to be always seeking God's gracious imputation in Christ.[93]

As reviewed, the notion of *simul* implies the notion of "progress" or "making progress,"[94] not as a human work for Luther, but as God's work.

---

86. AE 25:433–34; WA 56:441.13—442.22.

87. AE 25:332; WA 56:3438-21. This theological concept developed during the Patristic era, particularly in the fifth century (e.g., the Council of Ephesus (431) and the Council of Chalcedon (451)). On this subject during the Reformation, see Cross, *Communicatio idiomatum*.

88. AE 25:260; WA 56:272.19–20.

89. Rupp, *Righteousness of God*, 183.

90. AE 25:251–52; WA 56:16–21.

91. AE 25:268; WA 56:280.17–18.

92. Luther terms it "trusting despair" (*fiducialis desperatio*). Hamm, *Early Luther*, 97–100.

93. AE 25:268; WA 56:281.5–9. See also Oberman, *Reformation*, 102.

94. Carey, "Luther and the Legacy of Augustine," 42.

That "the righteous shall live by faith" (Romans 1:17) thus means for Luther that one receives by faith the external righteousness of God in a continual progress as "from faith to faith."[95] The notion of progress must be kept in mind until the ultimate destination is reached. The analogies of healing and a journey in the *Lectures on Romans* illustrate affirmatively that one is justified with God's imputation (i.e., the instantaneous effect of the external righteousness of God that corresponds to the forgiveness of sins) and is thus entirely righteous in hope (i.e., "the beginning of righteousness"),[96] but the same person is still a sinner in fact. Meantime, everyone in faith is in a process towards complete healing and in a journey towards the destination (i.e., the continual effect of the external righteousness of God that corresponds to the removal of sin), always in seeking righteousness, and always in confessing unrighteousness before God.[97]

Sermons with the Theme of Three Stages (1516/17)

In his sermon on October 5, 1516, Luther addresses the three stages concerning the Christian life in faith. The early stage begins with baptism; faith in the intermediate stage trusts solely in the word of God; and a Christian in the last stage has willing obedience to accept and follow God's will.[98] In a similar vein, in his sermon on the *Pater Noster* (October 12, 1516)[99] Luther

---

95. AE 25:153; WA 56:173.11–12.

96. AE 25:260; WA 56:272.19–20. Luther's notion of the "beginning of righteousness" (*initium iustitie*), which is found earlier in the *Dictata* (AE 10:267; WA 55II:296.3–4), continues to appear in his later years. In his *Lectures on Isaiah* lectured from July 1527 to February 1530, for instance, Luther stresses that a Christian only begins to have the righteousness of God in this life. "A Christian is not yet perfect, but he is a Christian who *has, that is, who begins to have,* the righteousness of God . . . Therefore, however perfect and absolute the teaching of Christ is that affirms that all our sins belong to Christ, *it is not perfect in our life*. It is enough for us to have begun and to be in the state of reaching after what is before us." Emphases added. AE 17:224 WA 31II:434.26–28, 31–34. Ch 53:5. In addition, Luther uses the term "the beginning of salvation" in an equivalent sense. In his later lectures on Galatians, he notes, "This is the beginning of salvation. By this means [the gospel] we are delivered from sin and justified, and eternal life is granted to us, not for our own merits and works but for our faith, by which we take hold of Christ." AE 26:132; WA 40I:232.21–23. Lectured in 1531/35. Furthermore, Luther employs in the same lectures the analogy of leaven to express the same theological notion, which will be discussed later in this chapter. AE 26:350; WA 40I:537.21–22, 25.

97. AE 25:260; WA 56:272.16–21.

98. Wicks, *Man Yearning for Grace*, 162. WA 1:88.19.

99. WA 1:93.11–32.

addresses three phases in the Christian life, which appears to be similar to the sermon of Jordan of Quedlinburg (d. 1380)[100]: the beginners (*incipientes*); those making progress (*proficientes*); and the perfect (*perfecti*).[101] Luther illustrates that the first phase is likened to the people of Israel who begin a new journey of Exodus; the second phase to the people of Israel's daily journey of spiritual battles in the desert; and the third phase to the saints in heaven—the destination.[102] To a large extent, Luther's sermon on the *Pater Noster* resonates with his *Lectures on Romans*, particularly with respect to the three middle stages in motion drawn from Aristotle's physics, as well as the last stage in perfection.[103]

In his sermon on January 1, 1517, Luther also treats the subject of the removal of sin with the theme of Jesus' circumcision as the sign of healing for original sin. In emphasis on faith, Luther articulates the subject of the righteousness of faith with respect to the Christian life.[104] In brief, the righteousness of God is not only that which comes from outside (*extra nos*) wherein one is considered righteous, but also that which continues to be living, active, and alive through faith alone in a Christian.[105]

Luther's three sermons reviewed above highlight three phases of the Christian life (i.e., beginning, progressing, and arriving in the destination) with emphasis on faith actively engaging in life. As regards Luther's theology of justification, no matter how mature his perspective is, his theology treats two aspects simultaneously: the forgiveness of sin and the removal of sin. Luther does not isolate from forgiveness the notion of a continual effect that corresponds to the removal of sin, partly because Luther likens

---

100. Jordanus de Saxonia, an Augustinian hermit.

101. Saak notes that Luther might have read Jordan's sermon. Saak, *Luther and Reformation*, 57.

102. Saak, *Luther and Reformation*, 232–33. WA 1:93.11-32.

103. AE 25:433–34; WA 56:441.13—442.22. Saak argues that Luther's passive interpretation of the righteousness of God originated from the Aristotelian concept (e.g., the last stage in motion); therefore, it is not part of his Reformation insight or discovery. Saak, *Luther and Reformation*, 198–201. Despite Saak's claim, Luther in fact discusses the passive interpretation more frequently based on the philology of Hebrew language. AE 10:65; WA 55II:76.21–32. In addition, Luther's notion of passivity in which one is made righteous is claimed explicitly in the analogy of healing, that of wedding, and the German mystic notion of the joyous exchange and the soul's passivity before God from Tauler. Wicks, *Man Yearning for Grace*, 144; WA 56:378.13.

104. Wicks, *Man Yearning for Grace*, 159–61.

105. Sermon on February 24, 1517 on Matt. 11:25. Wicks, *Man Yearning for Grace*, 161–62.

the Christian life to a journey towards the destination, also partly because faith, which is imperfect in this journey, continues to grow daily. Meantime, God reckons the imperfect righteousness of faith as perfect righteousness, which appears distinctively in his mature theology (e.g., *Lectures on Galatians*, 1531/35).

Between 1518 and 1520

Sermo de Poenitentia, 1518[106]

Noticeable in 1518 is his greater emphasis on faith that trusts in the *promise* of forgiveness for justification. Luther's attention on faith that trusts in the promise already appears in his *Lectures on Romans* with the analogy of healing. A striking difference in 1518, as well as in his *Lectures on Hebrews* (1517/18),[107] however, is captured in his statement concerning faith and the sacrament. Reinterpreting the effect of the sacrament, Luther asserts in the *Explanations*,[108] also at the Diet of Augsburg (1518), that it is not sacrament, but *faith* in the sacrament that *justifies*.[109] In his *Sermo de poenitentia* written before Easter 1518, Luther addresses the same subject wherein he distinguishes faith from both contrition and the sacrament. Luther's principal emphasis lies on faith that trusts in the word of Christ as true, certain, and sufficient,[110] based on which he further differentiates faith from contrition as well as from participating in the sacrament without faith in the promise.[111]

About this time occurs a remarkable shift in Luther's perspective. Up until now, Luther framed his theology of justification more or less in the premise of repentance or self-accusation.[112] Now, Luther defines faith in reference to *certainty*,[113] underscoring that faith that solely trusts in the

---

106. WA 1:319–24.

107. Wicks, *Man Yearning for Grace*, 212. See also Rittgers, *Reformation of Suffering*, 102–4.

108. AE 31:107; WA 1:544.4–41. Thesis Seven.

109. Lohse, *Martin Luther*, 149; Lohse, *Martin Luther's Theology*, 112; Wicks, *Man Yearning for Grace*, 7.

110. WA 1:324.6–7.

111. WA 1:324.13, 15–17.

112. Hamm, *Early Luther*, 109.

113. Wicks, *Man Yearning for Grace*, 6, 214–15. See also Rex, *Making of Luther*, 69–99.

promise of forgiveness is "the beginning of a process" in the transformation of the whole person.[114] In this theological reorientation, Luther continues to articulate the effect and function of faith. The more radically he articulates it, the more accurately he clarifies it in the light of his theology of justification by faith alone.[115]

Sermon on Two Kinds of Righteousness (1519)[116]

Compared to the previous lectures and sermons, Luther's *Sermon on the Two Kinds of Righteousness*[117] exhibits his further developed articulation on the subject of righteousness with the distinction between the notion of *external*—from without—and *internal*—from within.[118] Luther terms the first righteousness the "alien righteousness," "the righteousness of Christ," or the "infinite righteousness" which accentuates the connotation of the external righteousness given solely by faith.[119] Concerning the second righteousness, he terms it the "proper righteousness," "our own actual righteousness," or "the proper righteousness of God" given from within.[120] The

---

114. Lohse, *Martin Luther*, 163.

115. "Through no attitude on your part will you become worthy, through no works will you be prepared for the sacrament, but through faith alone, for only faith in the word of Christ justifies, makes a person alive, worthy, and well prepared. Without faith all other things are acts of presumption and desperation. The just person lives not by his attitude but by faith . . . When, however, you believe Christ's words, you honor it and thereby are righteous." AE 31:271; WA 2:14.5–7, 11–12. *Proceedings at Augburg* (1518). In the *Freedom of a Christian*, Luther also addresses this subject of honoring Christ by trusting him. AE 31:350. WA 7:53.34–36.

116. *Sermo de duplici iustitia*. WA 2:145–52.

117. Prior to the *Two Kinds of Righteousness*, Luther addressed the same theme in the *Sermon on the Threefold Righteousness* (*Sermo de Triplici Iusticia*, 1518). WA 2:43–47.

118. Luther also distinguishes—not separate—them and claims that there is "one righteousness" (*una iustitia simplex fidei et operum*), as he clarifies later in his Table Talk. "Therefore a separation of the righteousness of faith and of works is not to be allowed, as if the two were different righteousnesses, as commonly taught by the sophists. Otherwise they are justly separated. But there is simply one righteousness of faith and works, just as God and man are one Person and body and soul are one human being. For if you separate the two, faith quickly perishes and works remain—a twofold godless hypocrisy. For if there are good works, they come from faith and are done by faith; if there is faith, it reveals itself and is active. [In] John 15:4–5 it is said: The branch that remains in the vine bears fruit." WA Tr 2:247:10–16. (1534, No. 1886), in Plass, *What Luther Says*, 1231.3919.

119. AE 31:297–99; WA 2:145.9—146.35.

120. AE 31:299–300; WA 2:146.36–147.23. Later in his *Disputation Concerning*

alien (or external) righteousness of Christ is given on two occasions: first, in baptism, and second, whenever one is truly repentant.[121] This is a clue to understanding Luther's theology of justification in general, and this sermon in particular. Using baptismal terminology, Luther describes the first kind of righteousness in two respects: one, an *instantaneous* effect in which all sins are swallowed up "in a moment"; consequently, no sin remains in those who receive Christ's righteousness.[122] The other is a *continual* effect whereby Christ daily removes the old Adam in a Christian.[123]

Unmistakable is Luther's use of baptismal terminology to underscore that it is the work of God, not a human work, which makes one to be righteous before God. As reviewed earlier, Luther places baptism as the point of departure of a spiritual journey, and in baptism one dies with Christ's death and arises with new life in Christ. In explicating this baptismal effect, Luther employs the analogy of marriage in German mysticism, and addresses the concept of joyous exchange in reference to the alien righteousness: "Through faith in Christ, therefore, Christ's righteousness becomes our righteousness and all that he has becomes ours; rather, he himself becomes ours."[124] In the effect of this union, no sin exists in a person baptized with Christ; all that a bridegroom has is transferred to a bride, and vice versa. This is the *instantaneous* effect of the first righteousness which corresponds to the forgiveness of sin by faith alone in the promise of Christ. In the *Freedom of A Christian* (1520)[125] Luther reiterates the instantaneous effect of the righteousness of God, and terms it "complete salvation" and "so great a righteousness that they will need nothing more to become righteous,"[126] affirming that "faith alone, without works, justifies, frees, and saves."[127]

Apparent in the *Sermon on the Two Kinds of Righteousness* is the *continual* effect of the *alien* or external righteousness in the notion of union

---

Justification (1536), Luther articulates the distinction of the two kinds of righteousness and discusses the two kinds of justification—perfect justification by imputation and imperfect justification by works, not by faith. *Disputation* 280, cited in Erich Seeberg, *Luthers Theologie*, 2:407, in Viladesau, *Triumph of the Cross*, 112n30.

121. AE 31:297; WA 2:145.14–15.

122. "This is an infinite righteousness, and one that swallows up all sins in a moment, for it is impossible that sin should exist in Christ." AE 31:298; WA 2:146.12–14.

123. AE 31:299; WA 2:146.32–35.

124. AE 31:297–98; WA 2:145.18–21, 145.31—146.2, 8–9.

125. *Tractatus de libertate christiana*. AE 31:333–77; WA 7:49–73.

126. AE 31:347–48; WA 7:52.12–13, 17–19.

127. AE 31:348; WA 7:52.22–24.

where Christ daily removes the old Adam in the baptized person, as well as whenever one is truly repentant. Later in the *Large Catechism* and in the *Small Catechism* alike,[128] Luther explains it in the section of the "significance" of baptism, as well as the "power and effect" of baptism:

> These two parts, being dipped under the water and emerging from it, point to the power and effect of baptism, which is nothing else than the slaying of the old Adam and the resurrection of the new creature, both of which must continue in us our whole life long. Thus a Christian life is nothing else than a daily baptism, begun once and continuing ever after. For we must keep at it without ceasing, always purging whatever pertains to the old Adam, so that whatever belongs to the new creature may come forth.[129]

In a similar vein, Luther addresses in his 1519 sermon the continual effect of the alien righteousness: "Christ daily drives out the old Adam more and more in accordance with the extent to which faith and knowledge of Christ grow. For alien righteousness is not instilled all at once, but it begins, makes progress, and is finally perfected at the end through death."[130] In this theological discourse, without necessarily adopting the terminology of *simul iustus et peccator*, the sermon alludes to the notion of *simul* where a baptized Christian is both *righteous* in union with Christ through faith, and a *sinner* with the old Adam that still remains. The former corresponds to the instantaneous effect of the external righteousness of God that has begun in baptism whereas the latter accords with the continual effect of the same righteousness in progress in the power and effect of baptism until its completion. In so doing, Luther frames his statement of the continual effect of the alien righteousness of Christ within the three stages of a journey towards the destination.

Luther's emphasis on unconditional justification by faith alone accentuates the significance and effect of the gospel to the extent that faith that trusts the word of God brings one to the complete righteousness of Christ.

---

128. "It signifies that the old creature in us with all sins and evil desires is to be drowned and die through daily contrition and repentance, and on the other hand that daily a new person is to come forth and rise up to live before God in righteousness and purity forever." *Small Catechism* (1529), in *BC²* 360.12; WA 30I:257.18-24.

129. *Large Catechism* (1529), in *BC²* 465.65; WA 30I:220.18-25.

130. Et ita Christus expellit de die in diem magis et magis, secundum quod crescit illa fides et cognitio Christi. Non enim tota simul infunditur, sed incipit, proficit et perficitur tandem in fine per mortem. AE 31:299; WA 2:146.32-35. *Sermon on the Two Kinds of Righteousness*.

This is one of Luther's exemplary theological discourses that address both the *forgiveness* of sin—the *instantaneous* effect of the alien righteousness of God—and the *removal* of sin—the *continual* effect. Luther later terms the dual effects of the external righteousness of God "spiritual justification" (*iustificatio spiritualis*),[131] particularly in the aspect of the healing of sin.[132]

After 1521

We now review the following three works of Luther to trace further development of his theology of justification. Luther's mature theology accentuates the certainty of the gospel of forgiveness wherein faith secures salvation by means of God's imputation. Equally significant in his mature theology is his consistency in emphasis on the continual removal of sin in progress. In this respect, the analogy of leaven, as well as the analogy of healing, not only illustrates the notion of *simul* but also profoundly illuminates the continual effect of the external righteousness of God. In brief, Luther's mature theology of justification continues to maintain the notion of the instantaneous and continual effects of the external righteousness of God, and articulates it particularly in the distinction between law and gospel.

Against Latomus (1521)[133]

In *Against Latomus* written in the Wartburg Castle, Luther treats the subject of a twofold evil—external ("wrath, death, and being accursed") and internal (e.g., "sin and corruption of nature"),[134] and asserts that under grace sin is fully forgiven; therefore, there is no wrath under grace.[135] Here Luther addresses the twofold effect of the alien righteousness, framing it with the distinction of God's grace and God's gift of faith.[136] Luther expounds on the

---

131. AE 34:162; WA 39I:93.8. *Disputation Concerning Justification* (1536).

132. AE 34:156; WA 39I:86.10. AE 34:181; WA 39I:113.11–12.

133. *Rationis Latomianae confutatio.* AE 32:137–260; WA 8:43–128.

134. AE 32:224–28; WA 8:104.22—107.12.

135. AE 32:229; WA 8:107.13–16.

136. "Observe that this faith is the gift of God, which the grace of God obtains for us, and which purging away sin, makes us saved and certain—not because of our works, but because of Christ's—so that we can stand and endure in eternity . . ." AE 32:236; WA 8:112.12–15. See also AE 32:227–28; WA 8:106.20–28. In this context, Luther notes that God's righteousness is his gift (*donum dei*), "namely, faith in Christ" (*fides Christi*). AE

subject of faith with greater respect to the continual effect, and employs the analogy of the leaven to illustrate the process of healing: "Everything is forgiven through grace, but as yet not everything is healed through the gift [of faith]. The gift has been infused, the leaven has been added to the mixture. It works so as to purge away the sin for which a person has already been forgiven . . ."[137] The leaven—the gift of faith—has been added to the dough (i.e., sin is forgiven by grace through faith), and it continues to spread throughout the dough wherein the removal of sin is now in effect in progress. The analogy of leaven appears again in the later *Lectures on Galatians* where Luther presents the leaven itself as Christ, the true object of faith, to which we turn.

Lectures on Galatians (1531/35)[138]

In his *Preface of 1535* to the *Lectures on Galatians*,[139] Luther succinctly notes what the doctrine of justification by faith alone signifies. It is a "faith in Christ"[140] who is "our only righteousness"[141] through whom "we are redeemed from sin, death, and the devil and endowed with eternal life."[142] With a brief introduction of other kinds of righteousness (e.g., political and ceremonial), Luther treats two kinds of righteousness, the theme which he addressed earlier in his 1519 *Sermon on the Two Kinds of Righteousness*.[143]

32:227; WA 8:106.1–2.

137. AE 32:229; WA 8:107.21–23.

138. *Argumentum Epistolae S. Pauli ad Galatas*. AE 26:4—27:144; WA 40I:41.14—40II:184.11. The WA begins with the *Annotationes Martini Lutheri In Epistolam Pauli ad Galatas*, which the AE translates without a designated title. AE 26:3; WA 40I:39.1—40.13.

139. *Commentarius in Epistolam ad Galatas: Praefatio D. Martini Lutheri*. AE 27:145–49; WA 40I:33–36.

140. AE 27:145; WA 40I:33.7.

141. AE 27:149; WA 40I:33.23.

142. AE 27:145; WA 40I:33.19–20.

143. Approaching the subject from a different angle with the distinction of law and gospel, Luther articulates it as active righteousness and passive righteousness. Luther terms the former "the active righteousness of the Law" and the latter "the passive righteousness of Christ," "the righteousness of faith," "Christian righteousness," and "the righteousness of grace, mercy, and the forgiveness of sin." AE 26:4–9; WA 40I:40.14—48.33. Luther also calls it the "most excellent righteousness" since God reckons a sinner righteous by faith alone without works; the righteousness of God that one passively receives. AE 26:4; WA 40I:41.14–16. Luther defines this proper distinction of these two kinds of righteousness as "our theology" (*nostra theologia*). AE 26:7; WA 40I:45.24.

Luther's Perception

The outstanding feature of the later *Lectures on Galatians* is Luther's articulation of the subject with respect to the distinction between law and gospel. This so-called "fundamental hermeneutical presupposition"[144] of Luther highlights the contrast that the law accuses and kills, but the gospel comforts and makes alive. There is no middle ground; one is *either* entirely condemned under the law *or* entirely righteous in the gospel. By the same token, between the two kinds of righteousness there is no middle ground; one is *either* justified entirely by the righteousness of the gospel *or* condemned entirely by that of the law.[145]

In these lectures, Luther treats the subject of the two kinds of righteousness differently from his 1519 sermon. While the latter approaches the subject in the distinction of the external (or alien) righteousness and the internal (or proper) righteousness, the former employs the distinction between law and gospel. This is not a hypothetical speculation or theory, however. It is Luther's Reformation theology fundamentally rooted in his reading of St Paul's epistle and his experience of *Anfechtungen*.[146] Under the law that demands perfect obedience towards God and accuses any shortfalls,[147] Luther in his early years struggled with such an image of God.[148] Having discovered the gospel of faith in Christ, Luther exhorts afflicted consciences to pay close attention, not to their sins, but to the gospel wherein all their sins are transferred to Christ.[149] That is, in the righteousness of Christ all are completely dead to the law and thus to sin,[150] the teaching of which Luther avows: "This is our theology."[151]

In this theology, Christ is the only rescuer of wounded consciences from the accusation of the law and sins.[152] Against the law and the devil Christ protects them by becoming the law to accuse the law, sin to nullify the power of sin, and death to conquer death.[153] With Christ a Christian is

---

144. Kolb, *Martin Luther*, 50.
145. AE 26:9; WA 40I:48.30–31. AE 26:203; WA 40I:329.22–23.
146. AE 26:10; WA 40I:49.31–34.
147. AE 26:148; WA 40I:257.22–23.
148. AE 26:154; WA 40I:265.17–19.
149. AE 26:132; WA 40I:232.18–20. AE 26:162; WA 40I:276.18–19.
150. AE 26:158; WA 40I:271.29–31.
151. AE 26:161; WA 40I:275.17.
152. AE 26:160–61; WA 40I:274.27–34. For those assaulted by the accusation of the devil, Luther stresses the assuring righteousness of Christ. AE 26:162; WA 40I:276.29–32.
153. "While He is the Law, He is liberty; while He is sin, He is righteousness; and while He is death, He is life." AE 26:163; WA 40I:278.24–25.

not only crucified but also made alive yet through faith.[154] In this union, Christ lives in a believer, and vice versa.[155] Through faith alone they become "as one person."[156] Luther describes it as "a double life," for Christians possess simultaneously both their own life and an "alien" life—the former being "a mask of life" and the latter being an alien yet true life, namely, "Christ." Therefore, "Christ . . . is truly my Life," affirms Luther.[157]

For Luther, the "true meaning of justification" is living by faith in Christ who has abolished the righteousness of the law,[158] who has rescued a sinner from sin and justified, and who has obtained eternal life, which *is* "the beginning of salvation."[159] In this passive righteousness of faith, God reckons a sinner who believes in Christ righteous. Faith and God's imputation are thus the two integral parts of Christian righteousness.[160] Luther's statement in these lectures that the righteousness of faith is the beginning of salvation that awaits its completion resonates, to a certain extent, with his 1519 *Sermon on the Two Kinds of Righteousness*. Luther's mature theology accentuates that God's imputation secures the assurance of the gospel. Faith is still weak; therefore, Luther terms it "imperfect righteousness" (*iustitia imperfecta*).[161] By God's imputation, however, what is imperfect is now reckoned perfect righteousness. Luther reiterates: "God reckons this [righteousness of] *imperfect faith* as perfect righteousness for the sake of Christ, His Son, who suffered for the sins of the world and in whom I begin to believe.[162] . . . I begin to take hold of Christ; and on His account God

---

154. AE 26:165; WA 40I:281.19–20, 23–24.

155. AE 26:167; WA 40I:283.32.

156. AE 26:168; WA 40I:285.24–26.

157. AE 26:170; WA 40I:287.28–29, 288.24–26.

158. AE 26:172; WA 40I:290.33—291.13.

159. AE 26:132; WA 40I:232.21–23.

160. AE 26:229–30; WA 40I:364.11–24. "We conclude, therefore, that righteousness does indeed begin through faith and that through it we have the first fruits of the Spirit. But because faith is weak, it is not perfected without the imputation of God. Hence faith begins righteousness, but imputation perfects it until the day of Christ." AE 26:230; WA 40I:364.24–28.

161. AE 26:232; WA 40I:367.19–22.

162. [Q]uod Deus reputat *istam imperfectam fidem* ad iustitiam perfectam propter Christum, filium suum, passum pro peccatis mundi, in quem coepi credere. AE 26:231; WA 40I:366.29–30, 367.11. Emphases added in the text and the footnote.

reckons *imperfect righteousness* as perfect righteousness and sin as not sin, even though it really is sin."[163]

With greater emphasis on God's imputation, Luther's mature theology continues to maintain the aspect of the continual—rather *continuous*—effect of the alien righteousness of God. The continual effect in Christ that "begins, makes progress, and is finally perfected at the end through death"[164] is now simply described as the "daily coming of Christ" which augments the notion of the joyous exchange.[165] Luther reaffirms:

> . . . He [Christ] comes to us spiritually every day, causing us to grow in faith and in our knowledge of Him. Thus the conscience takes hold of Christ more perfectly day by day; and day by day the law of flesh and sin, the fear of death, and whatever other evils the Law brings with it are diminishing . . .[166] He comes to us *spiritually without interruption* and *continually smothers and kills* these things in us . . .[167] But Christ comes *spiritually as we gradually acknowledge and understand more and more* what has been granted to us by Him.[168]

The analogy of the leaven clearly amplifies the comforting and assuring effect of the gospel, and explicitly accentuates the continual effect in progress:

---

163. Propter quem reputat Deus *iustitiam imperfectam* pro iustitia perfecta et peccatum pro non peccato quod tamen vere peccatum est. AE 26:232; WA 40I:367.19-21. Emphases added in the text and the footnote. See also AE 26:230; WA 40I:364.25-28. Luther underscores that faith, or we in faith, cannot take hold of Christ perfectly. AE 26:349; WA 40I:535.26-30.

164. "Christ daily drives out the old Adam more and more in accordance with the extent to which faith and knowledge of Christ grow. For alien righteousness is not instilled all at once, but it begins, makes progress, and is finally perfected at the end through death." AE 31:299; WA 2:146.32-24.

165. "But it is always encouraged by the daily coming of Christ." AE 26:349 WA 40I:536.25-26.

166. AE 26:350; WA 40I:536.27-30.

167. AE 26:350; WA 40I:537.33-34. Emphasis added.

168. AE 26:351; WA 40I:538.30-33. Emphasis added. "In addition, Christ comes spiritually every day; through the Word of the Gospel faith also comes every day; and when faith is present, our custodian, with his gloomy and grievous task, is also forced to yield." AE 26:351; WA 40I:538.33-34. "With His own blood, to be sure, He redeemed and sanctified all men just once. But because we are not yet perfectly pure but remnants of sin still cling to our flesh and the flesh wars against the spirit, therefore He comes spiritually every day; day by day He completes the time set by the Father more and more, abrogating and abolishing the Law." AE 26:360; WA 40I:550.25-29.

> Thus we have received the first fruits of the Spirit (Rom. 8:23), and the leaven hidden in the lump; the whole lump has not yet been leavened, but *it is beginning to be leavened. If I look at the leaven, I see nothing but the leaven;* but if I look at the mass of the lump, there is not merely the leaven anymore. *Thus if I look at Christ, I am completely holy and pure, and I know nothing at all about the Law;* for Christ *is* my leaven.[169]

Leavening has certainly begun but is not completed yet. When looking at the entire dough, one has no profound assuring comfort of justification or righteousness. When looking at the leaven through faith, however, the same person finds *certainty* of justification and righteousness. Thus, fixing his eyes on the leaven, Luther contends, "I refuse to look at anything except this Christ."[170]

Disputation Concerning Justification (1536)[171]

Luther in this disputation discusses his theology of justification in reference to original sin before and after baptism. As far as the substance of original sin (*peccatum originale*) is concerned, it still remains after baptism; therefore, the removal of sin is required; but as far as God's imputation is concerned, it is already removed in Christ.[172] Unambiguous is Luther's logic: since original sin remains until the moment of death,[173] necessary is daily healing of sin. No human works can cure this spiritual condition; it is faith that heals, for "faith alone justifies, alone saves, and leads to the kingdom";[174] therefore, "justification is healing for sin."[175] In this respect, Luther terms his theology "spiritual theology" (*theologia spiritualis*) and the two kinds of righteousness "spiritual justification" (*iustificatio spiritualis*).[176] As if recall-

---

169. AE 26:350; WA 40I:537.21–25. Emphases added.

170. AE 26:182; WA 40I:304.9–10.

171. *Die Disputation de iustificatione*. AE 34:151–96; WA 39I:82–126. See the title in WA 39I:vii, 78.

172. AE 34:181; WA 39I:112.8–9.

173. AE 34:180; WA 39I:111.20–22.

174. AE 34:190; WA 39I:121.31–32.

175. [Iustificatio] est enim sanatio peccati. AE 34:156; WA 39I:86.10. *Fourth Disputation [Concerning the passage Rom. 3:28]*, Thesis Twenty-nine. See also AE 34:181; WA 39I:113.11–12.

176. AE 34:168–69; WA 39I:99.24–31. AE 34:162; WA 39I:93.8. On Ps. 90:3 (1534/35), Luther also notes, "But because the doctors of the church usually took into

ing his *Sermon on the Two Kinds of Righteousness* (1519),[177] as well as the *Lectures on Galatians* (1531/35), Luther in this disputation reiterates:

> Forgiveness of sins is not a matter of a passing work or action, but of perpetual duration. For the forgiveness of sins begins in baptism and remains with us all the way to death, until we arise from the dead, and leads us into life eternal. So we live continually under the remission of sins. Christ is truly and constantly the liberator from our sins, is called our Savior, and saves us by taking away our sins. *If, however, he saves us always and continually, then we are constantly sinners*. Since we are daily sinners, sin is also now necessarily in our mortal body.[178]
>
> On no condition is sin a passing phase, but *we are justified daily* by the unmerited forgiveness of sins and by the justification of God's mercy. *Sin remains, then, perpetually in this life*, until the hour of the last judgment comes and then *at last we shall be made perfectly righteous*.[179]

With the analogy of a journey Luther asserts that "a man who is justified is not yet a righteous man, but is in the very movement or journey toward righteousness."[180] Luther underscores the notion of *simul iustus et peccator*, and reinforces the continual effect of the alien—external—righteousness: "Therefore, whoever is justified is still a sinner; and yet he is considered fully and perfectly righteous by God who pardons and is merciful."[181]

As reviewed, Luther's theology of justification was in a long process of development from the notion of self-accusation to God's imputation

---

account only carnal considerations and were unable to apply Scripture to those more latent and *spiritual corruptions* of human nature, they also deal quite carelessly with the most important doctrines of Scripture. We shall let them have their way. But we shall be guided by the true and real sense of the Hebrew text." AE 13:95; WA 40III:515.21–25. Emphasis added.

177. A sinner forgiven is righteous in two kinds of righteousness: "inward righteousness" before God and "outward righteousness" before neighbor. Using the Aristotelian terminology, Luther interprets the former as the "efficient cause of justification" and the latter as the "effective cause." AE 34:161–62; WA 39I:92.26—93.16.

178. AE 34:164; WA 39I:94.37—95.8. Emphasis added.

179. AE 34:167; WA 39I:98.7–11. Emphases added.

180. AE 34:152; WA 39I:83.16–17.

181. AE 34:152–53; WA 39I:83.18–19. By his expression of "considered fully and perfectly righteous," Luther refers to a twofold aspect of the righteousness of Christ: first, it covers Christians from God's wrath and judgment like an "umbrella" that protects; second, the righteousness of Christ is from outside (*extra nos*) as a gift, not as a quality of virtue. AE 34:153; WA 39I:83.22–25.

that reckons the imperfect righteousness of faith as perfect righteousness in the distinction of law and gospel. With several different features in this development, three aspects remain in *continuity*: first, Luther's theological reorientation constantly views justification not as a human work or merits but as God's work by means of the gift of faith alone. Second, Luther's theology of justification is not a speculative theology or theory but an existential hermeneutical theology that interacts with a human being living in spiritual afflictions in daily newness of life. Third, Luther discusses the subject of justification not only with regard to an instantaneous effect of the external righteousness of God with respect to the forgiveness of sin (i.e., baptism), but also with regard to a continual effect in progress with respect to the removal of sin (i.e., whenever one is truly repentant).[182] Carey rightly comments:

> Thus justification is always a process according to Luther's theology, but in his mature thought the goal of the process, the righteousness of God in Christ, is already present in us by faith—and not, as in his early lectures, by a faith that believes the accusation in the word of God and agrees that we deserve damnation. Rather, faith means that we gladly take hold of a word of grace, through which we receive nothing less than Christ himself. It is a faith that finds righteousness not hidden under condemnation but in the love of the bridegroom whom it joyfully embraces, assured by his promise that it can sing, "My beloved is mine and I am his."[183]

Justification is God's gracious act towards a sinful human being in faith, and righteousness is God's gift of grace. The significance of this divine act is God's imputation in which a sinner is reckoned fully righteous in Christ. Yet this is the beginning of righteousness; a Christian, who is *already entirely and perfectly* healthy in faith that trusts in the promise, *continues to be healed until* full restoration is made.

---

182. Luther's notion of progress in his theology of justification by faith alone, however, is different from the notion of a qualitative progress. Nor is it similar to that of John Wesley. Hall, "Theology of the Cross," 73–80.

183. Carey, "Luther and the Legacy of Augustine," 54. See also Lohse's comments with acknowledgement of Luther's theology of justification that involves the aspect of renewal. Lohse, *Martin Luther's Theology*, 262–64. Hamm also underlines the same perspective. "... the application of the vocabulary of mysticism offers us the chance to understand Luther's Christology and theology of justification not only in their forensic sense (as in the tradition of Anselm of Canterbury) but also in their holistic relevance to life, experience, and piety." Hamm, *Early Luther*, 232. See also Rittgers, *Reformation of Suffering*, 109–10.

Luther's Perception

Four Significances of the Continual Effect in Luther's Theology of Justification

This section draws particular attention to four significances of the continual effect of the external righteousness of God, which sets out the frame of reference for further discussions in the following section. The first and foremost significance is that the notion of a continual effect in progress implies the anticipation of its final destination or completion.[184] Luther employs two analogies—spiritual journey and healing—to underline the primary significance. The analogy of a spiritual journey illustrates three reference points: first, the point of departure through baptism; second, continuation in moving toward the destination; and third, eternal rest in the final destination.[185] Similarly, the analogy of healing also reinforces the concept of the three reference points, the last of which is the notion of complete health.[186] The final reference point in both analogies signifies the consummation of what is hoped for on the Last Day—being fully and entirely righteous before God with the righteousness of Christ. Justification by faith alone that begins in baptism is the beginning of righteousness.[187] While the battle with the old Adam ends at death, death itself is *not* the destination *until* the perfect righteousness of Christ imputed to the believers in Christ by faith is fully revealed on the Day of Resurrection of the dead.[188]

---

184. As discussed above, this aspect appears throughout Luther's works. As regards this perspective of Luther's in the *Dictata*, see also Ozment, *Homo Spiritualis*, 134–38.

185. AE 11:494; WA 55II:971.2293-95. See also Luther's three sermons (October 5 and 12, 1516, and January 1, 1517) discussed earlier under "Sermons with the Theme of Three Stages" in this chapter.

186. "Thus original sin is restless even in us, but since we are under the doctor, under Christ, and live mindful of our illness, we shall be blessed. For that poison decreases more and more from day to day and we always wipe out, wash, and cleanse the poison, with the poison becoming less until it is totally extinguished by fire in the judgment. In the meantime we endure the cure of a living physician, that is, of Christ. We hear the Word, pray, read. As much as we can we recover through the Word." AE 34:182; WA 39I:113.20-26. Also, AE 34:156; WA 39I:86.10. *Disputation Concerning Justification* (1536).

187. Wicks, *Man Yearning for Grace*, 70. AE 10:267; WA 55II:296.3-4. See also AE 25:260; WA 56:272.21.

188. AE 31:358; WA 7:59.34-60.1. *The Freedom of A Christian* (1520). By the same token, God's imputation is required until the Day of Christ. AE 26:230; WA 40I:364.24-28. *Lectures on Galatians* (1531/35). In the *Explanations* (1518) as well as in the Leipzig Debate, Luther argues that souls in purgatory continue to sin in fear, and thus suffer due to a lack of trust in Christ.

Luther's View of Purgatory

The notion of the final destination lays out a theological framework within which the distinction of "in fact" (*in re*—here and now) and "in hope" (*in spe*—there in the consummation) plays a key role in Luther's understanding of justification. For Luther, as Carey rightly comments, what shall be seen and obtained at the final destination is already present here and now[189] insofar as God's imputation of grace is in effect. Luther's theological assertion of God's imputation, however, does not fail to acknowledge that there is still more to come on the Day of Christ.[190] In Luther's theology God's eternal decree remains to be pronounced on the Last Day while it is present here and now in certainty through faith alone that trusts in the promise of Christ. Luther's notion of postmortem torment in purgatory alludes to this process toward the destination reoriented in his theology of justification.

Second, the notion of a continual effect in Luther's theology of justification refers to a continual growth in faith. Luther denies the theology of *habitus* which claims that a qualitative disposition of a believer satisfies God who demands righteousness, and asserts instead the theology of justification by faith that trusts in the promise of Christ. In Luther's theological reorientation is an irreversible shift between what was taught to be the cause of justification (i.e., quality) and what he discovered (i.e., faith). Nothing is claimed to be good as far as a qualitative disposition of a human being is concerned, for what is truly good comes only from outside as a gift of God, namely, Christ.[191] Just as grace is not a quality or disposition in oneself but a gift that comes from God, so is righteousness that one receives in passivity by faith alone. That a Christian in union with Christ, therefore, possesses the righteousness of Christ means that Christ, while living in a Christian, still owns righteousness, in a strict sense.[192] In this respect, justification for Luther is not a qualitative term but a relational term.[193] This distinction between the increase of a qualitative virtue and the increase in

---

189. Carey, "Luther and the Legacy of Augustine," 54.

190. Cf. Saak claims that in Luther's justification by faith alone God's decree of salvation to be pronounced on the day of the ultimate consummation is "collapsed into a temporal, knowable pronouncement based on faith." Saak, *Luther and Reformation*, 222.

191. AE 25:267; WA 56:279.22–24.

192. Bayer, *Living By Faith*, 68.

193. Hamm, *Early Luther*, 99. Luther's analogy of fire and iron also illustrates his theology of justification in a relational term in that Christ's righteousness, which is transferred to a human being, never becomes part of human nature or quality. Hamm, *Early Luther*, 212–13. See also Kolb, *Martin Luther*, 79.

faith is critical in understanding how Luther perceived purgatory in his theology of justification. Souls suffering in purgatory primarily require the infusion of grace in order for them to endure the cross and increase in faith and love in Christ (e.g., the *Explanations* and the *Leipzig Debate*). This process in purgatory has no connotation of quality but that of relation with Christ in faith.

Third, the notion of a continual effect signifies Luther's notion of the imperfect righteousness of faith. In the Aristotelian notion, a "motion" signifies a certain act that has begun which is still incomplete, and indicates a process, standing between two reference points simultaneously (i.e., the point of departure and the point of arrival). In the *Dictata*, Luther integrates the Aristotelian concept of motion into his theology of justification, and states that a person in self-accusation in humility is simultaneously between the two spiritual reference points—being sinful and being forgiven.[194] In the *Lectures on Romans*, Luther further asserts that just as nothing stands still but is continuously moving forward in a spiritual movement of progress, so is the state of the righteous always being penitent and always being justified by faith alone.[195] From the same perspective Luther understands Revelation 22:11 "Let him who is righteous still be justified."

Luther's mature theology continues to maintain the continual effect in progress. The analogy of the leaven in the later *Lectures on Galatians* (1531/35) signifies both the instantaneous and the continual effects of justifying grace. Within the distinction between law and gospel, the instantaneous effect of the gospel reinforces Luther's theology of justification to secure the *certainty* of perfect righteousness in a journey toward the eternal destination, and stresses that without God's imputation the righteousness of faith is nothing but imperfect.[196] Unequivocal is Luther's profound assertion that the righteousness of faith is imperfect righteousness, but God reckons it as perfect righteousness. Luther's intense emphasis on the effect of the gospel in which a sinner is entirely righteous does *not* eliminate the aspect of a *continual* effect in his theology of justification. With these two distinguished effects—instantaneous and continual—with respect to forgiveness and the removal of sin respectively, Luther maintains his notion of *simultaneity*—"righteous and a sinner at once." Luther thus asserts that "a

---

194. AE 11:494–95; WA 55II:971.2294–99.

195. By this statement, Luther refers to Bernard of Clairvaux. AE 25:433–34; WA 56:441.13—442.22.

196. AE 26:230; WA 40I:364.24–28.

man *who is justified* is not yet a righteous man, but *is in* the very movement or journey toward righteousness."[197]

Luther's notion of purgatory is indispensably pertinent to that of the imperfect righteousness of faith in a continual process. Among the three types of dying souls in the *Explanations* (1518), for instance, Luther understands purgatory with respect to faith in the sense that a soul dying with imperfect faith departs for purgatory in order to continue to grow in faith and love in Christ.[198] By the time Luther affirms in his mature theology that the imperfect righteousness of faith is reckoned as perfect righteousness by God's imputation (1531),[199] Luther has already accepted the postmortem condition of souls in peaceful rest in replacement of the notion of postmortem torment (1525/26).[200]

Fourth, Luther's notion of continual progress is intertwined with that of a spiritual journey of the cross. Principally, Luther's theology of justification presupposes a human condition of *Anfechtung*.[201] Prior to God's proper work in the effect of the gospel, God's alien work in the law demands perfection and brings judgment. In this respect, the *tentatio* of suffering and affliction is quintessential in understanding a spiritual journey. Luther himself experienced in the cloister such spiritual afflictions as "near despair,"[202] and termed it God's alien work to judge, accuse, and condemn, which brings one to humiliation[203] for justification. The term "trusting despair" underlines Luther's dynamic notion of spiritual afflictions in the sphere of justification.[204] Until reaching the ultimate destination, every step in newness of life is likened to a difficult path of journeying such as that of the people of Israel in the desert.[205]

---

197. AE 34:152; WA 39I:83.16–17. *Disputation Concerning Justification* (1536). Emphases added.

198. AE 31:131–32; WA 1:559.11–37.

199. AE 26:232; WA 40I:367.19–22.

200. AE 15:147; WA 20:160.26–29.

201. AE 27:22; WA 40II:25.23–26.

202. Brecht, *Martin Luther*, 1:82; Hamm, *Early Luther*, 42.

203. AE 10:406; WA 55II:435.43–60. Ps. 72:1.

204. Hamm, *Early Luther*, 32, 56.

205. Saak, *Luther and Reformation*, 232–33. Sermon on the *Pater Noster* (October 12, 1516). In a broad spectrum, the late medieval consolation literature (e.g., *Consolatorium theologicum*, 1509) by Johannes von Dambach (d. 1372) and *De consolatione theologiae* (1418) by Jean Gerson (d. 1429)) treats the subject of suffering as a divine instrument with which one is led to heaven. See Rittgers, *Reformation of Suffering*, 55–62.

Luther's notion of postmortem torment alludes to this spiritual battle. In describing the torment of souls in purgatory, Luther seems to recollect his former experiences of *Anfechtungen* where he felt stretched out with Christ suffering on the cross. For Luther purgatory is a spiritual battle in *Anfechtung* with bearing the cross in the sense that souls in purgatory suffer dreadful fear to grow in faith and love in Christ. Luther not only understood this spiritual *tentatio* as "the cross,"[206] but also likened the *entire life* of a Christian life to *enduring the cross*.[207] These four significances of the continual effect in Luther's theology of justification are the key notions within which Luther perceived purgatory, to which subject we now turn for further discussions.

LUTHER'S VIEW OF PURGATORY IN JUSTIFICATION BY FAITH ALONE

Overview

The *Ninety-five Theses* exhibit Luther's disputations against contemporary religious practices that accommodate a way to bypass the punishments of purgatory by means of indulgences. Unequivocal is Luther's warning that such widely accepted practices of indulgences which claim redemption of souls from purgatory are not only spiritually dangerous but also pastorally harmful.[208] In response, Luther contended with several disputations on the subject of newness of life in faith,[209] which include that, first, the entire Christian life is in the continuation of repentance; second, one is justified, not by the sacrament, but by faith in the sacrament; third, the efficacy of the papal power has no jurisdiction over the souls in purgatory except for

---

206. Hamm, *Early Luther*, 44.

207. Rupp, *Righteousness of God*, 207, 208, 210.

208. Thesis Forty-nine notes, "[P]apal indulgences are . . . very harmful if they [Christians] lose their fear of God because of them." AE 31:29–30; WA 1:235.34. Thesis Ninety-five also echoes Luther's concern. AE 31:33; WA 1:238.20–21. Prior to composing the *Ninety-five Theses*, Luther addressed the same concern. In a series of sermons on the Ten Commandments, especially on February 24, 1517, for instance, Luther notes that security and freedom associated with indulgences are dangerous. WA 1:138.12—141.38, in Saak, *Luther and the Reformation*, 279. Thesis Fourteen–Thesis Seventeen, Aland, "Sermon on Indulgence and Grace, 1518," 65–66. See also Thesis Fifty-eight in the *Explanations*. AE 31:220; WA 1:610.21–23. AE 31:128–30; WA 1:557.33—558.18.

209. Hamm, *Early Luther*, 105–6.

intercession in their behalf; and fourth, the canonical laws are inapplicable both to the dying and to the souls in purgatory.

In the *Explanations*, Luther debates in defense the subject of purgatory, and attempts to answer the question as to what punishments souls suffer in purgatory. Prior to his disputations, Luther admits that he has a lack of "experience" to discuss the subject.[210] He then lays out his premise and arguments within the theological framework of his theology of justification. Luther does not deny that souls in purgatory suffer other punishments,[211] but he contends that purgatory is not merely "a workshop of punishment."[212] In a strict sense, souls in purgatory suffer, not the penalty that they incurred prior to death for the incompletion of satisfaction, but the dread and fear due to a lack of faith that trusts in God.[213] The increase of grace is the only solution for the souls in purgatory whereby faith and love in Christ continue to grow to the extent to which they willingly accept their sufferings as God's will to bear the cross.

As regards the quest of how Luther accommodates both the notion of purgatory and justification by faith alone, the following section examines the *Explanations* based on the following premises: first, compared to his earlier lectures, the *Explanations* demonstrates Luther's advancement in his theology of justification, to a certain extent; second, in the *Explanations* Luther explicitly addresses his theses concerning the punishments of purgatory and treats the subject intensely; and third, until his attacks on the doctrine of purgatory (1521/22), if not immediately after his conviction about the papacy as the Antichrist, Luther to a large extent continues to hold his view of purgatory presented in the *Explanations*, and in this respect, the current examination excludes the *Leipzig Debate* since its content on the subject of purgatory mirrors that of the *Explanations*.

In examining the *Explanations*, we also acknowledge that, first, the *Explanations* consist in the major theses (e.g., Theses One to Four) and the proposals (e.g., Theses Five to Ninety-five);[214] second, Luther treats the subject of purgatory as part of his theological proposals or opinions in an academic setting and not as doctrine; and third, as far as the subject of the punishments of purgatory is concerned, Luther acknowledges that it is one

210. AE 31:123; WA 1:554.15-22.
211. AE 31:178; WA 1:586.12-13.
212. AE 31:135; WA 1:561.28-29.
213. AE 31:141-42; WA 1:565.7-49.
214. *From Conflict to Communion*, 26.22.

of the subjects that are "debatable" and also "dubious," to a certain extent.[215] Within these premises and acknowledgment, the following section examines the *Explanations* to find the way in which Luther perceived purgatory and articulated the subject in the framework of his theology of justification.

Justification by Faith Alone in the *Explanations*

The section limits the examination of the *Explanations* to four theses—Seven, Thirty-seven, Thirty-eighty, and Fifty-eight—to validate that the *Explanations* are a qualified primary source for the examination of Luther's perception of purgatory in light of his theology of justification by faith alone.[216]

Thesis Seven: *Fides Sacramenti Iustificat*[217]

In Thesis Seven,[218] Luther addresses the subject of faith that solely trusts in the promise of forgiveness, and explains it with the notion of a twofold work of God—alien and proper—on the basis of the distinction between law and gospel. In the former, a Christian experiences God's hiddenness in *Anfechtung*, and in the latter the same person receives certainty of forgiveness by faith alone. In reference to God's unexpected and alien operation for salvation that King David experienced (Psalm 18:15), for instance,[219] Luther states: "I declare: When God begins to justify a man, he first of all condemns him; him whom he wishes to raise up, he destroys; him whom he wishes to heal, he smites; and the one to whom he wishes to give life, he kills."[220] This *Anfechtung* or *tentatio* in which one feels smitten, destroyed, and even killed in a spiritual agony is an acute spiritual temptation wherein one experiences condemnation under God's wrath and *uncertainty* about

---

215. AE 31:123; WA 1:554.15–22.

216. Luther prepared the *Explanations* in the winter of 1517/18. Lohse notes that it is recognized as Luther's first authentic Reformation writing. "This [the *Explanations*] has properly been referred to as Luther's first true Reformation writing. The significance of the *Explanations* does not lie in their external form, which simply follows the *Ninety-five Theses* point-for-point, but rather in their content: Luther's new understanding of grace, the sacraments, faith, justification, and ecclesiastical authority is much more clearly and sharply presented here than in the *Ninety-five Theses*." Lohse, *Martin Luther*, 125.

217. "Faith in the Sacrament Justifies."

218. AE 31:98–107; WA 1:539.32—545.9.

219. AE 31:99; WA 1:540.16–18.

220. AE 31:99; WA 1:540.8–10.

the presence of grace.²²¹ As if recalling his experience, Luther describes this *tentatio* that "man [in *Anfechtung*] knows so little about his justification that he believes he is very near condemnation."²²² In this judgment and condemnation, however, is "the beginning of salvation."²²³ One who repents with "true contrition of heart and humility of spirit"²²⁴ receives the "peace of conscience"²²⁵ in the certainty of forgiveness through the words of absolution.²²⁶

Furthermore, with the analogy of healing Luther presents Christ as the one who "justifies and heals," and affirms that by faith alone one is justified and healed:

> The Lord causes his saints to marvel in such a way that no one would have confidence in the one who justifies and heals him, if he did not believe that he was justified and healed; just as the sick man would not believe that the doctor cuts his body out of a desire to heal his infirmity, if he were not so persuaded by good friends.²²⁷

Laying a great emphasis on the gift of faith that trusts in the word of promise,²²⁸ Luther further states, "Therefore, we are justified by faith, and by faith also we receive peace, not by works, penance, or confessions."²²⁹ Luther makes a final remark: "Therefore it is not the sacrament, but faith in the sacrament, that justifies,"²³⁰ the view against which Cajetan warns later at his interview with Luther during the Diet of Augsburg,²³¹ which is then condemned in the bull *Exsurge Domine*. Prior to that, Luther's statement

---

221. AE 31:99, 100; WA 540.8–10, 31.

222. AE 31:100, WA 1:540.30–31.

223. AE 31:99; WA 1:540.18–19.

224. AE 31:99; WA 1:540.24–25.

225. AE 31:100; WA 1:541.5.

226. "For faith born of this word [of absolution] will bring peace of conscience... For you will have peace only as long as you believe in the word of that one who promised... Christ is our peace, but only through faith." AE 31:100; WA 1:541.5–9.

227. AE 31:104–5; WA 1:543.27–30.

228. "For the remission of sin and the gift of grace are not enough; one must also believe that one's sin has been remitted... So great a matter is the word of Christ and man's faith in him." AE 31:104; WA 1:543.23–24. AE 31:105; WA 1:543.40—544.1.

229. AE 31:105; WA 1:544.7–8.

230. Oportet enim accedentem credere, deinde non sacramentum sed fides sacramenti iustificat. AE 31:107; WA 1:544.40–41.

231. Olivier, *Trial of Luther*, 51; Wicks, *Cajetan Responds*, 23.

reappears in his *Sermo de poenitentia* (1518) where he reaffirms that faith takes the promise of God as true, and also that faith alone justifies.

Thesis Thirty-Seven: *Unio cum Christo*

In Thesis Thirty-seven,[232] Luther addresses the subject of union with Christ (*unio cum Christo*). Luther alleges that both "to be a Christian" and "to possess Christ" are inseparable acts in which one receives "all the benefits of Christ."[233] With the notion of joyous exchange Luther asserts that Christians receive Christ's righteousness "through the unity of the Spirit by faith in him," and that all their sins are "swallowed up in him."[234] Luther's statement is parallel to his *Sermon on the Two Kinds of Righteousness* which would be composed about a year later (1519) in two respects: terminology and scriptural references. In his 1519 sermon, Luther reasserts the notion of joyous exchange where Christ's righteousness and a Christian's sins are exchanged, the notion of which he notes: "This is an infinite righteousness, and one that swallows up all sins in a moment."[235] Luther's emphasis in the *Explanations* lies clearly on the same theological perspective where he says, "Indeed, this most pleasant participation in the benefits of Christ and joyful changes of life do not take place *except by faith*."[236] In brief, with the notion of union with Christ Luther contends that both to be a Christian and to possess Christ are fundamentally interrelated, and with the analogy of joyous exchange he highlights the way in which a Christian receives the benefits of Christ.

---

232. AE 31:189–91; WA 1:593.3—593.38.

233. AE 31:189–90; WA 1:593:7–8. Of this union Luther says, "By faith in Christ, a Christian is made one spirit and one body with Christ." AE 31:190; WA 1:593.14–15.

234. AE 31:190; WA 1:593.22-24. ". . . by means of faith our sins become no longer ours but Christ's upon whom God placed the sins of all of us . . . All the righteousness of Christ becomes ours." AE 31:190; WA 1:593.25–28.

235. To augment the statement, Luther employs the passages of Scripture among which three are particularly identical between the *Explanations* and his 1519 sermon: Gen. 2:24 and Eph. 5:31–32 with respect to a union with Christ, and Rom. 8:32 with respect to receiving Christ's benefits in this union. AE 31:297–98; WA 2:145.18–21, 145.3—146.2, 8–9.

236. AE 31:190–91; WA 1:593.30–31. Emphasis added.

Thesis Thirty-Eight: *Fides Verbi Christi Iustificat*[237]

Thesis Thirty-eight[238] demonstrates a certain development in Luther's perspective between the *Ninety-five Theses* and the *Explanations*. In the *Ninety-five Theses*, Luther initially acknowledged "the papal remission and blessings" as "the proclamation of the divine remission";[239] however, in the *Explanations* he retrieves his stance and refurbishes his thesis in accordance with his theological presupposition that one receives forgiveness solely by faith that trusts in the promise of Christ spoken through the words of absolution. In the *Explanations*, as Hamm comments, Luther makes a clear distinction between repentance and justification[240] to the extent that the former indicates only the "beginning of grace," the stage of which is "certainly close to justification."[241] In the *Explanations*, Luther contends that "[t]herefore it is neither the sacrament nor the priest, but faith in the word of Christ spoken through the priest and his office which justifies you,"[242] and argues that one is justified not by penitence but by faith that trusts in the promise of Christ.[243]

Thesis Fifty-Eight: *Iusticia Christi et Meritum Eius Iustificat et Remittit Peccata*[244]

In Thesis Fifty-eight,[245] rejecting the theological notion and practices of seeking to be justified by indulgences or human works of righteousness,[246] Luther argues that it is Christ's righteousness and merit that justify and

---

237. "Faith in the Word of Christ Justifies."
238. AE 31:191–96; WA 1:593.39—596.39.
239. AE 31:191; WA 1:593.40–41.
240. Hamm, *Early Luther*, 101–9.
241. AE 31:193; WA 1:595.12–13.
242. AE 31:194; WA 1:595.33–34.
243. "That man's very faith causes him to be truly pardoned . . . I tell you, faith in that word of Christ makes you truly baptized, whatever feeling you may have about your penitence." AE 31:193; WA 1:594.39, 40–41. "Therefore penitence is not as necessary as faith. In this respect faith in absolution receives incomparably more benefit than does zeal in penitence." AE 31:194; WA 1:595.21–23.
244. "Christ's Righteousness and His Merit Justify and Remit Sins."
245. AE 31:212–28; WA 1:605.26—614.37.
246. AE 31:220; WA 1:610.21–23.

remit sins.[247] Explaining how the merits of Christ work for Christians, Luther returns to the subject of God's alien work, and reaffirms that Christians are conformed to the image of Christ by bearing the cross of sufferings.[248] In other words, one is justified, not by human works, but by Christ's righteousness and merits on the cross. In this regard, Luther compares a theologian of glory and a theologian of the cross, the subject that becomes the main thesis of his *Heidelberg Disputation* (April 26, 1518), which will be discussed in the next chapter.

As reviewed, noticeable in the four theses of the *Explanations* is Luther's theology of justification in accentuation on trusting the promise of forgiveness. With the analogy of marriage Luther articulates the concept of joyous exchange that all sins are swallowed up in Christ, and Christ's righteousness is transferred to a Christian. Luther further clarifies that penitence is not the cause of justification, nor does he identify repentance and justification as a single equivalent event. Both are essentially interrelated in the sense that repentance is necessary, but a penitent is justified only by faith that trusts in Christ's promise. By the same token, Luther contends that it is Christ's righteousness that justifies a penitent who then continues to take up the cross of suffering in conformity to the image of Christ. Within this theological framework Luther argues that the justified souls in purgatory continue to require the grace of God to endure the cross and continue to grow in faith and love in Christ.

LUTHER'S PERCEPTION OF PURGATORY IN HIS THEOLOGY OF JUSTIFICATION IN THE *EXPLANATIONS*

Concerning the major question as to how Luther accommodates both purgatory and justification by faith alone, we now further examine the *Explanations* with particular regard to the four significances of the continual effect of the external righteousness of God, and discuss Luther's reasoning on purgatory within the framework of his theology of justification.

---

247. AE 31:224; WA 1:613.1–2.
248. AE 31:225; WA 1:613.11–19.

Purgatory as a Spiritual Journey of Faith to the Destination

In Luther's theology of justification, the continual effect for the present moment signifies a journey to the final destination. Concerning the subject of salvation and entry into heaven, Luther asserts on the basis of Revelation 21:27[249] that no one can enter heaven without perfect spiritual health, namely, being purely cleansed from sins.[250] With that statement, Luther criticizes the on-going practices of ensuring exemption from the punishments of purgatory by means of indulgences without proper teaching on faith and repentance.[251] Contending that Christians, who are still sinners, require both suffering and repentance, Luther opposes such perceptions and practices that instigate avoidance of Christian suffering and the negligence of repentance.

In reference to Revelation 21:27, Luther addresses the subject of perfection as requirement for entry into heaven, and redefines what spiritual perfection is. Employing the terminology of healing, and alluding to the analogy of health, Luther espouses that one is justified and healed by trusting the words of promise of Christ.[252] Luther's analogy of healing signifies perfect restoration to eternal peace, and underlines the perfect spiritual health in faith.[253] "Therefore, we are justified by faith," says Luther, "and by faith also we receive peace, not by works, penance, or confessions."[254] If

---

249. "For nothing unclean shall enter heaven," translated as in AE 31:153; WA 1:572.14.

250. AE 31:153; WA 1:572.13-14. Thesis Twenty-four in the *Explanations*. See also AE 31:154; WA 1:572.14-15. In his *Sermon on the Tenth Sunday after Trinity* (July 27, 1516), on the basis of 1 Cor. 15:50 Luther proposed that what is required in purgatory is the healing for guilt and the increase of love in God. WA 1:65.9-33, in Saak, *Luther and Reformation*, 273. Cf. In terms of the year of Luther's composition of the sermon, however, Wicks argues that the title of the document is "Treatise on Indulgences" written early in the fall of 1517. Wicks, "Martin Luther's Treatise on Indulgences," 489.

251. See "Overview" in chapter 4.

252. AE 31:104-5; WA 1:543.27-30. Also in the *Defense* (1521), Luther addresses the subject with respect to the removal of sin, and asserts now as an article of faith that sin that remains after baptism prevents one from entering heaven, which requires forgiveness: "Christ cleanses his church through the baptism of water and the gospel, that he may lead home a bride, the glorious church, 'without spot or wrinkle or any such thing.'" AE 32:19-31; WA 7:329.9—345.26, 345.27-36, 347.1-34, 349.1-12. The Second and Third Articles.

253. Luther understands spiritual health as "faith in or love in Christ." AE 31:124; WA 1:555.4-5. Luther's view of faith and love will be treated in the next section.

254. AE 31:105; WA 1:544.7-8.

Luther's statement is taken into consideration in the context of purgatory, peace in rest will be given, not in purgatory but in the final destination of a spiritual journey of faith, the notion of which is modified from 1521/22 onwards at the time of his attacks on the doctrine of purgatory.

Luther's illustration of three types of dying souls (e.g., first, dying without faith; second, dying with perfect faith; and third, dying with imperfect faith) elucidates his theological reasoning that distinguishes between the blessed or perfect and the imperfect.[255] Whereas the second type of dying soul *trusts* in God entirely above all things, and willingly accepts death as God's will, the third type that is dying in weak faith not only loves the earthly life, but also experiences fear of death and judgment.[256] The key notion that divides all three types is the distinction between *faith* that trusts in God wholeheartedly and *distrust* or lack of trust that causes fear which constitutes the punishment of purgatory.[257] In this regard, and based on Revelation 21:27, Luther proposes necessity of growth in faith in purgatory prior to entry into the destination.

Purgatory Where Faith and Love in Christ Continually Grow

The continual effect also involves faith and love, not as qualitative virtues to possess, but as a gift of God and its fruit in a continual growth. In emphasis on the growth,[258] Luther makes a twofold assertion that faith grows only in bearing the cross, and that a Christian enters heaven only through the cross of tribulations.[259]

Rejecting the scholastic view that satisfaction (i.e., fasting, almsgiving, and praying) requires its completion prior to entering heaven,[260] Luther *redefines* the technical term "satisfaction," and argues that God is almost always satisfied with "a contrite heart" and the cross of sufferings, which is

---

255. AE 31:131–32; WA 1:559.11–37. While Luther simply uses the traditional notion of the state of dying souls, he reinterprets it in his theological orientation of justification. See Chemnitz, *Examination of the Council of Trent*, pt. 4, topic 3, sec. 1.3, 228.

256. AE 31:131–32; WA 1:559.11–37.

257. AE 31:124–25; WA 1:555.6–25.

258. Luther notes that his theses on purgatory and its punishments stress the necessity for souls in purgatory to be perfectly healed by grace. AE 31:178; WA 1:586.12–13.

259. AE 31:251; WA 1:628.23–28.

260. Aland, "Sermon on Indulgence and Grace, 1518," 63–67.

newness of life in faith.²⁶¹ This is one of the examples which demonstrate how Luther redefines theological and technical terms and concepts within the framework and perspective of his theology of justification.²⁶² Similarly, Luther perceives purgatory as postmortem spiritual afflictions of bearing the cross, willingly accepting it as God's will.

Just as Luther understands righteousness and faith, not as a qualitative disposition, but as a gift of God, so does he perceive what love is in this respect. To love God is not a certain quality required to earn God's grace, but the fruit of faith produced by God's grace.²⁶³ It is a willing spirit of a Christian to love God above all things and accept God's will, even to death. Luther thus proposes spiritual health with reference to "faith in or love in Christ";²⁶⁴ conversely, by weak spiritual health Luther refers to a lack of trust and love in Christ.²⁶⁵

This can be understood in the sphere of a function of faith. In the *Freedom* of 1520, for instance, Luther addresses the threefold function of faith that justifies, honors, and unites.²⁶⁶ Concerning the second function, Luther notes that "it honors him whom it trusts with the most reverent and

---

261. AE 31:94; WA 1:537.10-11. AE 31:95; WA 1:538.2-6. With reference to satisfaction, Luther interprets Micah 6:8 and claims that the satisfaction God requires is "to do justice, and to love kindness, and to walk humbly with your God." He summarizes that "God requires ... justice, compassion, and fear. This, as I have said, means a new life." AE 31:96-97; WA 1:538.27-28, 34.

262. Luther's use of theological and technical terms is flexible, and sometimes even "imprecise," as Cargill Thompson points out: "Luther's language is often extremely imprecise: he had little regard for verbal exactness, while he frequently employs even technical theological terms in a variety of ways. Usually it is clear from the context in what sense he is using a particular term in a given instance; however, the fact that the same word or phrase can have several connotations makes the task of trying to expound his thought an extremely difficult undertaking for modern scholars, since it is often hard to define precisely what he means by a specific phrase or concept." Thompson, "Two Kingdoms and Two Regiments," 165, quoted in Stephenson, "Luther's Eucharistic Writings of 1523 to 1528," 273-74. On Luther's use of the term "purgatory," see "Chronological Overview" in chapter 3.

263. AE 34:168; WA 39I:98.24-29. *Disputation Concerning Justification* (1536).

264. AE 31:124; WA 1:555.4-5. With respect to spiritual health or growth, see also Luther's *Dictata* on a threefold purpose of suffering that God is with the afflicted to teach, strengthen, and comfort them. It is implied that the threefold purpose of affliction aims to help Christians grow in faith and love in Christ. AE 10:48-51; WA 55II:56.19—62.5. On Ps. 4:1.

265. AE 31:124; WA 1:555.4-5. AE 31:133; WA 1:560.8-11. See also AE 31:124-25; WA 1:555.6-25.

266. AE 31:348-53; WA 7:52.20—56.14.

highest regard since it considers him trustful and trustworthy."[267] Just as faith honors God whom it trusts, so does it love God whom it trusts above all. Luther later explicates it succinctly in the Small Catechism where he explains the meaning of the First Commandment: "We are to fear, love, and trust [in] God above all things."[268] The old Adam hinders this fruit of faith;[269] therefore, faith is to increase, and healing is required. In brief, faith bears its fruit of love; in return, love "as a fully trusting love"[270] bears witness to faith.[271]

Purgatory for the Frailty of Faith that Causes Fear

The continual effect not only implies the frailty of faith but also signifies the imperfect righteousness of faith. As regards the imperfect righteousness of faith, which necessitates God's imputation, we reviewed earlier in a broad context of Luther's theology of justification that for the sake of Christ God reckons the imperfect righteousness of faith as perfect righteousness,[272] and that the analogy of leaven and the notion of *simul* (i.e., *simul iustus et peccator*) coincide with the continual effect of the external righteousness of God.[273] Let us now draw attention to the notion of the frailty of faith addressed in the *Explanations*.

Luther argues that the frailty of faith is not made perfect instantly at death.[274] Instead, a soul that dies in fear without fully trusting in God or accepting death as God's will, not only has guilt for the lack of trust and love in God, but also suffers dread and fear in purgatory.[275] With respect to the fear with which souls in purgatory suffer, Luther asserts based on 1 John 4:18 that *perfect love* dispels fear.[276] While this statement seems to

---

267. AE 31:350. WA 7:53.34–36.
268. "The Ten Commandments," Small Catechism in BC^2 351.2; WA 30I:284.2–3.
269. AE 31:135; WA 1:561.29–32. See also AE 31:123; WA 1:554.26—555.25.
270. Hamm, *Early Luther*, 248.
271. Lohse, *Martin Luther's Theology*, 278. WA 39II:248.11–15.
272. AE 26:232; WA 40I:367.19–21.
273. See "Four Significances of the Continual Effect in Luther's Theology of Justification" earlier in this chapter.
274. AE 31:133; WA 1:560.20–21.
275. AE 31:136; WA 1:562.12–13. AE 31:126; WA 1:556.6–7. See also AE 31:154; WA 1:572.14–15.
276. AE 31:124; WA 1:554.26–32.

underline the subject of love, not necessarily faith, a particular point needs to be addressed for clarification. In his theological reorientation, in which faith—not love—takes the central role in his theology of justification,[277] Luther is consistent in asserting how to resolve the issue of fear and trembling at death and in purgatory, namely, "by faith" in Christ. Luther notes: "[T]he thesis is clear enough. If anyone is snatched away by death before he has attained that perfect love which drives out fear, he necessarily dies in fear and trembling until love is perfected and able to cast out fear. This fear which I mention is that conscience which is evil and disturbed because of *a weak point in faith* . . . [S]uch dread is a punishment of purgatory, indeed the greatest punishment."[278] The root cause of fear is the *frailty*, weakness, or *imperfection* of faith on account of which the dying souls, as well as souls in purgatory, cannot love God above all things. Addressing the subject of newness of life in 1 John 4:18, Luther employs a traditional analogy of health, and stresses that spiritual health for souls in purgatory is "faith in or love in Christ."[279]

As discussed, the analogy of health implies a continual progress towards perfect health. To increase love for God means to increase faith that trusts in God, which necessitates the infused grace of God.[280] Otherwise, the condition of purgatory remains without difference from hell[281] except for the duration[282] since souls in purgatory remain with guilt, namely, "the fear of punishment and the lack of love,"[283] which God alone remits.[284] Therefore, when Luther discusses the subject of fear with related to a lack of love (e.g., "perfect love dispels fear" as in 1 John 4:18), he speaks about faith in his theology of justification.[285]

---

277. Hamm, *Early Luther*, 59–84.

278. AE 31:124, 126; WA 1:555.6–10, 556.6–7. Emphasis added.

279. AE 31:124; WA 1:555.4–5.

280. AE 31:131–36; WA 1:559.6—561.42. AE 31:124; WA 1:555.4–5.

281. AE 31:136; WA 1:562.12.

282. AE 31:130; WA 1:558.33.

283. AE 31:136; WA 1:562.13–14.

284. AE 31:242; WA 1:622.35–36.

285. This technique in using theological terms resonates with Luther's way of addressing the subject of justification and sanctification. See Bayer, *Living By Faith*, 58–59. Conversely, Luther also terms "the seven holy possessions of the church," which essentially include the sacrament of baptism and the office of the keys, "the seven principal parts of Christian *sanctification*." AE 41:166; WA 50:643.4–5. Emphasis added.

Purgatory as the Cross of Suffering

The final significance of the continual effect in Luther's theology of justification, with which we attempt to trace how Luther holds at once both purgatory and justification by faith alone, is his perception of purgatory as the cross of souls. Luther uses the term "cross" in several senses. First, the cross indicates "true inner repentance," which Luther terms "the hatred of self" (*odium sui*).[286] As indicated in Thesis One, "When our Lord and Master Jesus Christ said, 'Repent' [Matt. 4:17], he willed the entire life of believers to be one of repentance,"[287] one must bear the cross of repentance until the last moment so as to enter heaven.[288] Second, in the same vein, Luther also terms it "the cross and mortification of suffering" with respect to the "voluntary and evangelical punishment" and the "need of salvation."[289] Third, bearing the cross also means seeking to accept the will of God, even suffering and death. In this respect, the term "resignation" is intertwined with the notion of the cross.[290]

Therefore, if God's will is not to remove the cross of sufferings but to administer it, and if souls in purgatory accept the will of God, not reluctantly but willingly, suffering in purgatory is "the cross of souls."[291] A baptized Christian should be ready to bear the cross, stresses Luther, so as to "be conformed to the image of the Son of God."[292] This notion of *conformity* resonates with Luther's description of *Anfechtung* about which he states: "All that remains is the stark-naked desire for help and a terrible groaning, but it does not know where to turn for help. In this instance *the person is stretched out with Christ* so that all his bones may be counted, and every

---

286. AE 31:88; WA 1:533.35–36.

287. AE 31:83; WA 1:530.16–17.

288. AE 31:89; WA 1:534.3–4.

289. Luther explains this category of punishment based on 1 Cor. 11:31 and relates it as "spiritual penance" commanded by God. AE 31:90; WA 1:534.33–35. "This thesis is evident from reason. The cross of repentance must continue until, according to the Apostle, the body of sin is destroyed [Rom. 6:6] and the inveterate first Adam, along with its image, perishes, and the new Adam is perfect in the image of God. But sin remains until death, although it diminishes daily through the renewing of the mind." AE 31:89; WA 1:534.11–15.

290. AE 31:137 WA 1:562.20–25.

291. AE 31:153; WA 1:571.34–36.

292. AE 31:225; WA 1:613.11–19. Late medieval German passion mysticism treats the theme of suffering with respect to purification from sin and thus an existential purgatory for growth in love for God. Rittgers, *Reformation of Suffering*, 73–74.

corner of the soul is filled with the greatest bitterness, dread, trembling, and sorrow in such a manner that all these last forever."[293] With this statement of suffering in great intensity Luther aims to underscore the incomparable degree of torments in purgatory,[294] as well as God's alien operation for salvation. Luther espouses that the cross of spiritual afflictions is necessary for justification, not as a cause but as God's alien operation for justification where one is accused to be justified in faith.

Just as *tentatio* or *Anfechtung* is the cross of souls in purgatory, so is the "groaning" of the suffering souls in purgatory "a hymn of the cross."[295] The work of God appears to be strange, for the justified, weak souls rather suffer in purgatory, but the purpose of this alien work is to lead them to grow in faith and love in Christ.[296] Luther thus underscores that purgatory increases love for God and perfects it, and stresses that "purgatory perfects love most of all."[297] This is the continual effect of justifying grace in progress until its completion.

Salient is Luther's underlying argument that faith and the cross are not to be divorced, for they are mutually complementary.[298] No one is justified by the cross, but solely by faith that trusts in the promise of God; however, for Luther faith is not a metaphysical notion or theory that does not treat *Anfechtung* as the cross. Luther, therefore, states: "Even if God could make all men perfect by grace, perhaps without punishments, nevertheless he has not decided to do it, but rather *has decided that all men should conform to the image of his Son, that is to the cross* [Cf. Rom. 8:29]."[299]

---

293. AE 31:129; WA 1:558.4-8. Emphasis added.

294. AE 31:129-30; WA 1:558.12-14.

295. On "a hymn of the cross" (*crucis hymnus*), see AE 31:226; WA 1:614.1-4. On "groaning" (*gemitus*), see AE 31:129; WA 1:558.3-6. AE 31:131; WA 1:558.39—559.1. In the same vein, Luther uses the expression of "the song of the cross" (*canticum crucis*) during the Leipzig Debate. WA 2:333.25-27.

296. AE 31:137; WA 1:562.20-25. AE 31:145; WA 1:567.15-19. See also AE 31:124; WA 1:555.4-5.

297. AE 31:137; WA 1:563.2.

298. Leppin claims that in Luther mysticism and Scripture are not "mutually exclusive" but "complementary." Leppin, "Luther's Roots," 58.

299. AE 31:153; WA 1:571.34-36. Emphasis added. Concerning the "voluntary and evangelical punishment," Luther understands it as "the cross and mortification of suffering . . . commanded by Christ both with respect to the nature of spiritual penance and certainly with respect to the need of salvation." AE 31:90; WA 1:534.33-35. Concerning the significance of suffering in Luther's soteriology, see also Rittgers, *Reformation of Suffering*, 104-10.

When it is read in reference to the souls suffering in purgatory, Luther's statement illuminates his theological reorientation where he upholds both purgatory and justification by faith alone in such a way that the former is perceived and defined by the latter in conjunction with the cross. Thesis Ninety-five, where Luther makes a final remark that one enters heaven "through many tribulations,"[300] echoes the statement above in clarity, just as Thesis One depicts the *Christian life in reality*: "[T]he entire life of believers to be one of repentance."[301]

CONCLUSION

Luther integrated the subject of purgatory with the notion of a continual effect of justifying grace. For Luther purgatory is not just for punishments that were incurred prior to death due to incompletion of satisfaction. Nor is it a postmortem condition of peace and rest, at least until he redefines it in 1521/22, for souls in purgatory suffer torments in the dread and fear due to a lack of faith and trust. Luther perceived the condition of purgatory with respect to spiritual afflictions, and termed it "the cross of souls" both in the *Explanations* and during the debate with Eck in Leipzig. Souls in purgatory are always in motion, just as a human being in this life, either moving forward or falling away from trusting and loving in Christ. Until his attacks on the formal doctrine of purgatory (1521/22), Luther considered postmortem torments in purgatory essential for a continual growth in faith which corresponds to the removal of sin prior to a soul's entry into the eternal destination (Revelation 21:27).

The subject of Luther's perception of purgatory in view of his theology of justification raises a question as to what significance there is with respect to before and after his dismissal of the notion of postmortem torment (e.g., 1525/26). This can be addressed in terms of continuity and discontinuity. In accordance with his reading of Scripture (e.g., Revelation 21:27), Luther held that without perfect spiritual health no one can enter the eternal destination. It is the first half of the *continuity* between before and after 1525/26 where perfection is essentially required to enter the eternal destination. On the Last Day, God judges between good and evil, the righteous and the unrighteous. Salvation will be offered to the righteous, and the condemnation to the unrighteous. In this regard, the distinction between the young

---

300. AE 31:251; WA 1:628.23–28.
301. AE 31:83; WA 1:530.16–17.

Luther and the mature Luther is irrelevant. Since Luther's discovery of a new theological insight (i.e., *Anfechtungen* prior to *Dictata*), his perception of God's way of salvation is consistent, that is, not by a set of qualitative virtues but by a gift of faith alone. Luther terms it the righteousness of faith, in which is the beginning of salvation. This incipient righteousness is imperfect, and one who dies with fear in this imperfect righteousness (i.e., weakness in faith) departs for purgatory to continue to grow in faith and love in Christ. Even after dismissing the notion of postmortem torment—purgatory—in 1525/26, Luther maintained his theological assertion that the incipient righteousness of faith is imperfect, which is the second half of the *continuity* before and after his dismissal of the notion of purgatory.

A significant shift in Luther's perspective is captured only after his dismissal of the notion of postmortem torment (1525/26), if not at the time of his attacks on the doctrine of purgatory (1521/22), that God reckons this imperfect righteousness of faith as perfect righteousness (1531/35). This is the first half of *discontinuity* between before and after the dismissal of his notion of purgatory wherein the perfect righteousness of Christ is imputed through faith alone to cover all sins entirely. When a Christian dies, therefore, the soul rests in peace without due sufferings of labor, which is the second half of the *discontinuity*. Accepting the expression of the Scripture (e.g., the departing souls return to the forefathers of faith), Luther frames the image of life hereafter in a peaceful rest and sleep in the bosom of Christ—the promise of God—until the Day of Christ.[302]

On the one hand, Luther's view of purgatory in the *Explanations* confirms that his theology of justification lays a fundamental theological framework that provides certainty to his theological inquiry amid his existential *tentatio* of sufferings. For Luther, theology is not a philosophical speculation but an existential inquiry for certainty of how to be justified before God. No sooner had his doubts about the pope as the Antichrist been confirmed in 1520 than Luther began to attack the formal doctrine of purgatory. Nor was there any noticeable shift beforehand concerning his notion of purgatory other than his inquiry and speculation in his early lectures on Galatians about the contemporary scriptural references to purgatory. Only during his attacks on the doctrine of purgatory (1521/22), Luther's perception of purgatory began to be reoriented from postmortem torment to antemortem torment except for few souls. After the dismissal of his notion of postmortem torment, Luther's theological concept of God's

---

302. AE 4:308–18; WA 43:357.6—364.18. See also AE 7:293–94; WA 44:517.13–30.

imputation plays a key role in providing certainty to the Christians suffering in existential afflictions, even the fear of death.

On the other hand, the continuity and discontinuity mentioned above underlines not only what is significant in examining Luther's view of purgatory, but also what has been *a missing piece* in understanding Luther. The subject of Luther's view of purgatory has not received due attention in Luther scholarship. While it is relatively a minor subject, it is inextricably interrelated with other major theological subjects such as justification by faith alone. It can be further argued that minor theological subjects in Luther's theology may continue to be examined in order to find small missing pieces and optimize the readers' lens so as to assist them to have a full picture in understanding Luther's theology.

I have thus far attempted to answer why it took so long for Luther to deny purgatory, and how he could hold purgatory while asserting justification by faith alone. In explicating theology in general and his theology of justification in particular, Luther is consistent, as well as persistent, in doing theology, maintaining the fundamental presupposition of his theology—a believer suffering in afflictions before God. The terms and concepts that he frequently employs—such as God's hiddenness in *Anfechtung*, resignation in conformity with Christ, and the analogies of leaven, healing, and a journey—not only articulate God's justifying grace with the distinction between forgiveness and the removal of sin (i.e., the instantaneous and continual effects of the external—alien—righteousness of God), but also indicate that Luther's theology does essentially treat the subject of suffering—the cross. With the final questions of "What was Luther's intention in treating the subject of the punishments of purgatory in the *Explanations*, and how did he accomplish it?" the following chapter will treat Luther's theological interpretation of sufferings of *Anfechtung* as "the cross," a concept which is profoundly demonstrated in the theology of the cross (*theologia crucis*).

5

Purgatory as the Cross
Luther's Theological Interpretation of Suffering

> "The crisis of the Western world turns not least on a philosophy and program of education which try to redeem man by bypassing the cross. In acting against the cross, they act against the truth."
>
> —Benedict XVI

> "Lord, put Your cross before our eyes
> As each of us here lives and dies,
> Grant us Your passion so to view
> That we may put our trust in You."
>
> —Kurt E. Reinhardt

INTRODUCTION

THIS CHAPTER ATTEMPTS TO answer the question "Why is it significant to examine Luther's view of purgatory despite his denial of purgatory, after all?" In other words, "What was Luther's intention and purpose in treating the subject of the punishments of purgatory in the *Explanations*, and how did he maneuver it?" In answering the question, I propose that Luther's view of purgatory exhibits his theological interpretation of suffering and the cross, a theological insight which appears in the form of the theology of the cross. That is, in the *Explanations* of 1518 Luther articulates his view of purgatory in the framework of the theology of the cross.

Undertaking the task, I establish the major premise as a point of departure that while Luther refers to John Tauler to support his view of postmortem torment considering the notion of suffering as a foretaste of hell, Luther's view itself precedes his acquaintance with Tauler's sermons. To establish this premise, I will compare the *Dictata* (1513–1515) and the *Explanations* (1518), and discuss the notion of tasting hell in this life in both documents. As for the minor premise, I propose that Tauler's role in Luther's disputations is twofold: first, to *represent* a tradition of German theology in defense of the Wittenberg theology and Luther's propositions on the subject of the punishments of purgatory; second, to *dispute* the opponents' criticism of Luther, as well as their scholastic tradition and their biblical reference to purgatory. With regard to the minor premise, I concur with Ozment's viewpoint that Luther's use of Tauler's theology is to defend the Wittenberg theology,[1] and with Brecht's stance that tradition played a significant role in the field of theology at that time,[2] a notion alluded to in Luther's *Preface to the Complete Edition of A German Theology* (1518).[3] Subsequently, following a review of Luther's theology of the cross in the *Heidelberg Disputation*, we will revisit the *Dictata* and the *Explanations* to discuss Luther's notion of suffering as a foretaste of hell in the framework of the theology of the cross.

The current chapter assumes the following limitations: first, with regard to Tauler's view of suffering and purgatory, the primary source is the sermons of Tauler translated into English. Second, the *Heidelberg Disputation* is the primary source in examining Luther's theology of the cross. Third, Luther's theological perception of suffering involves his adaptation to mystical theology, but the perimeter of the current review on mystical theology is the notion of union with Christ (*unio cum Christo*) in Tauler's sermons.

---

1. Ozment, *Age of Reform*, 240; see 240n54. WA 1:379.5–6.

2. Brecht, *Martin Luther*, 1:141.

3. *Vorrede zu der vollständigen Ausgabe der "deutschen Theologie"* was published in June 1518. AE 31:75–76; WA 1:378–79.

LUTHER'S *ANFECHTUNG*

Luther's Existential Orientation

Luther's theology neither rejects the role of reason (e.g., the Declaration of the *Explanations*)[4] nor entertains metaphysical speculations for the sake of theoretical notions (e.g., *Heidelberg Disputation*).[5] Presupposing a human being in the *Sitz im Leben*,[6] Luther's theology maintains an "existential significance" and attempts to answer the queries encountered in its *Sitz im Leben*.[7] Luther's well-known statement, "*Experience* alone makes the theologian"[8] echoes this *existential* orientation.[9] In this context, Luther's theology draws close attention to human suffering of fear, uncertainty, and despair, and practices faith. The fear of death, a subject which Luther frequently addresses, for instance,[10] is a reminder that a human being is an existential being that experiences fear, despair, and death.[11] Luther's sermon in 1522 exhibits his theological perspective: "The summons of death comes to us all, and no one can die for another. Every one must fight his own death by himself, alone. We can shout into another's ears, but every one must himself be prepared for the time of death, for I will not be with you then, nor you with me. Therefore every one must himself know and be armed with the chief things which concern a Christian."[12]

---

4. AE 31:83; WA 1:529.29—530.3. See "Declaration of the *Explanations*: Two Principles and Three Categories of Authorities" in this chapter concerning Luther's theological methodology presented particularly in the *Explanations*. Luther takes the "judgment of reason and experience" as the third category of authority.

5. AE 39-70; WA 1:353.1—374.31.

6. The term used in biblical criticism refers to the "social context" or the "place in life." See *Oxford Reference* and *Oxford Biblical Studies Online*.

7. Lohse, *Martin Luther*, 18-19.

8. *Sola experientia facit theologum*. AE 54:7; WA Tr 1:16.10-11. Emphasis added. Bayer, *Martin Luther's Theology*, 21-22. See also Rittgers, "Luther's Engagement in Pastoral Care," 469.

9. Throughout this chapter, the term "existential" denotes a human "experience" of suffering and afflictions.

10. Luther treats the subject in his sermons, lectures, letters, and treatises throughout his entire career. *A Sermon on Preparing to Die* (1519) is one of the examples, as well as the *Explanations* of 1518. See also Karant-Nunn, "Martin Luther on Death and Dying."

11. Barth, *Theology of Martin Luther*, 381-94.

12. The First Sermon, March 9, 1522, Invocavit Sunday. AE 51:70; WA 10III:1.7—2.2, quoted in Barth, *Theology of Martin Luther*, 382.

Purgatory as the Cross

In this existential orientation, Luther's theology comprises a twofold quintessential component: knowledge of sinful humanity and that of God who justifies a sinner. In a strict sense, the term a "sinner" or a person "guilty of sin and condemned" describes the essence of Luther's theological anthropology.[13] Luther stresses that ". . . a theologian discusses man as a sinner. In theology, this is the essence of man."[14] Sin, or *knowledge* of sin, is not a metaphysical notion, but an existential realization in experience. Luther notes that "It [knowledge of sin] is a true *feeling*, a true *experience*, and a very serious *struggle* of the heart, as he [David] testifies when he says (v. 3), 'I *know* (that is, I feel or experience) my transgressions.'"[15] By "knowledge" in this sense, Luther employs a Hebraic connotation of knowledge.[16]

Luther's assertion of knowledge of sin as "a true experience" further implies that the consequence of sin is essentially existential. Humanity is by nature "subject to eternal death,"[17] and this knowledge *is* real. For this reason, without struggling with the consequence of sin, no proper or profound discussion of theology is possible. Luther reiterates, "The knowledge of sin is itself the feeling of sin, and the sinful man is the one who is oppressed by his conscience and tossed to and fro, not knowing where to turn."[18] For Luther, *Anfechtung* itself is a sign of an existential being where one is brought near to despair.[19] When struggling with the angst of *Anfechtung*, it is not enough to assume that God exists. On the contrary, it is necessary

---

13. "The proper subject of theology is man guilty of sin and condemned, and God the Justifier and Savior of man the sinner." AE 12:311; WA 40II:328.17–18. *Commentary on Psalm 51 (Enarratio Psalmi LI)* lectured in 1532, printed in 1538. Regarding Luther's notion of existential *Anfechtung* as a chief constituent of his theological anthropology, see Slenczka, "Luther's Anthropology," 222–32. As Roper notes, the "real knots" that Luther struggled with were "his lack of love of God and his fear of judgment." Roper, *Martin Luther*, 53.

14. AE 12:310; WA 40II:327.20–21.

15. AE 12:310; WA 40II:326.34–37. Emphases added.

16. AE 12:310; WA 40II:326.37.

17. AE 12:308; WA 40II:322.25.

18. [N]esciens quo se vertat. AE 12:310; WA 40II:327.16. Emphasis added. Analogously, the *Anfechtung* account in the *Explanations* (1518) also describes, "*nescit unde petat auxilium*," that is, if literally translated, "The soul does not know from where help reaches or comes." Luther's expression seems to resonate with Ps. 120:1 in Vulgate (i.e., Psalm 121:1 in English translation), ". . . unde veniet auxilium mihi," or "From where does help come to me?" if translated literally. See AE 31:129; WA 1:558.18.

19. Luther notes, "When this happens, despair follows, casting him into hell." AE 12:311; WA 40II:327.23.

to *know*—not merely intellectually but existentially—that *God* who exists is found *in suffering* just as God was there at the crucifixion of Christ. "Therefore, a godly mind is not shocked to hear that God is present in death or hell, both of which are more horrible and foul than either a hole or a sewer. Indeed, since Scripture testifies that God is everywhere and fills all things [Jer. 23:24], a godly mind not only says that He is in those places, but must need to learn and know that he *is* there."[20]

In this respect, Luther's theology is principally existential as opposed to notional. Just as sin and its consequences are real for Luther, so is God who justifies a condemned sinner solely by faith in the crucified Christ. Luther notes this dialectic notion, "Though I am a sinner in myself, I am not a sinner in Christ."[21] For Luther, theological anthropology (i.e., a sinner before God) and existential theology (i.e., God who is found in suffering justifies a sinner) are complementary and essential to be always retained, for they are inseparable. When they are separated from each other, theology becomes a theory and a metaphysical notion. As Dragseth rightly comments, "For Luther the idea of being righteous cannot be divorced from the awareness of death,"[22] the dialectic concept in Luther's theology is principally existential: uncertainty and certainty, eternal death and eternal life, and a human being who is a sinner yet righteous before God. This is Luther's theology, the way in which he exercises his faith in the *Sitz im Leben*.

The Term *Anfechtung*

Scholars unanimously agree that there is no equivalent term in English for the *Anfechtung*. It corresponds to *tentatio* in Latin, not as "temptation" in the sense of "enticement,"[23] but as "estrangement,"[24] "assault,"[25] or "on trial."[26] The root of the term means "'assail,' 'combat' or 'bodily struggle,'"[27] such as

---

20. AE 33:47; WA 18:623.14–17. Emphasis added. See Steven Paulson's brief summary on Luther's view of God. Paulson, "Luther's Doctrine of God," 187–200.
21. AE 12:311; WA 40II:327.31–32.
22. Dragseth, *The Devil's Whore*, 138.
23. Westhelle, "God against God," 275
24. Rittgers, "Luther's Engagement in Pastoral Care," 469.
25. McGrath, *Luther's Theology of the Cross*, 224.
26. Westhelle, "God against God," 275–76.
27. Ngien, *Luther's Theology of the Cross*, 31.

Luther's accidental injury from falling on a dagger in his early years,[28] as well as his physical and mental illness in his last years.[29] It also denotes a "severe torment of the inner spirit and conscience"[30] and "unremitting spiritual conflict which never ends until death."[31] Luther's *Anfechtung* or the notion of "agonizing struggle"[32] is not an academic notion[33] but an existential term drawn from his experience of "doubts and afflictions" in great intensity.[34]

Luther's Experience of *Anfechtung*

In a narrow sense, Luther's *Anfechtung* was noticeable not only before but also *after* his discovery of the gospel,[35] particularly between 1517 and 1521, a period Olivier describes in terms of Luther's lonely and intensive trials in conflict with Rome[36] under the so-called "*Causa Lutheri*" (*Luther Affair* or *die Luthersache*).[37] In a broad sense, however, Luther's entire life was a period of *Anfechtung*, and so Luther understood it.[38]

In his early years in the monastery, prior to the discovery of the gospel, Luther frequently experienced the *Anfechtung* of uncertainty, the spiritual affliction that oppressed him with fear of God's wrath and death, in addition to struggling with a sense of inadequacy before God. Luther was at war with himself in his quest of where to find a gracious God, but his "existential wrestling" continued without success in finding relief.[39] The

---

28. Whitford, *Luther*, 23; Jonas et al., *Last Days of Luther*, 9. See also Roper, *Martin Luther*, 33

29. Lohse, *Martin Luther*, 39.

30. The translator's note in von Loewenich, *Martin Luther*, 54.

31. Rupp, *The Righteousness of God*, 105.

32. Bayer, *Martin Luther's Theology*, 20–21.

33. Vogelsang, *Der angefochtene Christus bei Luther*, 4, quoted in Rupp, *Righteousness of God*, 106.

34. Hamm, *Early Luther*, 27. On Luther's use of the term in various contexts, see Scaer, "The Concept of *Anfechtung*," 15–30.

35. Lohse, *Martin Luther*, 25.

36. Olivier, *Trial of Luther*, 57.

37. Among the publications on this subject are Olivier, *Trial of Luther*; Fabisch and Iserloh, eds., *Dokumente zur Causa Lutheri (1517–1521)*; Kohnle, *Reichstag und Reformation*; and Borth, *Die Luthersache (causa Lutheri) 1517–1524*. See also Wicks, *Cajetan Responds*.

38. Rupp, *Righteousness of God*, 105. See also Roper, *Martin Luther*, 44–47, 53–54.

39. Schilling, *Martin Luther*, 68–74.

greater efforts he put to acquire forgiveness to be righteous before God, the greater intensity of the *Anfechtung* he encountered and wrestled with.

Luther's acquaintance with Scripture, following Staupitz's advice, came to be a decisive turning point for him. Luther examined Scripture in seeking the answer for his quest.[40] Schilling comments: "The essence of Luder's interest in Scripture did not lie, however, in history or philology or grammar. He understood the Bible in existential terms, the only way he could make sense of his devotional predicament, his crisis about life itself . . . [H]is uniqueness stemmed from the existential radicality with which the Bible was heard and given context, its *Sitz im Leben*."[41] Thereafter, Luther began to translate in the *Dictata* his own existential suffering into biblical terminology,[42] and it became a source of "the theological harvest of his *Anfechtung* in the cloister"[43] and a "process of fermentation"[44] in his theological discovery. Luther's discovery of the meaning of *Anfechtung* was laid more significantly in the notion of "God-forsakenness"—an experience of hell in this life.[45]

Luther's *Anfechtung* as a Foretaste of Hell in the *Dictata* and the *Explanations*

Luther's notion of *Anfechtung* as a foretaste of hell, or such sufferings as tasting hell in this life, appears not only in the *Explanations* (1518) but also in the *Dictata*. In the former, as if recalling his personal experience of spiritual estrangement and agony, Luther describes:

> I myself 'knew a man' [II Cor. 12:2] who claimed that he had often suffered these punishments, in fact over a very brief period of time. Yet they were so great and so much like hell . . . In this moment . . . the soul cannot believe that it can ever be redeemed other than that the punishment is not yet completely felt . . . All that remains is the stark-naked desire for help and a terrible groaning, but it does not know where to turn for help. In this instance the person is stretched out with Christ so that all his bones may be

40. Lohse, *Martin Luther*, 27, 75.
41. Schilling, *Martin Luther*, 76–77.
42. Slenczka, "Luther's Anthropology," 215.
43. Hamm, *Early Luther*, 45.
44. Lohse, *Martin Luther's Theology*, 53.
45. Hamm, *Early Luther*, 224–25.

counted, and every corner of the soul is filled with the greatest bitterness, dread, trembling, and sorrow in such a manner that all these last forever.[46]

Luther's description of *Anfechtung* accentuates his notion that the punishments of purgatory seem incomparable with such "unbearable and inconsolable trembling" in a foretaste of hell.[47] Souls in purgatory are "already at the gate, at the threshold of condemnation and at the entrance of hell,"[48] the inner or spiritual condition of which Luther terms "near despair."[49]

Luther's early lectures of the *Dictata*[50] also capture the notion of a foretaste of hell in the present life, where he notes that "all the saints" experience hell emotionally.[51]

> For they [all the saints] die as far as the desire and purpose to commit sin is concerned. Similarly, they descend into hell as far as the attitude toward its punishments is concerned. *Thus all the prayers of the Psalms which are uttered in the person of Christ as being in hell, are also uttered in the person of the saints, as descending to hell in their mind and heart . . .* Therefore he prays here, "Draw Me out, set Me free." All these are the most earnest prayers also of those who are occupied with meditating on hell, *just as they are the prayers of Christ who was literally in hell.*[52]

In this lecture, Luther relates the subject of suffering to the experience of tasting hell, particularly Christ's experience. These prayers are Christ's utterances in hell, and all the saints who follow him also descend into hell but emotionally. Luther highlights this descent for the disciple:

> Therefore go down with Jacob weeping to hell (Gen. 37:35). Mark this sign for yourself: When you are lukewarm and not in hell with your heart, know that there is danger for you, and

---

46. AE 31:129; WA 1:557.33—558.18. Thesis Fifteen.

47. AE 31:129–30; WA 1:558.12–14.

48. AE 31:130; WA 1:558.19–23.

49. AE 31:130; WA 1:558.21–23. See also AE 31:27; WA 1:234.6, 8. Recollecting his own experience of *Anfechtungen*, Luther describes later, "I myself was offended more than once, and brought to the very depth and abyss of despair, so that I wished I had never been created a man, . . ." AE 33:190; WA 18:719.9–12. *The Bondage of the Will* of 1525.

50. The *Dictata* seemed to have begun in mid-August 1513 and ended in the fall of or late in 1515. AE 10:x; 11:ix.

51. AE 10:367–74; WA 55II:400.477—407.703. On Ps. 69:16.

52. AE 10:372; WA 55II:404.617–26. On Ps. 69:16. Emphases added.

peace and security are lying in ambush for you to bring you to destruction . . . Therefore Christ descended once, and all should follow Him wherever He might go, for He has commanded that we should follow Him. But if we are to do so in all other matters, why not also in this?[53]

Several points are worth noting with respect to the notion of suffering as a foretaste of hell in the *Dictata* and the *Explanations*: first, in explicating Psalm 69:16 Luther states that what is called "the sign of the prophet Jonah"—suffering—is "a sign of God's grace."[54] Analogously, Luther addresses the persecution of the church on earth in reference to "purification" or "cleansing."[55] Later in the *Explanations*, Luther also defines the purpose of the postmortem tormenting condition, and asserts that the term "purgatory" denotes cleansing or purification, for which reason it is called purgatory (*purgatorium*), not "punitory" (*punitorium*).[56] Souls in purgatory, therefore, suffer torments for cleansing, not merely because of the penalties incurred before death.[57] Second, concerning those who tasted hell in this life, Luther in the *Dictata* underlines several biblical references including Hezekiah, David, Jonah,[58] and Jacob,[59] a list which appears again in the *Explanations* for the same purpose.[60] Third, in contrast to the saints

---

53. AE 10:373; WA 55II:405.650-52, 655-57. Luther's notion of a foretaste of hell also appears in his *Seven Penitential Psalms* (*Die sieben ßuspsalmen*) first in 1517 (WA 1:161.2-6) and then in 1525 (WA 18:481.24-25). Both editions are almost identical in terms of Luther's description of the subject. The AE translates the latter edition: "This [feeling of being forsaken and rejected by God] is a sample or foretaste of the pains of hell and everlasting damnation; . . ." AE 14:142. See also Rittgers, *Reformation of Suffering*, 100.

54. AE 10:373; WA 55II:405.657-58. On Ps. 60:8, Luther also notes that ". . . every trial is a sign of a loving God." AE 10:283; WA 55II:312.89. This seems to be Luther's recollection of his experience of being or feeling forsaken in dark *Anfechtung* where he then found a gracious God in suffering.

55. AE 10:283; WA 55II:312.78-93. AE 10:291-92; WA 55II:322.341-44.

56. AE 31:135; WA 1:561.28-29.

57. AE 31:144; WA 1:566.29-30.

58. Is. 38:10, 17; Ps. 130:1 and 1 Sam. 2:6; and Jonah 2:3, respectively. AE 10:371-73; WA 55II:403.593—405.640.

59. In reference to Gen. 37:35, AE 10:373; WA 55II:405.650.

60. In the *Explanations*, Luther mentions only David and Hezekiah, not Jonah, and adds Christ, Abraham, Moses, and Job in the *Defense* of 1521, and notes four names Abraham, Isaac, Jacob, and Joseph in the *Lectures on Genesis*, 41:1-7 (1543-1545). AE 31:128; WA 1:557.15-24; AE 32:95; WA 7:451.10-15; and AE 7:133; WA 44:392.21-22, respectively.

who tasted hell in this life, Luther stresses the type of "worldly men" who "live in their own goodness and do not descend to hell with the Lord, but rather ascend to the heavens."[61] The contrast of this statement resembles that of a theologian of glory and a theologian of the cross in the *Heidelberg Disputation*, a subject which will be discussed later in this chapter.[62] Fourth, in this particular lecture Luther does not seem to make explicit the linking of the two notions of a foretaste of hell and the suffering of purgatory, but on Psalm 69:3 in the *Dictata*, Luther employs the term "purgatory" and alludes to the notion of both postmortem and existential sufferings.[63] Just as "the mouth of death" could not swallow up Jesus, Luther emphasizes, "the pit of hell or purgatory" will not shut up the elect as in the resurrection of the dead, which also means, tropologically speaking in Luther's expression of existential suffering, "*through repentance* the mouth of hell and the way out are open."[64]

Significant is Luther's use of the term "purgatory" or "the mouth of hell" regarding the notion of a foretaste of hell for two reasons. First, *prior to* his acquaintance with Tauler, Luther already addresses the subject of suffering in light of the notion of a foretaste of hell and purgatory.[65] In the *Dictata*, Luther does not link the two notions as explicitly as in the *Explanations* or in the *Defense* (1521). It can still be argued, however, that such a suggestion is strongly implied in his interpretation, which appears more explicitly in the *Explanations* and in the *Defense*. Second, it proves that it is not Tauler who initially and primarily influenced Luther on the matter of suffering perceived as a foretaste of hell and purgatory. Nonetheless, Luther refers to Tauler in this regard, particularly in the *Explanations* (e.g., Thesis Fifteen) and the *Defense* (e.g., the Thirty-seventh Article). With

---

61. Luther underscores the same viewpoint in his *Preface to the Theologia Deutsch*. See also Podmore, *Struggling with God*, 97.

62. The former "looks upon the invisible things of God" while the latter "comprehends the visible and manifest things of God seen through suffering and the cross." AE 31:40; WA 1:354.17–20.

63. AE 10:363; WA 55II:396.372-74.

64. AE 10:364; WA 55II:396.379—397.391. Emphasis added.

65. According to Vogelsang, Luther must have lectured on Ps. 69 in the autumn of 1514 prior to his annotations on Tauler's sermons from early 1515. Vogelsang, *Der junge Luther*, 40, quoted in German, "Martin Luther's First Psalm Lectures," 4n2. Regarding Luther's annotations on Tauler's sermons, see Ozment, "Aid to Luther's Marginal Comments," 305. See also WA 9:95–104.

this finding, we raise a question as to what particular role Tauler plays in Luther's disputations.

LUTHER'S ACQUAINTANCE WITH AND USE OF TAULER

John Tauler

John Tauler (d. 1361), a pupil of Meister Eckhart von Hochheim (d. 1328),[66] was a German mystic, "less speculative, more vernacular" than his mentor.[67] Tauler's preaching career began in Strasbourg around 1330, but within a decade he was exiled with his fellow Dominicans in Basel where he became acquainted with a circle of clergy known as the "Friends of God" (*Gottesfreunde*). Upon returning to Strasbourg in 1343, he ministered to people in his hometown amid a series of outbreaks of earthquakes, fire, and the Black Death.

As for his works, no formal treatises are known either in Latin or German other than sermons. His sermons in German were first printed in Leipzig in 1498, and they were reprinted a decade later at Augsburg with several editions thereafter. Fifty years later, his sermons translated into Latin were first published at Cologne, with subsequent editions afterwards.[68] Distinctive from his contemporaries is Tauler's notion of union, in that while maintaining a common mystical theme of deification, he stresses particularly the way in which one is united with God, not by an ecclesiastical means (i.e., priests), but by individual spiritual afflictions.[69]

---

66. Meister Eckhart was a German Dominican mystic whose particular interest lay in the notion of the mystical union between an individual soul and God. Schürmann, "Meister Eckhart," Encyclopaedia Britannica.

67. Podmore, *Struggling with God*, 89. Podmore references McGinn, *The Harvest of Mysticism*.

68. "Johannes Tauler" in World Heritage Encyclopedia Edition.

69. Francke, "Medieval German Mysticism," 118–19. Francke also notes, "None of the mystics has conceived of the *unio mystica*, the sinking of deified man in the infinite, in so genuinely human a manner, or in terms so far raised above all exclusively ecclesiastical views." Francke, "Medieval German Mysticism," 119. Cf. Concerning the subject of penance, Luther stresses the aspect of an internal penance, as well as the notion and practice of the private confession before a priest. Leppin, "Luther's Roots," 56.

Tauler in Luther's Writings

John Tauler's sermons, as well as a German theological tract (hereinafter *German Theology*) written by a Frankfurter,[70] made a significant impression on Luther,[71] particularly on the theme of the dying of the old Adam and arising of a new man.[72] When publishing a portion of *German Theology* (i.e., chapters 7–26) on December 4, 1516,[73] Luther considered the booklet a succinct summary of Tauler's theology, and ranked it next to Scripture and Augustine.[74] Ten days later, Luther writes a letter to Spalatin recommending his consideration,[75] and the publication of the entire booklet follows in early June of 1518.[76] Meantime, Luther's references to Tauler appear occasionally in his sermons and letters. In his sermon on Sexagesima Sunday (February 15, 1517), for instance, Luther mentions Tauler when rejecting self-love.[77] Also, in a letter to Staupitz (March 31, 1518), Luther underscores that Tauler's booklet—referring to *German Theology*, however—influenced him, and he notes, "I really followed Tauler's theology and his booklet, which you gave me recently, printed by our Christian, Aurifaber."[78]

---

70. Brecht notes that the Frankfurter is "a curator of the House of the Order of Teutonic Knights in Frankfurt on the Main." Brecht, *Martin Luther*, 1:141. *German Theology* (*Eyn theologia deutsch*) confirmed Luther's theology that had already been developed. Jones, review of *Der 'Frankfurter' / 'Theologia Deutsch,'* 158.

71. Hamm, *Early Luther*, 225–26.

72. WA 1:153, quoted in Leppin, "Luther's Roots," 57. Concerning the aspect of dying, Luther later notes, "One becomes a theologian by living, rather by dying and being condemned, not by understanding, reading, or speculating." WA 5:163.28-29 (*Operationes in Psalmos*, 1519–1521), quoted in Leppin, "Luther's Roots," 55. Leppin comments that here "by dying" Luther refers to Tauler and the *Theologia Deutsch*. Cf. Luther's notion of dying for living seems to resonate with his reading of Galatians 2. Gorman comments, "... here in Galatians 2, as in Romans 6, faith is a death experience that, paradoxically, engenders life—life to God, life in Christ (v. 17), Christ's life within (v. 20)." Michael J. Gorman, *Cruciformity*, 138.

73. WA Br 1:79.58-64, quoted in Wicks, *Man Yearning for Grace*, 144. See also Leppin, "Luther's Roots," 56.

74. Brecht, *Martin Luther*, 1:139, 141. Leppin also comments that for Luther mysticism and Scripture are mutually "complementary." Leppin, "Luther's Roots," 58.

75. Wicks, *Man Yearning for Grace*, 144–45.

76. Brecht, *Martin Luther*, 1:141. See also Rittgers, *Reformation of Suffering*, 98n121.

77. Wicks, *Man Yearning for Grace*, 145. See Tauler's Sermon for Sexagesima Sunday in *Sermons and Conferences*, 160–63.

78. WA Br. 1:160, 8–9, quoted in Leppin, "Luther's Roots," 57; Leppin, *Martin Luther*, 25. By "Christian Aurifaber," Luther refers to Christian Döring. WA Br 1:160n5.

Luther's View of Purgatory

As far as Luther's acquaintance with Tauler's sermons is concerned, it was Johann Lang who had first received Tauler's sermons from a Wittenberg woman, who then passed it on to Luther.[79] Reading line by line, Luther annotates Tauler's sermons from early 1515 until mid-1516, selectively about twenty sermons.[80] In the annotations, however, Luther makes no single reference to the subject of purgatory. When reading Tauler's sermons, perhaps Luther might have paid attention only to the themes related to his experiences of *Anfechtungen*, self-condemnation, and resignation. Luther's marginal notes on Tauler's sermons affirm that Tauler's theology is "an experienced wisdom."[81] Subsequently, in his *Lectures on Romans*, sometime in May 1516, Luther refers to Tauler on the notion of the soul's passivity[82] in the context of God's artistic work of molding.[83] Then, in the *Explanations* and in the *Defense* Luther refers to Tauler on the subject of purgatory and the afflictions of the *Anfechtung*.[84]

Anfechtung: Tauler's Sermons in Harmony with Luther's View

While seeking a non-scholastic theological method, Luther discovers Tauler and begins to have high regard for him almost instantly,[85] with respect to the quality of his theology close to that of the fathers, in general,[86] and his theological insight drawn from his experience of spiritual afflictions,

---

79. Brecht, *Martin Luther*, 1:137. As for Luther's letter to Lang in October 1516, see Wicks, *Man Yearning for Grace*, 144. In early 1515, prior to this occurrence, Luther encountered with the preachers of "upper-Rhenish mysticism" associated with German mystics such as Meister Eckhart, John Tauler, and Henry Suso (d. 1366). Leppin, "Luther's Roots," 55–56.

80. Ozment, "Aid to Luther's Marginal Comments," 305–11. See also WA 9:95–104.

81. *Sapientia experimentalis*. WA 9:28.21, Rittgers, "Luther's Engagement in Pastoral Care," 469. See also Bayer, *Martin Luther's Theology*, 30. The American Edition translates the phrase "a wisdom of experience." AE 31:73.

82. Wicks, *Man Yearning for Grace*, 144; Brecht, *Martin Luther*, 1:137.

83. AE 25:367–68; WA 56:378.13–17. On Rom. 8:26. See Tauler's sermon for Easter Monday (Luke 24:32) in *Sermons and Conferences*, 257.

84. AE 32:95; WA 7:451.16–18.

85. Ozment, *Age of Reform*, 240. Leppin also points out that Luther attacked scholastic theology on the basis of mysticism. Leppin, "Luther's Roots," 57. See also Dennis Ngien, *Suffering of God*, 43.

86. Luther underscores it in his letter to George Spalatin (December 14, 1516). AE 48:35–36; WA Br 1.79.58–64.

in particular.[87] The content of Tauler's sermons is not distinctively new to Luther, however. During the later section of his lectures on Romans and the early phase of the indulgence controversy, for instance,[88] Luther learns that Tauler's mysticism confirms his theology of humility.[89] Tauler's theme of God's alien work that appears contrary to human expectation (i.e., the *Anfechtung*),[90] for another instance, confirms Luther's concept of God's alien work in the *Dictata*.[91]

With regard to the notion of union with Christ, Tauler stresses that Christ takes an active role, and the believers, taking the passive role, resign themselves entirely to God.[92] In Tauler's theology, both human passivity and resignation are the principal component, which is in harmony with Luther's notion, and which Luther terms a "naked faith."[93] Combined with a christocentric interpretation, which is Luther's hermeneutical principle not found in Tauler,[94] the notion of joyous exchange assures certainty for Luther to the extent to which a believer's union with Christ through faith is considered as "the justification of the ungodly."[95] Luther stresses that knowing Christ's passion means living in it by faith, not merely theorizing it intellectually.[96] "One

---

87. Brecht, *Martin Luther*, 1:137.

88. Wicks, *Man Yearning for Grace*, 145.

89. Brecht, *Martin Luther*, 1:137, 139. On the subject of the old Adam remaining after forgiveness, Luther also notices that Tauler, as well as the *German Theology*, concurs with his viewpoint. Wicks, *Man Yearning for Grace*, 151. Hoffman also comments that Luther's interest in Tauler's sermons and the *German Theology* was for the fact that both documents confirmed Luther's viewpoint. Hoffman, *Theology of Heart*, 105.

90. Hamm, *Early Luther*, 226.

91. Psalm 91:7; 92:4. Wicks, *Man Yearning for Grace*, 145–46; see also Brecht, *Martin Luther*, 1:138. Leppin points out that the concept continues to appear, first, in the *Ninety-five Theses* with respect to the notion of true repentance; then, in the *Heidelberg Disputation* with respect to the notion of *opus alienum dei*; and also in the *Antinomian Disputation* with respect to the notion of "*desperatio*." Leppin, "Luther's Transformation," 120; Rittgers, *Reformation of Suffering*, 111.

92. Wicks, *Man Yearning for Grace*, 146–47.

93. *Nuda fides in Deum*. WA 9:102.35, quoted in Wicks, *Man Yearning for Grace*, 147–48. In the *Heidelberg Disputation*, Luther reiterates it with the term "naked" or "bare" (*nudus*) that "our life is hidden in God (i.e. in the bare confidence in his mercy." AE 31:44; WA 1:357.3. The notion of self-accusation and resignation also appears in the *Seven Penitential Psalms*. See Brecht, *Martin Luther*, 1:143–44.

94. Wicks, *Man Yearning for Grace*, 152.

95. Hamm, *Early Luther*, 201–4.

96. Wicks, *Man Yearning for Grace*, 149.

becomes a theologian by living, rather by dying and being condemned," asserts Luther, "not by understanding, reading, or speculating."[97]

Tauler's Role in Luther's View of Purgatory

Declaration of the *Explanations*:
Two Principles and Three Categories of Authorities

In discussing the role of Tauler in Luther's disputations on purgatory, it is necessary to review the Declaration (*Protestatio*) with which Luther begins the *Explanations* for the purpose of defending himself in the prospect of persecution and death.[98] In the Declaration, Luther highlights two principles: first, it is the methodology of his disputation in which three particular categories of authorities are employed in a hierarchical order: Scripture, tradition, and a judgment of reason and experience. Concerning the first principle, Luther declares:

> First, I testify that I desire to say or maintain absolutely nothing except, first of all, what is in the Holy Scriptures and can be maintained from them; and then what is in and from the writings of the church fathers and is accepted by the Roman church and preserved both in the canons and the papal decrees. But if any proposition cannot be proved or disproved from them I shall simply maintain it, for the sake of debate, on the basis of the judgment of reason and experience, always, however, without violating the judgment of any of my superiors in these matters.[99]

The second principle is the right of Christian freedom to refute or accept theological opinions according to one's judgment.[100] If a proposition can neither be proved nor disproved by the first two categories of authorities, then the third category engages in the debate. The proposition on the punishments of purgatory is the case, for instance. This will be discussed in detail in a moment, but suffice it to note here that, first, Scripture is silent on the subject—in the way in which the opponents claim purgatory with

---

97. WA 5:163.28-29 (*Operationes in Psalmos*, 1519-1521), quoted in Leppin, "Luther's Roots," 55.

98. Luther was convinced in 1518 that his death (or "martyrdom") was impending under the threat of the papacy. Roper, *Martin Luther*, 109-11.

99. AE 31:83; WA 1:529.29—530.3.

100. AE 31:83; WA 1:529.29—530.12.

reference to the Scripture[101]—and, second, there is no unanimous agreement among the church fathers and no official teaching accepted by the Church in Rome on this particular subject.[102] This is the context in which Luther treats the subject within the perimeter of the third category (i.e., the judgment of reason and experience),[103] and further proposes:

> it does not seem proved, either by reason or Scripture, that souls in purgatory are outside the state of merit, that is, unable to grow in love;[104]
>
> Nor does it seem proved that souls in purgatory, at least not all of them, are certain and assured of their own salvation, even if we ourselves may be entirely certain of it.[105]

Regarding the second principle, Luther insists on the right of Christian freedom in order to maintain fair theological debates and defend without hindrance his dispositions against the opponents' criticism and accusations, and equally refute their arguments and claims. Luther declares:

---

101. Luther criticizes the opponents' methodology and their biblical reference to purgatory, and argues, "For it is better to state that this authority [Scripture] says nothing at all about this matter [of purgatory], than, in seeking to understand in both connections, to give the impression that it is by no means reliable." AE 31:139; WA 1:564.8–11. Unlike his opponents, Luther's argument on purgatory takes a different approach: first, Scripture speaks about those who tasted hell in this life; thus, it is certain that such punishments are imposed on the souls in purgatory. AE 31:140; WA 1:564.16–17.

102. With regard to the church fathers, Luther underlines the same viewpoint in the Leipzig Debate. WA 2:330.23–35. As for the official teaching of the Roman Church, however, Luther seems to pay no particular attention to the Second General Council of Lyons (1274) or the Council of Florence (1438-1439; July 6, 1439 on "purgatorial punishment" (*poenis purgatoriis*)). The Second General Council of Lyons confirms the definition of postmortem purgation defined in Innocent IV's letter sent to the Bishop of Tusculum (March 6, 1254). CCDD 1304:336. On the other hand, the Eastern Church does not agree with the Western Church in this regard, of which Luther was aware. See AE 32:96; WA 7:452.1–4. The *Defense* (1521).

103. Thesis Fifteen: "This fear or horror is sufficient in itself, to say nothing of other things, to constitute the penalty of purgatory, since it is very near the horror of despair." AE 31:125–30; WA 1:555.26—558.23. Thesis Sixteen: "Hell, purgatory, and heaven seem to differ the same as despair, fear, and assurance of salvation." AE 31:130; WA 1:558.25–26.

104. AE 31:136–40; WA 1: 562.1—564.31. Thesis Eighteen.

105. AE 31:140–45; WA 1:564.32—567.24. Thesis Nineteen. Luther addresses it in *Asterisci Lutheri adversus obeliscos Eccii* as well. WA 1:294.16, quoted in Vercruysse, "Luther's Theology of the Cross," 527. See also WA 2:332.38—333.2.

> I add one consideration and insist upon it according to the right of Christian liberty, that is, that I wish to refute or accept, according to my own judgment, the mere opinions of St. Thomas, Bonaventura, or other scholastics or canonists which are maintained without text or proof. I shall do this according to the advice of Paul to "test everything, hold fast to that which is good" [I Thess. 5:21], although I know the feeling of Thomists who want St. Thomas to be approved by the church in everything. The weight of St. Thomas' authority is known well enough. From this declaration I believe that it is made sufficiently clear that I can err, but also that I shall not be considered a heretic for that reason, no matter how much those who think and wish differently should rage or be consumed with anger.[106]

Concerning the second principle, Luther reiterates that opinions of the scholastic tradition cannot take precedence over other traditions, particularly a German tradition in this case. This is the ground on which Luther references Tauler on the subject of the punishments of purgatory.

Analysis: Luther's Reference to Tauler

Regarding his thesis that fear or horror itself is the punishment of purgatory,[107] Luther argues that some individuals have suffered the punishments in this life, namely, the "punishments of hell as fear, trembling, dread, and flight,"[108] and makes use of the three categories of authorities as proposed. First, from the primary authority (i.e., Scripture) Luther lists several references such as David[109] and Hezekiah.[110] Second, as for the subsequent level of authority (i.e., tradition), which played a major role in the field of theology,[111] Luther uses Tauler to defend his proposition.

> How many there are even today who taste those punishments! For what else does John Tauler teach in his German sermons than the sufferings of these punishments of which he also cites some examples? Indeed, I know that this teacher is unknown to the schools of theologians and is probably despised by them; but even

---

106. AE 31:83; WA 1:530.3–12.
107. See Thesis Fifteen. AE 31:125–30; WA 1:555.26—558.23.
108. AE 31:128; WA 1:557.15–24. AE 31:126; WA 1:556.6–10.
109. Ps. 28:1; 71:20; 88:33; 94:17; 141:7.
110. Isa. 38:10, 13.
111. Brecht, *Martin Luther*, 1:141.

though he has written entirely in the German vernacular, I have found in him more solid and sincere theology than is found in all the scholastic teachers of all the universities or than can be found in their propositions.[112]

As for the third authority of the judgment of reason or experience, Luther addresses the *Anfechtung* account—presumably his own—which begins with "I myself 'knew a man,'"[113] and stresses that postmortem torment in purgatory seems much greater than such dreadful suffering of *Anfechtung*.[114]

The composition of the *Defense* of 1521 is another occasion where Luther references Tauler. During this critical stage of transition in the Reformation, Luther redefines purgatory as a foretaste of hell in this life. What used to be taken into account in describing the postmortem *punishments* of purgatory is now considered as *purgatory itself* in this life:

> The existence of purgatory I have never denied. I still hold that it exists, as I have written and admitted many times, though I have found no way of proving it incontrovertibly from Scripture or reason. I find in Scripture that Christ, Abraham, Jacob, Moses, Job, David, Hezekiah, and some others tasted hell in this life. This I think was purgatory, and it seems not beyond belief that some of the dead suffer in like manner. *Tauler has much to say about it* and, in short, I myself have come to the conclusion that there is a purgatory, but I cannot force anybody else to come to the same result.[115]

In this particular thesis, Luther seems to employ Tauler in reference to *both* the notion of postmortem torments only for few souls[116] *and* existential suffering.[117] The *Defense* also demonstrates a sequential pattern resembling

---

112. AE 31:128–29; WA 1:557.25–32.

113. AE 31:129–30; WA 1:557.33—558.18. With this *Anfechtung* account, Luther might have possibly referred to Tauler. See "The *Explanations* (1518)" later in this chapter.

114. AE 31:129–30; WA 1:558.12–14.

115. AE 32:95; WA 7:451.11–18. Emphasis added. Regarding Luther's use of theological terms, see "Luther's Use of the Term 'Purgatory'" in chapter 3, and "Purgatory where Faith and Love in Christ Continually Grow" in chapter 4.

116. "[I]t seems not beyond belief that some of the dead suffer in like manner." AE 32:95; WA 7:451.16. Regarding Luther's view that purgatory is only for few souls, see AE 52:181; WA 10I 1:589.8–9. Luther's letter to von Amsdorf (January 13, 1522).

117. "[S]ome others tasted hell in this life. This I think was purgatory." AE 32:95; WA 7:451.15. The formality of the reference to the subject of suffering in the *Defense* (1521) is congruent with that to Tauler in the *Explanations* (1518) where Tauler represents the second category of authority (i.e., tradition). AE 31:128–29; WA 1:557.25–32.

that of the Declaration of the *Explanations* on the three categories of authorities.[118] Concerning the third authority of the judgment of reason or experience, however, Luther does not elaborate in this particular article, but makes a concluding remark with his redefined view of purgatory instead.[119]

In addition, in the *Lectures on Genesis* Luther references Tauler concerning the theme of the cross of suffering. Based on Tauler's statement, "Man should know that he has done great damage if he does not wait for God's work," Luther stresses that God's work of crucifying, mortifying and destroying the old Adam to nothingness occurs only "through suffering and the cross."[120] Luther's biblical references for his assertion include some of the individuals mentioned earlier in the *Dictata*, the *Explanations*, and the *Defense* who experienced sufferings in great intensity.[121] In this lecture, Luther does not follow the three categories of authorities in a sequential pattern; instead, he addresses Tauler prior to the biblical reference.

Analysis: Authority of Tradition

With the second category (i.e., tradition as represented by Tauler) in the *Explanations* and in the *Defense*, Luther defends the Wittenberg theology as rooted in an ancient tradition.[122] In this stance, Tauler was "a major ally

---

118. First, while the Scripture is silent on the subject of purgatory in the way the opponents claim, it speaks about the punishments of hell and those who tasted them in this life. Second, Tauler represents a tradition of German theology. AE 32:95; WA 7:451.11–18.

119. There are two possible reasons for Luther's silence on the authority of experience: first, Luther perhaps considers it unnecessary to address the subject with his reference to Tauler for both postmortem torment and a foretaste of hell in this article; second, it is perhaps redundant since he already addressed the subject earlier in the Fourth Article: "The question whether this great fear is a purgatory, I have left undecided, not knowing how to prove or disprove it; *we shall learn from our own experience. Besides, our lack of knowledge on this point makes no difference. Nevertheless, I think Scripture shows that the pains of hell (which all of them identify with purgatory) are fear, terror, horror, the desire to flee, and despair.*" AE 32:31; WA 7:349.30–34; emphases added.

120. AE 7:133; WA 44:397.9–20. On Gen. 41:1–7.

121. AE 7:133; WA 44:397.21–25 for Genesis; AE 10:371–73; WA 55II:403.593–405.640 for the *Dictata*; AE 31:128–29; WA 1:557.15–24 for the *Explanations*; and AE 32:95; WA 7:451.11–18 for the *Defense*.

122. AE 31:75–76; WA 1:378–79. The *Preface to the Complete Edition of a German Theology* (1518). See also Ozment, *Age of Reform*, 240 and 240n54, as well as Brecht, *Martin Luther*, 1:139, 141.

if not a major source" for Luther,[123] and Luther underlines it in the *Preface to the Complete Edition of a German Theology* (published in June 1518):

> I now for the first time become aware of the fact that a few of us highly educated Wittenberg theologians speak disgracefully, as though we want to undertake entirely new things, as though there had been no people previously or elsewhere . . . It is obvious that such matters as are contained in this book have not been discussed in our universities for a long time, with the result that the holy Word of God has not only been laid under the bench but has almost been destroyed by dust and filth.
>
> Let anyone who wishes read this little book, and then let him say whether theology is original with us or ancient, for this book is certainly not new.[124]

Furthermore, by means of the same authority Luther disputes the opponents' authority of tradition (i.e., Thomas Aquinas),[125] contending that it is not to be considered as a universal or superior authority next to the Scripture.[126]

Here is the critical punch line of Luther's argument against his opponents: "It is evident, therefore, that *this authority* [opponent's biblical reference] is directly opposed to purgatory, indeed by his ambiguity it makes a hell out of purgatory."[127] With this statement Luther makes it explicit that his opponents' claim on the authority of Scripture for purgatory—the way in which they use Scripture in reference to the subject—and their teachings about purgatory create "ambiguity," doubts, and "distortion,"[128] causing "purgatory" to be represented and conceived as "punitory."[129] In contrast, Luther claims that his propositions—the way he proposes—are suitably and satisfactorily rooted in the Scripture:

> In positing this as most likely true concerning the whole matter of the punishments of purgatory, I am moved to do so, first of all, because of the nature of dread and anxiety, then because Scripture

---

123. Ozment, "Aid to Luther's Marginal Comments," 305.

124. AE 31:75-76; WA 1:378.23—379.7.

125. By "Aquinas" Luther refers to the scholastic methodology that presupposes philosophy for the foundation of theology.

126. AE 31:83; WA 1:530.8-9.

127. AE 31:140; WA 1:564.27-29. Emphasis added.

128. AE 31:135; WA 1:561.28-38. See also AE 31:139-40; WA 1:564.4-21.

129. AE 31:135; WA 1:561.29.

attributes this punishment to the damned, and, finally, because the whole church says that the punishments of hell and of purgatory are the same. Therefore I believe that this opinion of ours is sufficiently rooted in the Scripture.[130]

He further claims that his reference to the same authority is arguably "better arguments" with "better examples of Scripture," the point of which he underscores in the conclusion: "If there are any who can produce better arguments concerning these matters, I shall not be jealous of them. I insist only that the one who does so should base his arguments on better examples of Scripture without veiling himself in the smoky opinions of men."[131]

Luther's disputations distinguish two types of theology between the wisdom of the world (i.e., philosophy) and that of Scripture, contending that the former is the theology of glory and the latter theology of the cross; the former is scholastic theology,[132] for instance, and the latter German theology.[133] Luther contends that his opponents' claims based on scholastic theology—which promotes the sales of indulgences and consequently depreciates the cross of existential suffering—must be refuted, and the teaching of the church needs to be amended for the proper spiritual care of the church. Luther makes it definite in the *Explanations*:

> The church needs a reformation which is not the work of one man, namely, the pope, or of many men, namely the cardinals, both of which the most recent council has demonstrated, but it is the work of the whole world, indeed it is the work of God alone. However, only God who has created time knows the time for this reformation. In the meantime we cannot deny such manifest wrongs. The power of the keys is abused and enslaved to greed and ambition. The raging abyss has received added impetus. We cannot stop it.[134]

In this polemical and pragmatic use of Tauler with reference to German theology, Luther underscores the following remarks: first, the tradition of scholastic theology treats the subject of the punishments of purgatory

---

130. AE 31:143–45; WA 1:566.24–28.

131. AE 31:145; WA 1:567.22–24.

132. Ebeling, *Luther*, 231.

133. Moltmann notes that Luther's theology of the cross attacks, not medieval catholic theology as a whole, but the theology of glory that he recognized in it, which is "man's inhuman concern for self-deification through knowledge and works." Jürgen Moltmann, *Crucified God*, 71. Lohse also notes that Luther's statement should be understood in the context of a battle with Rome. Lohse, *Martin Luther's Theology*, 38–39.

134. AE 31:250; WA 1:627.27–31.

ambiguously, but the tradition of German theology addresses the subject profoundly in light of "a wisdom of experience";[135] and second, with German theology as the ground of his proposals, his disputations are more persuasive than his opponents. Luther argues: "If there is anyone who does not believe that ["the inner fire is much more terrible than the outer fire" (e.g., the *Anfechtung* account)], we do not beg him to do so, but we have merely proved that these preachers of indulgences speak with too much audacity about many things of which they know nothing or else doubt. For one ought to *believe those who are experienced in these matters* rather than those who are inexperienced."[136]

Luther and Tauler: Convergences and Divergences

Having discussed Tauler's role in Luther's view of purgatory, it is fair to examine how close Luther's theological stance is to Tauler's. In a nutshell, there are noticeable parallels between Luther and Tauler, particularly with respect to uncertainty about salvation amid the storms of *Anfechtungen*; the notion of union with Christ; experiencing the pains of hell in this life; and the notion of *Anfechtung* perceived as the cross. Luther notes in his letter to George Spalatin (December 14, 1516) how impressive and profound Tauler's sermons are:

> I shall add my advice: if reading a pure and solid theology, which is available in German and is of a quality closest to that of the Fathers, might please you, then get for yourself the sermons of John Tauler, the Dominican. I am enclosing for you, so to speak, the essence of them all. I have seen no theological work in Latin or German that is more sound and more in harmony with the gospel than this. Taste it and see how sweet the Lord is after you have first tried and realized how bitter is whatever we are.[137]

---

135. AE 31:73.
136. AE 31:130; WA 1:558.15–18. Emphasis added.
137. AE 48:35–36; WA Br 1.79.58–64.

Luther's View of Purgatory

Convergence

Uncertainty of Salvation

In the sermon on the Feast of Many Holy Martyrs, Tauler addresses two ways wherein one becomes acquainted with and acquires the knowledge of God's saving grace and love: one in joy and the other in spiritual afflictions.[138] When all spiritual joys are withheld, believers continue to remain in God's grace. However, their tormenting afflictions and suppressing burdens overwhelm them to the extent that they become uncertain about God's saving grace. Tauler describes: "[T]hey are solely embarrassed, and know not which way to turn for relief, for God seems to them to have quite given them up. They can but stand fast in faith, hope, and charity, in a very thick darkness of soul ... By all these tribulations they are utterly worn out, and know not what they shall do."[139]

Luther's description of the *Anfechtung* in which one experiences "uncertainty" of salvation is strikingly parallel to Tauler's: "At such a time God seems terribly angry ... All that remains is the stark-naked desire for help and a terrible groaning, but it does not know where to turn for help ... [E]very corner of the soul is filled with the greatest bitterness, dread, trembling, and sorrow in such a manner that all these last forever."[140] On the matter of "uncertainty" of salvation in the punishments of hell or a foretaste of hell in this life, Luther refers to both Scripture[141] and Tauler,[142] as well as to the third category of authority, and notes: "That's what *those who have experienced it* say."[143]

---

138. Tauler, *Sermons and Conferences*, 739.
139. Tauler, *Sermons and Conferences*, 740.
140. AE 31:129; WA 1:557.37–38, 558.4–5, 6–8.
141. AE 31:128–29; WA 1:557.15–24. See also AE 31:141; WA 1:565.6–12.
142. AE 31:128–29; WA 1:557.25–32.
143. AE 31:141; WA 1:565.6–13. Emphasis added. Luther attempts to clarify his statement: "First, I have said that not all are certain. Secondly, perhaps it is better, according to the aforesaid, to say that they have not actually been certain, but that, because of their great desire for help, they are, so to speak, certain; and as though they were certain, they have asked to be helped quickly. So they rather imagine they are certain and timidly presume that they are certain as if they know for sure." AE 31:142; WA 1:565.30–34.

Purgatory as the Cross

Notion of Existential Pains of Hell

Both Luther and Tauler perceive suffering in relation to the notion of a foretaste of hell. With the statement, "The pains of hell itself seem less to them [believers] than the torture this causes, this and their other interior tribulations,"[144] Tauler insinuates that the suffering of *Anfechtung* is no less than experiencing the pains of hell. In the same vein, Luther addresses the subject with reference to Tauler:

> Some individuals have tasted these punishments in this life, especially those of hell. Therefore we must believe even more that they are imposed upon the dead in purgatory.
>
> How many there are even today who taste those punishments! For what else does John Tauler teach in his German sermons than the sufferings of these punishments of which he also cites some examples?[145]

Tauler's passion mysticism and his view of spiritual afflictions as the purgatorial pains of hell in this life confirm Luther's notion of *Anfechtungen* perceived as a foretaste of hell.[146] When Luther struggled with uncertainty of salvation in the dreadful fear of God's judgment, he related his afflictions with the passion of the crucified Christ. He then began to grasp what it means to be united with Christ through faith amid *Anfechtungen*; that is, trusting in "*Christus pro me*" in the midst of a spiritual anguish of near despair.[147] In this respect, faith for Luther is beyond intellectual knowledge or a theory of God's existence; it is a deep trust in Christ in the *Sitz im Leben* of affliction. Luther's theology is, thus, inextricably interwoven with his spiritual agony—the pains of hell in this life,[148] the notion of which Luther terms "the cross."

---

144. Tauler, *Sermons*, 741.

145. AE 31:128–29; WA 1:557.15–16, 25–27.

146. Vogelsang, "Weltbild und Kreuzestheologie," 94–99, quoted in Packull, "Luther and Medieval Mysticism," 81.

147. Hamm, *Early Luther*, 51, 216.

148. Hamm, *Early Luther*, 218. Hamm terms it "a mysticism of *Anfechtung*" or "a mysticism of the cross." Hamm, *Early Luther*, 220–21.

Luther's View of Purgatory

Anfechtung as the Cross

In the First Sermon for the Fifth Sunday after Trinity,[149] Tauler illustrates *Anfechtung* with regard to the cross, and addresses the notion of union with God in three different degrees—"jubilation," "destitution," and "transformation."[150] As for the second degree, Tauler describes:

> Hard and strong food it is that this man needs—not the baby's bread and milk. Before him lies a desert road, dark and lonely, and as God leads him through it, He deprives him of all the solaces and joys that He ever gave him. The poor man is so confused that he knows nothing of God—*he does not know whether there is a God above him or not* . . . He seems to himself penned in between two steep walls, a sword before him, a spear behind him . . . *If hell could be added to this purgatory of his*, it would be—so it seems to him—a softening of his pain . . . But, alas, this poor soul is *in anguish so deep*, that *he no more can believe that all will yet be well with him* than he can believe that darkness shall be turned into light.
>
> This trial prepares a man for God's higher work in him more than all the devotions and pious practices that can be thought of. And when our Lord finds him well enough purified by hanging upon *this cross of insufferable agony*, He then comes to him to introduce him to the third degree.[151]

Tauler terms this *Anfechtung* of uncertainty "purgatory," the "cross of insufferable agony," describing it as "a sharp anguish of soul" and the "anguish of purgatory."[152] For Tauler, the cross means not only "the Christ crucified"[153] in an objective sense, but also a Christian's "daily suffering"[154] associated with self-denial and resignation in the love of God,[155] two major themes in Tauler's mystical theology.

---

149. Tauler, *Sermons*, 433–41. On 1 Pet 3:8.

150. Tauler, *Sermons*, 439–41.

151. Tauler, *Sermons*, 440–41. Emphases added.

152. "True, this course means a sharp anguish of soul; it is painful in the extreme to be tormented with unceasing yearnings after self-renunciation and simplicity: but it is the anguish of purgatory, whose cleansing fires are thus endured before their time." Tauler, *Sermons*, 568. Second Sermon for the Nineteenth Sunday after Trinity on Matthew 22:4.

153. Tauler, *Sermons*, 690, 692.

154. Tauler, *Sermons*, 701.

155. Tauler, *Sermons*, 701–2.

Purgatory as the Cross

In a similar vein, Luther illustrates *Anfechtung* in the *Explanations* with the image of the cross, delineating it as a participation in the cross of Christ.

> In this moment . . . the soul cannot believe that it can ever be redeemed other than that the punishment is not yet completely felt.[156] Yet the soul is eternal and is not able to think of itself as being temporal . . . In this instance *the person is stretched out with Christ* so that all his bones may be counted, and every corner of the soul is filled with the greatest bitterness, dread, trembling, and sorrow in such a manner that all these last forever.[157]

For Luther, a desperate spiritual crisis in the sphere of God's alien work is the cross of Christ in which a Christian—already united with Christ in faith—participates. Similar to Tauler who perceived self-denial and resignation as the cross of a Christian,[158] Luther's theological perception of "the cross" is extensive, encompassing such notions as self-condemnation, repentance, resignation, and suffering of *Anfechtung*.[159] It particularly underlines the aspect of "the *passio* of faith, a passive experience of being led along Christ's way of the cross"[160] in which one is conformed to Christ in a union. For Luther, *Anfechtung* is not merely about following Christ, but a sign of participating in the cross of Christ.[161]

Divergences

With these remarkable similarities, equally noticeable are several differences between Tauler and Luther. First, Tauler asserts that one becomes perfect by means of suffering, and stresses that "[t]hey [the suffering Christians] reckon themselves as the basest sinners in the world; in God's eyes they are the most spotless."[162] On the other hand, Luther articulates the notion of suffering uniquely in the framework of his theology of justification. It is faith alone by which one is justified before God and reckoned

---

156. Hamm comments that this uncertainty about punishment is related to mysticism (e.g., John Tauler). Hamm, *Early Luther*, 227n146; 228n147, 148.

157. AE 31:129; WA 1:558.1–3, 5–8; emphasis added.

158. Tauler, *Sermons*, 702.

159. See "Luther's Perception of Purgatory in His Theology of Justification in the *Explanations*" in chapter 4.

160. Hamm, *Early Luther*, 219.

161. Rupp, *Luther's Progress*, 43.

162. Tauler, *Sermons*, 741.

righteous in Christ while *Anfechtung* is necessary for both the preparation for justification and the growth of faith.[163] Second, Tauler claims that sufferings in this life shorten the length of time in purgatory proportionally,[164] but Luther makes no such claim except for the assertion that postmortem torment seems incomparable with the sufferings of tasting hell in this life.[165] Third, Tauler stresses a single way for union with Christ; that is, one becomes united with God by means of suffering,[166] whereas Luther stresses that one is united with Christ through suffering, on the one hand,[167] and that a Christian—already united with Christ by faith—participates in Christ's suffering through *Anfechtungen*, on the other.

Luther's Notion of *Anfechtung* as the Cross of Suffering

Luther's notion of *Anfechting* as the cross is identical to Tauler's mystical theology. This particular notion of Luther's, however, is primarily rooted in his theological interpretation of suffering *prior to* his acquaintance with Tauler. This section briefly examines Luther's illustration in the *Dictata* with which he addresses the theme of the cross of suffering. It not only substantiates our further discussions in the following section, but also demonstrates that Luther's notion of suffering as participating in the cross of Christ already emerges in the *Dictata*, the core of which is materialized later as the theology of the cross.

---

163. See "A Foretaste of Hell in *Theologia Crucis* and the Theology of Justification" later in this chapter. Rittgers also notes that Luther stresses the external righteousness of Christ whereas Tauler tends to focus on the inward experience of the "birth of God." Rittgers, *Reformation of Suffering*, 99.

164. Here are a couple of instances: in the Second Sermon for the Nineteenth Sunday after Trinity, Matthew 22:4, and Second Sermon for the Feast of the Exaltation of the Holy Cross, John 12:32. Tauler, *Sermons*, 565, 694 respectively. In addition to Tauler, the late medieval German mystics shared the notion of purgatorial suffering in this life (e.g., Mechthild of Magdeburg (d. 1285), Margaret Ebner (d. 1351), and Thomas à Kempis (d. 1471)). See Rittgers, *Reformation of Suffering*, 72–80, particularly 73n72.

165. AE 31:128; WA 1:557.15–16, and AE 31:130; WA 1:557.13–14.

166. Third Sermon for the Fifth Sunday after Trinity on Luke 5:3–10. Tauler, *Sermons*, 448.

167. Ngien, *Suffering of God*, 31.

Purgatory as the Cross

An Illustration in the *Dictata*: a Sparrow's Nest

On Psalm 84:3 in the *Dictata*, Luther illustrates the cross of suffering with the image of a bird building a nest with despised objects. Just as a bird's nest is a dwelling place, so is the cross of suffering for a Christian. Luther notes: "Rather make your nest out of scraps, leaves, dry twigs, little branches, mud, and other worthless materials."[168] On the verse of "Thy altars, O Lord,"[169] Luther elaborates that "the nest represents the altars of Christ, the cross and sufferings of Christ, which are those things that are mean and worthless in the world, humility, reproach, offscouring, perplexity, etc."[170] Here Luther illuminates the analogy in relation to the Christian life that participates in the cross of Christ, and contends that the world disdains the cross and treats it as valueless. Promoting a Christian's conformity to the crucified Christ,[171] Luther urges people not to avoid the cross but to take it up.

> To rejoice and boast in sufferings is to be in the nest. Thus the wisdom of the world is made foolish, so that there is rest in suffering and disturbance in peace. But only the turtledove finds these, and one who seeks them, that is, groans . . . Cross, winepress, nest, altar, all these are the same, except that the nest expresses choice and a willing taking up the cross . . . Who will still doubt that the cross of Christ is described and pictured by the hand of God in all creatures? Therefore *why try to escape* what every creature is teaching you? *Why not accept the cross* which is shown you everywhere? . . . So then, *be a sparrow and a swallow*, for such creatures choose the lowly things."[172]

---

168. AE 11:140; WA 55II:633.116-17. Luther quotes Augustine in reference to faith as a nest, and Bernard to the wounds of Christ, and notes, "[B]lessed is he who continually meditates on them [the wounds of Christ] and is contrite and does the works of penitence. Such a person is the sparrow that builds his nest and produces offspring in the cross of Christ." AE 11:140-41; WA 55II:633.130-32.

169. Luther notes that our altar is "Christ, Himself the Priest and the Sacrifice and our Altar, on which we are placed and offered to God the Father, and in Him we offer all our sacrifices," as well as "the mystical cross of Christ, on which all must be offered." AE 11:141; WA 55II:634.148-50, 635.155.

170. AE 11:141-42; WA 55II:635.158-60. On Ps. 84:3.

171. "They are our crosses and our sufferings and our altars, on which we present our bodies as a living sacrifice." AE 11:142; WA 55II:635.163-64. Conformity to the passion of Christ is the central theme in late medieval German passion mysticism. See Rittgers, *Reformation of Suffering*, 72-80, particularly 73.

172. AE 11:142; WA 55II:635.167-73, 176-80. Emphases added. By the same token, lecturing on Psalm 60:8 Luther treats the trials of persecution and underlines the

The materials that a bird collects to build a nest are worthless to the wisdom of the world. In a bird's nest is hidden, however, the wisdom of the cross, for it demonstrates a mystical dwelling place of a Christian. The cross of Christ crucified is for Luther "the mystical cross of Christ," a dwelling place in which Christians daily walk in newness of life, as well as the mystical altar on which they offer themselves up by conforming themselves to the crucified Christ and taking their crosses daily.[173]

In God is hidden the Christian life; likewise, in suffering is hidden *true rest*. What is valuable—suffering of the cross—is treated as worthless, but a gracious God is found only in the crucified Christ. The illustration of a bird nest in the *Dictata* thus sheds light on Luther's theological perception of suffering—the theology of the cross (*theologia crucis*) to which we turn.

THEOLOGIA CRUCIS: LUTHER'S INTERPRETATION OF SUFFERING

The theology of the cross, a principle of Luther's theological methodology,[174] exhibits his interpretation of suffering. Echoing Luther's statement that "the cross is our theology,"[175] as well as that the cross alone is the touchstone,[176] the theology of the cross, or its theological insight, is the "framework"[177] in which Luther perceived suffering and thus purgatory. In other words,

---

necessity and significance of suffering: "Why, then, do you try to run away from temptations and trials? For they are a sign that you are being prepared for glory and are being called to be a dish for all the saints, who will be refreshed by you in heaven." AE 10:287; WA 55II:317.215–17. This is the passage that Rittgers highlights in addressing the subject of suffering and salvation in the early Luther. See Rittgers, *Reformation of Suffering*, 84–110.

173. Luther used the term "mystical"—*crux Christi mystica*—in this lecture. AE 11:141; WA 55II:635.155.

174. Vercruysse, "Luther's Theology of the Cross," 524. Moltmann comments that the theology of the cross, which Luther developed as "the programme of critical and Reformation theology," is "the key signature for all Christian theology." Moltmann, *Crucified God*, 72.

175. *CRUX sola est nostra Theologia*. WA 2:319.3, quoted in Lohse, *Martin Luther's Theology*, 39; Kolb, *Martin Luther: Confessor*, 23. Also, in "XV Psalmos graduum, 1532/33" (published in 1540), WA 40III:193.6–7, 19–20, quoted in Kolb, "Luther on the Theology of the Cross," 34n2.

176. *CRUX probat omnia*. "[T]he cross puts everything to the test" or "preserves everything," WA 2:325.1 in Lohse, *Martin Luther's Theology*, 39. See also AE 34:286–87; WA 50:660.1–4.

177. Kolb, "Luther on the Theology of the Cross," 34.

Luther's view of the postmortem punishments of purgatory as the cross of suffering in which one tastes hell is his theological interpretation of *Anfechtung*. For our discussions, this section reviews the theology of the cross drawn from the *Heidelberg Disputation*, and subsequently revisits the texts of the *Dictata* and the *Explanations* to confirm Luther's articulation of his view of purgatory in the latter in the framework of the theology of the cross.

Heidelberg Disputation (1518)

In the *Heidelberg Disputation*,[178] Luther makes a distinction between a theologian of the cross and a theologian of glory. By the latter, Luther refers to his contemporary theologians who in their presuppositions claim that humanity by "doing what is in it" can assist and contribute to God's saving work. They consider suffering, not as God's saving work, argues Luther, but as that which is unnecessary and valueless, and thus to be avoided.[179] At the heart of the theology of glory are the sales of indulgences that promote avoidance of suffering.[180] Following the circulation of the *Ninety-five Theses* and under pressure from Rome, Staupitz invites Luther to present his theology to his fellow Augustinians. Adhering to Staupitz's advice not to debate such a controversial subject as indulgences, Luther selects the theology of the cross instead. The content of Luther's *Heidelberg Disputation*, however, is *not* entirely irrelevant to that of the *Ninety-five Theses*. Thesis Twenty of the former, "He deserves to be called a theologian ... who comprehends the visible and manifest things of God seen through suffering and the cross,"[181] for instance, resonates with the last two theses of the latter that highlight the axiom of the theology of the cross:

> Christians should be exhorted to be diligent in following Christ, their head, through penalties, death, and hell;
> And thus be confident of entering into heaven through many tribulations rather than through the false security of peace [Acts 14:22].[182]

---

178. AE 39–70; WA 1:353.1—374.31.

179. AE 31:40, 53; WA 1:362.20-34. Ebeling also notes that "the invisibility of the *Deus gloriosus* as perceived by reason is a glorification of the world." Ebeling, *Luther*, 227–28.

180. Analogously, Vercruysse points out a linkage between the theology of the cross and the controversy of indulgences. Vercruysse, "Luther's Theology of the Cross," 531.

181. AE 31:40; WA 1:354.19–20.

182. AE 31:33; WA 1:238:18–21. Theses Ninety-four and Ninety-five, respectively.

Against the contemporary practices of indulgences which promote depreciation of and prevention from suffering of purgatory, namely, the cross of souls, Luther denounces in the *Ninety-five Theses* such practices as a misplaced security of peace.[183] Unmistakable is Luther's underlying argument that Christians must consider both antemortem and postmortem sufferings as the cross, and that indulgences should not be treated in reference to the souls in purgatory. In the *Heidelberg Disputation*, Luther addresses the same agenda without discussing the subject of indulgences or employing its terminology.[184] Instead, Luther addresses the principal subject of his theology, and asserts that "God can be found only in suffering and the cross" in this life.[185]

The broad context of the indulgence controversy captures Luther's salient point treated in the *Heidelberg Disputation*: anyone who attempts in a misplaced security of peace to escape suffering and the cross by means of indulgences can neither find God nor be the "friend of the cross" (*amicus crucis*).[186] Vercruysse rightly comments: "Because of this choice [i.e., wrong preferences—works and glory to suffering and the cross—brought by the wrong understanding of God] he cannot but detest all kinds of sufferings and crosses. He is the enemy of the cross . . . In opposition to Christ he is Adam, who is built up by all these works."[187] The avoidance of suffering is, in fact, the ignorant rejection of God's saving act and an illusion of hope to be righteous before God by means of self-righteousness. God causes one to despair of such illusions so as to seek[188] and find God in the cross of suffering as in the crucified Christ.[189] Therefore, "He who does not know Christ does not know God hidden in suffering,"[190] and no one finds God unless one practices faith in the midst of *Anfechtungen*. This is God's alien and proper work for salvation.

183. Luther's phrase in Latin is "*securitatem pacis confidant*" which the American Edition translates as "the false security of peace." AE 31:33; WA 1:238.21.

184. Similarly, Vercruysse also notes that Luther's major point treated in the *Explanations* (i.e., the subject related to the Christian life) is a minor point in the *Heidelberg Disputation*, and what is a minor point addressed in the former (i.e., how to know a gracious God) is a major point in the latter. Vercruysse, "Luther's Theology of the Cross," 536.

185. AE 31:53; WA 1:362.28–29.

186. Vercruysse, "Luther's Theology of the Cross," 534–40. See also AE 31:53; WA 1:362.29.

187. Vercruysse, "Luther's Theology of the Cross," 537.

188. AE 31:51; WA 1:361.6–30.

189. AE 31:52–53; WA 1:362.1–33.

190. AE 31:53; WA 1:362.23–24.

Theologia Crucis: Term and Content[191]

The theology of the cross, which developed in Luther's biblical interpretation,[192] is the principal methodology and perspective of Luther's theology as a whole.[193] Two contrasting phrases elaborate Luther's theological methodology: "observes what is understood" (*intellecta conspicit*) and "understands what is seen" (*conspecta intelligit*), as McGrat translates, the latter of which represents Luther's theological method principally linked to his experience,[194] not just any type of experience but particularly that of the suffering of the cross or in "cruciform."[195] Several keywords constitute the concept of the theology of the cross, which include God's alien work, *Anfechtung* or *tentatio*, humility, conformity with Christ, resignation, the hiddenness of God,[196] terms and phrases already treated earlier. As discussed, faith and suffering are not to be separated in Luther, and his use of the term the "cross" of Christ is frequently interchangeable with the suffering of a Christian.[197] Principally and fundamentally, Luther's theology of faith is thus related to the theology of the cross, and vice versa.[198]

Luther treats in his *Lectures on Romans* the content of the theology of the cross where he addresses a twofold suffering under God's wrath and in his mercy, and further asserts that anyone who is unwilling to suffer is

---

191. In *Heidelberg Disputation*, as Vitor Westhelle rightly points out, Luther does not address a "theology" of the cross as an abstract concept but a "theologian" of the cross as a particular way in which one perceives and exercises faith. Westhelle, "Luther's *Theologia Crucis*," 156. See also Forde, *On Being*, 11. In this section, using the term the "theology" of the cross, I do not treat the subject of the cross in an abstract concept but draw attention to the way in which Luther perceived suffering.

192. Kolb, *Martin Luther*, 23. See also Wicks, *Luther*, 61–62.

193. Von Loewenich, *Martin Luther*, 13. Vercruysse, "Luther's Theology of the Cross," 524–25. Ngien, *The Suffering of God*, 42. See also Thiemann, "Luther's Theology of the Cross," 229–30. Furthermore, Kolb stresses that the function of the theology of the cross is not only "a hermeneutical framework" but also "an orientation for theological criticism." Kolb, "Luther on the Theology of the Cross," 44.

194. Both phrases are from Theses Nineteen and Twenty of the *Heidelberg Disputation* respectively. McGrath, *Luther's Theology of the Cross*, 204, 207.

195. Duttenhaver, "Suffering and Love, 99."

196. Ngien, *Suffering of God*, 31–32.

197. Chapter 4 discusses the subject. Westhelle also notes that Prenter identifies the cross of Christ and that of a Christian in a way that Christ and a Christian are in a mystical union, and Jon Sobrino views the subject in "an analogous relation." Westhelle, "Luther's *Theologia Crucis*," 159.

198. See McGrath, *Luther's Theology of the Cross*, particularly 125–232.

not a Christian but an enemy of the cross of Christ.[199] The term *"theologia crucis"* appears in the spring of 1518. In the *Asterisci Lutheri adversus obeliscos Eccii*, a response to Eck's *Obelisci*,[200] for instance, Luther criticizes Eck for his ignorance of the theology of the cross,[201] and in a similar vein Luther reproves him at the *Leipzig Debate*.[202] In the marginal glosses on Hebrews 12:11, Luther discusses the subject[203] and elaborates it in the *Heidelberg Disputations* and the *Explanations*.[204] In the *Operationes in Psalmos* (1519/22), Luther further demonstrates his theological articulation of the subject, particularly with respect to Christ's twofold work.[205] Throughout his career, Luther continues to use the term "the theology of the cross," conveying his theological perspective and hermeneutical method.[206]

In principle, Luther's theology of the cross exhibits the crux of his theological perspective that his theology of suffering is nothing but his theology of faith. For Luther faith and suffering are the way in which one discovers the truth and works of God hidden in suffering. Not all people in suffering find a gracious God, however, if they claim knowledge of God in a metaphysical sense. Only by means of faith one learns and obtains true knowledge of a gracious God hidden in suffering (e.g., God in the crucified Christ). Faith that trusts in Christ dwells in a Christian and is active amid spiritual agony and affliction. Therefore, to live by faith means to be conformed to Christ by bearing the cross of suffering.[207]

---

199. *Inimicus crucis Christi.* AE 25:288–90; WA 56:302.9—303.17. On Rom. 5:3. See also Vercruysse, "Luther's Theology of the Cross," 529. As discussed earlier, Luther's insight of the theology of the cross already appears in the *Dictata*. See "The *Dictata*" in this chapter.

200. WA 1:281–314.

201. Vercruysse, "Luther's Theology of the Cross," 527, 526–28.

202. WA 2:333.38—334.2. See chapter 3.

203. WA 57III:79.7–9. *Hebräervorlesung* 1517/18, quoted in von Loewenich, *Martin Luther*, 99. Also, Westhelle, "Luther's *Theologia Crucis*," 158.

204. Vercruysse, "Luther's Theology of the Cross," 528–30.

205. Wicks, *Luther*, 87. On Ps. 9.

206. Kolb, "Luther's Theology of the Cross," 69–85. Cf. On the other hand, Westhelle notes that Luther's use of the term continued until 1525. Afterwards, only its content remained in Luther's later writings. Westhelle, "Luther's *Theologia Crucis*," 164.

207. Wicks, *Man Yearning for Grace*, 207–8.

Luther's Notion of a Foretaste of Hell in *Theologia Crucis*

A Foretaste of Hell

In Thesis Four of the *Heidelberg Disputation*, Luther explains in discussion on the theology of the cross the notion of experiencing hell in this life. Suffering the pangs of hell, which appears to be evil to human reason, is in fact the "unattractive" work of God. With reference to 1 Samuel 2:6 Luther notes that the work of God "kills" and "brings down to Sheol" whereby one tastes hell in this life, "finding in ourselves nothing but sin, foolishness, death, and hell."[208] Where there is nothing but death and hell, there is no certainty of salvation; therefore, it is the taste of "near despair"—not total despair.[209] As far as the Christian life is concerned in this context, there is "no form or beauty" in it,[210] for in suffering it is "hidden in God," that is, "in the bare confidence in his mercy."[211]

In this paradox, faith is both existential and eschatological simultaneously. It is *existential* since it experiences the work of God in the *Sitz im Leben* "here and now," and it is *eschatological* as it gazes upon what will be revealed on the Day of Christ "there and then." Luther terms it "the alien work of God," which is "counterintuitive and paradoxical,"[212] that "humbles us thoroughly, making us despair, so that he may exalt us in his mercy, giving us hope."[213] In other words, the theology of the cross refers to the theology of faith, not in a sense of describing what the work of God or faith is in theoretical or metaphysical idealism, but in a sense of absolute trusting in God while experiencing "the unattractive work ... which *God does* in us."[214]

Unambiguous is the purpose of this work of God to make humans "despair" of their own ability by leading them "into hell" so that they might find God and recognize his way of salvation.[215] God accomplishes this, not through the manifestation of his glory and power, but "through the cross

---

208. AE 31:44; WA 1:356.36—357.4.

209. AE 31:13; WA 1:558.22.

210. Is. 53:2. AE 31:44; WA 1:357.2. Thesis Four.

211. *In nuda fiducia misericordiae eius.* AE 31:44; WA 1:357.3.

212. Rittgers, *Reformation of Suffering*, 111.

213. Luther notes that the expression of "the alien work of God" is drawn from Isa. 28:21 ("to do his deed—strange is his deed! And to work his work—alien is his work!"). AE 31:44; WA 1:357.6-8.

214. AE 31:44; WA 1:357.15-16. Emphasis added.

215. AE 31:51-52; WA 1:361.22-30.

and suffering."[216] The crucified Christ was the unmitigated manifestation of God's alien work on the cross, on the one hand, and "the weakness and folly of God" to human reason, on the other.[217] A gracious God, who is hidden, is discovered where he works, and the work of God appears but in suffering and on the cross. "For this reason true theology and recognition of God are in the crucified Christ,"[218] and therefore, "[h]e who does not know Christ does not know God hidden in suffering."[219] Nor is there certainty of salvation unless this work of God is perceived in faith.

Fundamentally, God has decided to be found only on the cross in the form of "the weakness and folly of God,"[220] and it is also his will that "all men should conform to the image of his Son, that is to the cross."[221] Luther's *Anfechtung* account in reference to the punishments of purgatory in the *Explanations*, for instance, is the description of God's unattractive work.[222] Such an experience of tasting hell engenders a sense of being forsaken, not for the purpose of total despair in a strict sense, but for the growth in faith and love in Christ,[223] for there is God's presence within God-forsakenness, the paradox not perceived except through faith alone.

A Foretaste of Hell against a Human Work and Certainty

The theology of the cross not only unfolds a particular way that God accomplishes his will, but also rejects human reason that speculates and refutes suffering and the cross as God's work. When Eck claims certainty of salvation of souls in purgatory, for instance, Luther contends that the separation itself of soul and body at the moment of death does not constitute certainty of salvation, and criticizes that such a view ignores the theology of

---

216. AE 31:55; WA 1:363.24–32. Althaus comments that by works in the theology of the glory Luther refers to God's works as well as humans'. Analogously, by suffering in the theology of the cross Luther refers to Christ's suffering as well as the Christians'. Althaus, *Theology of Martin Luther*, 26–27.

217. AE 31:52; WA 1:362.4–5.

218. AE 31:53; WA 1:362.18–19.

219. AE 31:53; WA 1:362.23–24.

220. AE 31:52; WA 1:362.4–5.

221. AE 31:153; WA 1:571.34–36.

222. AE 31:129; WA 1:557.34–35, 37–38, 558.5–8.

223. AE 31:137; WA 1:562.20–25. AE 31:145; WA 1:567.15–19.

the cross.²²⁴ Luther does not claim that no single soul in purgatory is certain of their salvation; however, he confutes that *all* souls are certain from the moment of their departure.²²⁵

In his criticism of Eck's claim, Luther makes a twofold argument: first, certainty of salvation is not a hypothetical subject to be treated by a metaphysical speculation, but a genuine, theological subject which cannot be discussed properly without the experience of sufferings and the cross; second, the theology of the cross rejects certainty relying on human imagination or reason without knowing—that is, *experiencing*—the work of God manifested in suffering. In the corollary of Thesis Six in the *Heidelberg Disputation*, Luther argues that one cannot be certain of God's grace by "doing what is in self."²²⁶ Fundamentally, free will "exists in name only," for in reality "it commits a mortal sin."²²⁷ With this twofold argument Luther contends that the unattractive work of God is necessary while it appears repugnant to human reason. By the same token, the postmortem *Anfechtung* of tasting hell in near despair in purgatory essentially teaches souls to trust and love in Christ to the point of full resignation to God's will and conformity to the image of the crucified Christ.

A Foretaste of Hell in *Theologia Crucis* and the Theology of Justification

Being forsaken, one realizes that God destroys self-reliance and self-righteousness. The cross and suffering in this respect "dethrones" such positivism of human work as a contribution to God's work for salvation and crucifies the old Adam.²²⁸ To be born anew, one thus must die, and "to die . . . means to feel death at hand"—a foretaste of hell.²²⁹

Luther addresses the subject of an alien work of God both as a "preparation of justification" by faith alone and as part of newness of life in faith.²³⁰

---

224. Luther addresses the subject in the *Asterisci Lutheri Adversus Obeliscos Eckii*. See Vercruysse, "Luther's Theology of the Cross," 527–28. The same theme reappears during the Leipzig Debate. WA 2:333.38—334.2. See chapter 3.

225. AE 31:140–45; WA 1:564.32—567.24. Also, WA 1:294.16. The *Asterisci Lutheri Adversus Obeliscos Eckii*, quoted in Vercruysse, "Luther's Theology of the Cross," 527. See also WA 2:332.38—333.2.

226. Again, it is in Latin *facere quod in se est*. AE 31:67–68; WA 1:373.6–35.

227. AE 31:40; WA 1:354.5–6.

228. AE 31:53; WA 1:362.20–33.

229. AE 31:55; WA 1:363.24–37.

230. Vercruysse, "Luther's Theology of the Cross," 532. With regard to Luther's

The former relates to God's work of the instantaneous effect of the external righteousness of God and the latter relates to that of the continual effect. From the perspective of the latter effect, God works in the suffering of *Anfechtung* for daily justification.[231] In such a spiritual crisis as being forsaken, faith discovers what—rather *who*—is hidden in it; it is a gracious God working for salvation with a new and genuine *certainty*. Luther asserts that "[h]e is not righteous who does much, but he who, without work, believes much in Christ."[232]

A theologian—or friend—of the cross, therefore, does not seek to be righteous before God with human work, "but seeks God" instead.[233] Luther addresses the subject in a christocentric sense that "justification by faith in Christ is sufficient to him."[234] This gift of faith "justifies"; that is, "through faith Christ is in us, indeed, one with us."[235] In this union with Christ, Christ's fulfillment of the law and the commands of God is transferred to a Christian as in joyous exchange.[236] Furthermore, a theologian or friend of the cross comprehends the alien and proper work of God in the perspective of love. The love of the human being emerges when it finds the object of love, but the love of God "does not find, but creates"[237] the object of love. God does *not find* who is lovable in a qualitative sense but *makes* the unlovable loved. Luther notes, "Therefore sinners are attractive because they are loved; they are not loved because they are attractive."[238] In other words, God *creates* the object of love by loving—that is, *justifying*—a sinner. Luther highlights: "This is the love of the cross, born of the cross, which turns in the direction where it does not find good which it may enjoy, but where it may confer good upon the bad and needy person."[239] God who

---

theology of the cross intertwined with his theology of justification, see also Althaus, *Theology of Martin Luther*, 32–34, as well as McGrath, *Luther's Theology of the Cross*, 125–232.

231. See also AE 34:167; WA 39I:98.7–11.

232. AE 31:41; WA 1:354.19–20. Thesis Twenty-five.

233. AE 31:56; WA 1:365.12–14.

234. AE 31:56; WA 1:365.14.

235. AE 31:56; WA 1:364.21–24.

236. "Christ is just and has fulfilled all the commands of God, wherefore we also fulfill everything through him since he was made ours through faith." AE 31:56; WA 1:364.24–26.

237. AE 31:57; WA 1:365.2–3.

238. AE 31:57; WA 1:365.11–12.

239. AE 31:57; WA 1:365.13–15.

loves sinners, therefore, *pardons* their sins in the instantaneous effect of the righteousness of God in baptism, and furthermore *removes* them daily in the continual effect.

Revisiting Luther's Notion of a Foretaste of Hell—the Cross

The *Dictata*

We have now reached at the final point to revisit the *Dictata* and the *Explanations*, and reread them in view of the theology of the cross, paying particular attention to Luther's articulation of the notion of suffering as a foretaste of hell.

In the *Dictata*, Luther already discusses at this early stage the subject of suffering in the perspective of the theology of the cross, and warns against the notion of peace and security that disdains suffering.[240] On Psalm 69:16 in the *Dictata*, Luther further notes:

> For they [the saints] die as far as the desire and purpose to commit sin is concerned. Similarly, they descend into hell as far as the attitude toward its punishments is concerned. Thus all the prayers of the Psalms which are uttered in the person of Christ as being in hell, are also uttered in the person of the saints, as descending to hell in their mind and heart . . . For that reason whoever does not die *with Christ* and descend to hell will never rise and ascend with Him. Therefore he prays here, "Draw Me out, set Me free." All these are the most earnest prayers also of those who are occupied with meditating on hell, just as they are the prayers of Christ who was literally in hell. Therefore it follows that worldly men, since they live in their own goodness and do not descend to hell with the Lord, but rather ascend to the heavens, will themselves finally descend and not ascend.[241]

The salient point of Luther's lectures can be summarized that the saints die "with Christ" as for the old Adam and descend into hell *with him* to ascend *with him*. In this statement, Luther addresses six aspects of the cross of suffering: first, Luther treats the subject of the suffering of a Christian; second, as far as the degree of suffering is concerned, it is no less than tasting hell in this life as Luther notes that "they descend into hell as far as the

---

240. AE 10:373; WA 55II:406.666–69.
241. AE 10:372; WA55II:404.617–28. Emphasis added.

attitude toward its punishments is concerned";[242] third, with the statement that "whoever does not die with Christ and descend to hell will never rise and ascend with Him," Luther makes a contrast between those who *do not* die with Christ and those who *do*, which resembles the contrast between a theologian of glory and a theologian of the cross; fourth, the phrase "with Christ" (*cum Christo*) also connotes the notion of "union with Christ" (*unio cum Christo*) with respect to the conformity to the image of the crucified Christ; fifth, it elucidates that the life of a Christian is hidden in the crucified Christ, of which Luther articulates: "Thus all the prayers of the Psalms which are uttered in the person of Christ as being in hell, are also uttered in the person of the saints, as descending to hell in their mind and heart";[243] and sixth, Luther addresses the subject of the cross of suffering as that which is perceived through faith in hope.[244] As reviewed, Luther's notion of suffering as a foretaste of hell in the *Dictata*, just as illustrated in the analogy of a sparrow's nest,[245] echoes his theological insight of the theology of the cross, which appears more explicitly in the *Explanations*.

The *Explanations* (1518)

While the *Explanations* treat the subject of the theology of the cross in a general sense, the *Anfechtung* account particularly addresses the cross of suffering as a foretaste of hell in light of the theology of the cross.

242. As discussed earlier, concerning the saints' descending into hell with Christ, Luther describes it as "the pit of hell or purgatory." AE 10:364; WA 55II:396.380-83. On Ps. 69:3.

243. It is worth noting that in Ps. 69:16 the fifth point is only implicit in this lecture; however, his lecture on Ps. 18:11 in the *Dictata* demonstrates his perspective on the *hiddenness* of God in the mystery of faith and Christ's incarnation. Concerning Verse 11, "The hiding place of God is darkness," Luther comments more explicitly: "In the first place, because He dwells in the riddle and darkness of faith. Second, because He dwells in an unapproachable light (1 Tim. 6:16), so that no mind can penetrate to Him . . . For thus God is hidden and beyond understanding. Third, this can be understood as referring to the mystery of the Incarnation. For He is concealed in humanity, which is His darkness . . . Fourth, this refers to the church or the blessed Virgin, for He was concealed in both and continues to be hidden in the church to the present . . . Fifth, it refers to the sacrament of the Eucharist, where He is most completely concealed. For that reason this can also be understood as referring to Christ's incarnation." AE 10:119-20; WA 55II:138.5—139.2. On Ps. 18:11.

244. AE 10:372; WA 55II:404.630-32.

245. AE 11:142; WA 55II:635.167-73, 176-80. On Ps. 84:3 in the *Dictata*. See "An Illustration in the *Dictata*: A Sparrow's Nest" in this chapter.

Purgatory as the Cross

> I myself 'knew a man' [II Cor. 12:2] who claimed that he had often suffered these punishments, in fact over a very brief period of time. Yet they were so great and so much like hell that no tongue could adequately express them, no pen could describe them, and one who had not himself experienced them could not believe them... At such a time God seems terribly angry, and with him the whole creation... All that remains is the stark-naked desire for help and a terrible groaning, but it does not know where to turn for help. In this instance the person is stretched out with Christ so that all his bones may be counted, and every corner of the soul is filled with the greatest bitterness, dread, trembling, and sorrow in such a manner that all these last forever.[246]

Luther addresses this *Anfechtung* account in the context of discussing the punishments of purgatory, using the three categories of authorities set out as the methodology in the Declaration. Luther underscores the first authority of the Scripture with reference to David and Hezekiah, followed by the second authority of tradition with Tauler representing Germany theology. Then, for the third authority of experience, Luther introduces the presumably autobiographical *Anfechtung* account.

Scholars concur almost unanimously that it is probably the account of Luther's own experience mainly because Luther's expression of "I myself 'knew a man'" resonates with St Paul's description of his own experience (2 Corinthians 12:2). However, it may be possible—while not making a particular claim—that with the expression Luther might have referred to Tauler for the following three reasons: first, Luther treats the subject of the punishments of purgatory in the perspective of "a wisdom of experience,"[247] referring to the German mystics, particularly Tauler.[248] Concerning the scholastic theologians, Luther comments that "these preachers of indulgences speak with too much audacity about many things of which they know nothing or else doubt."[249] Second, as for the subject of the punishments of purgatory, Luther admits that he has no sufficient experience to treat it properly.[250] Third, Luther seems to consider Tauler not only as an

---

246. AE 31:129; WA 1:557.33-35, 37-38; 558.4-8.

247. "For one ought to believe those who are experienced in these matters [of the punishments of purgatory] rather than those who are inexperienced." Thesis Fifteen of the *Explanations*, AE 31:130; WA 1:558.16-17.

248. AE 31:73.

249. AE 31:130; WA 1:558.16-17.

250. "One might ask, however, 'From which punishments, then, are souls released,

eminent theologian in the tradition of German theology,[251] but also as one of those who had much more profound experiences than he himself.[252] In this respect, with the *Anfechtung* account Luther might have referred to Tauler, delineating the pains of hell drawn from his own experiences, to a certain extent. In addition, the convergences between Luther and Tauler, as discussed earlier,[253] buttress this conjecture.

Whether or not Luther's *Anfechtung* account specifically refers to Tauler, it is inevitably convincing that the account itself illuminates several aspects of Luther's theology of the cross. First, it is Luther's notion of a Christian's existential suffering; second, as the context of this particular thesis indicates, the account explicitly enunciates that "they [punishments] were so great and so much like hell," which refers to a foretaste of hell experienced in this present life; third, it is also deeply rooted in the notion of union with Christ as it describes vividly concerning the pains of suffering that "the person is stretched out with Christ so that all his bones may be counted"; fourth, the whole account underlines the hiddenness of God in such a dreadful agony; and fifth, it implies that the *Anfechtung* of a foretaste of hell is not completely without hope as Luther insinuates, "All that remains is the stark-naked desire for help and a terrible groaning."[254]

Overall, it is unquestionable that Luther articulates in the *Dictata* and in the *Explanations* the notion of suffering as a foretaste of hell. In the former, Luther discusses it regarding the saints who descend into hell with Christ;[255]

---

or what punishments do they suffer in purgatory if they do not suffer anything which is included in the canonical law?' My response is, if I knew the answer to that, why would I need to discuss it or ask about it? *I am not experienced enough to know what God does with souls who have departed*, at least not as experienced as those innumerable redeemers of souls who make such sure pronouncements about everything as though it were impossible for them to be mere men." AE 31:123; WA 1:554.17-22; emphasis added.

251. "I have found in him more solid and sincere theology than is found in all the scholastic teachers of all the universities or than can be found in their propositions." AE 31:129; WA 1:557.29-32.

252. "For what else does John Tauler teach in his German sermons than the sufferings of these punishments of which he also cites some examples?" AE 31:128-29; WA 1:557.25-27.

253. See "Luther and Tauler: Convergences & Divergences" in this chapter.

254. AE 31:129; WA 1:558.4-5. Emphasis added. The term "groaning" (*gemitus*) in the *Explanations* has a positive connotation such as "the outward fruits of penance and of the Spirit" and the "sign" of hope from a third person's perspective. AE 31:87; WA 1:532.30-32 and AE 31:131; WA 1:558.40—559.1, respectively.

255. "He [Jesus] entered into hell, which opened its mouth, but it could not close its mouth on Him and hold Him. But the way out was entirely open to Him. The mouth of

in the latter, Luther elaborates the subject extensively, particularly in the context of disputing scholastic theology concerning the punishments of purgatory. Luther argues that the scholastic methodology based on Aristotelian philosophy is inadequate in discussing the subject of the punishments of purgatory, and defends his theses with a tradition of German mystical theology.[256] The theology of the cross is in this respect the framework and content of his disputations, in general, and that of his theological interpretation of the cross of suffering as a foretaste of hell, in particular.

After 1525/26

After his dismissal of the notion of postmortem torment in 1525/26, Luther seems to eschew using the term "purgatory" in general, and addressing the subject of purgatory, in particular, except for the composition of the *Recantation*,[257] as well as the *Confession* of 1528.[258] Nonetheless, Luther continues to use the term "*tentatio*" or "*Anfechtung*" in reference to Christian suffering not only as the training of faith but also as a true possession or mark of the Church.

In the *Preface to the Wittenberg Edition of Luther's German Writings* (1539),[259] for instance, Luther addresses a three-fold "correct way of studying theology" which he also terms "David's rules."[260] Based on Psalm 119, Luther addresses David's three rules of *oratio*, *meditatio*, and *tentatio*,[261] and

---

death received Him by the same death, but it could not shut Him up. So also the saints go into death, into the mouth of the deep, but they will not be shut up in it, because they will rise from the dead, and the pit of hell or purgatory cannot swallow them up and shut them up like the ungodly, whom the tempest has overwhelmed a second time (that is, in body and soul) . . . It is, however, understood tropologically, when the elect are not allowed to despair in sins when they are dead and in the mire of sins. But they will not be swallowed up by them, but through repentance the mouth of hell and the way out are open." AE 10:363-64; WA 55II:396.377—97.391. On Ps 69:3.

256. While Luther refuted the Aristotelian philosophy employed in scholastic theology, Luther did not reject Aristotle's philosophy in its entirety (e.g., Luther's use of Aristotle's logic). See Saak, *Luther and Reformation*, 154-201.

257. AE 61:217-44; WA 30II: 367.1—390.31.

258. Part Three. AE 37:369; WA 26:508.8-9.

259. AE 34:283-88; WA 50:657-61. *Vorrede zum 1. Bande der Wittenberger Ausgabe der deutschen Schriften*.

260. *Eine rechte weise in der Theologia zu studirn*. AE 34:285; WA 50:658.29-30. AE 34:287; WA 50:660.17, respectively.

261. In his theological construction Luther reoriented *Lectio Divina* (*lectio, meditatio,*

elaborates the subject in the theology of the cross. Regarding the first rule, Luther contrasts true wisdom and the wisdom of the world, the wisdom drawn from Scripture and that of other books, and wisdom from above and foolishness of human reason.[262] Luther contends that human reason and wisdom ought to be dethroned by tasting hell in suffering.[263] As for the second rule, Luther stresses doing theology "externally" and "outwardly" such as through reading, hearing, writing, and preaching the Word of God, not merely contemplating in heart and mind. On the third rule, Luther reiterates the aspect of experiencing *tentatio* or *Anfechtung*: "This is the *touchstone* which teaches you not only to know and understand, but also to experience how right, how true, how sweet, how lovely, how mighty, how comforting God's Word is, wisdom beyond all wisdom."[264] Noticeable is Luther's terminology employed in this treatise, which strongly resonates with his appraisal of German Theology that it is "an experienced wisdom."[265] This particular school of *Anfechtung* and *tentatio* makes one "a real theologian,"[266] and Luther similarly underscores in the *Table Talk* that "Experience alone makes the theologian."[267]

In the treatise of *On the Councils and the Church* of 1539, for another instance, Luther treats the subject of *Anfechtung* as part of the seven true marks or possessions of the church.[268] Luther presents them as the "seven true principal parts of the great holy possession whereby the Holy Spirit effects in us a daily sanctification and vivification in Christ, according to the first table of Moses."[269] The reason that Christians suffer in conformity

---

oratio, and *contemplatio*), a contemplative meditation practice in the Middle Ages. For the historical root of *Lectio Divina* and its practice of reading for contemplative meditation, see Sterponi, "Reading and Meditation," 667–89.

262. AE 34:285; WA 50:659.5–8.

263. AE 34:285; WA 50:659.8–10.

264. AE 34:286–87; WA 50:660.1–4; emphasis added.

265. WA 9:28.21, quoted in Rittgers, "Luther's Engagement in Pastoral Care," 469.

266. AE 34:287; WA 50:660.27.

267. "*Sola experientia facit theologum.*" AE 54:7; WA Tr 1:16.13, quoted in Lohse, *Martin Luther's Theology*, 21–22; Rittgers, "Luther's Engagement in Pastoral Care," 469.

268. AE 41:164–65; WA 50:641.35—643.5.

269. Luther preferred to use the term "seven sacraments" instead of "the seven true marks or possessions," "the seven principal parts of Christian sanctification," or "the seven holy possessions of the church"; however, he purposefully avoided the term "sacraments" to differentiate them from the seven sacraments traditionally taught in the Church of Rome. AE 41:165–66; WA 50:642.32—643.5.

to the image of the crucified Christ is, asserts Luther, simply "... to become like their head, Christ."[270]

Tentatio or *Anfechtung* as the cross, even tasting hell in this life, is not only that which trains faith in the *Sitz im Leben*, but also a true mark and possession of the church. Christians suffer, not *to be* who they are, but *to live* who they already are in Christ,[271] that is, living as a "Crosstian" (*Crucianus*).[272] To know Christ means not to have merely a historical knowledge of him but to have him in the suffering of *Anfechtung* in conformity to his cross. In the same vein, Christians—who find and know God in the crucified Christ—suffer "because they want to have none but Christ, and no other God"[273] as Luther writes it to Melanchthon, "Anyone who wants to have Christ must suffer."[274] To know Christ, therefore, is to bear the cross of suffering, daily walking in newness of life in *Anfechtung* as Luther avers, "[I]n that way we learn to believe in God, to trust him, to love him, and to place our hope in him."[275]

At one point in later years, Luther accentuates the role of this school of Christ with the term "purgatory." In the *Sermon Annotations*, as discussed earlier, Luther elaborates existential suffering as a foretaste of hell:

> The Papists and those who hung up contradictions boast that I have professed purgatory. *And I still profess it. But I profess the one that we often encounter in the psalms*, where the saints praise God because they have been freed from the lowest hell, from the darkness and the shadow of death, from the hand of hell, from the perils of hell, from the bands and gates of death and the life

---

270. AE 41:164–65; WA 50:642.1–6. Luther's statement echoes his Thesis Ninety-four of the *Ninety-five Theses*. AE 31:33; WA 1:238:18–19.

271. "[T]he only reason they must suffer is that they steadfastly adhere to Christ and God's word, enduring this for the sake of Christ." AE 41:165; WA 50:642.4–6. Luther insinuates it in the *Explanations* about the sufferings of the souls in purgatory, "It is evident, therefore, that they suffer, not because of the fear of punishment, but because of their love for righteousness." AE 31:145; WA 1:567.16–17.

272. The word "*Crucianus*" is Luther's *jeu de mots* of the word "*Christianus*." AE 5:274(n10); WA 43:617.33–35. See also Rittgers, *Reformation of Suffering*, 121.

273. AE 41:165; WA 50:642.15–16.

274. *Luther an Melanchthon* (June 29, 1530), WA Br 5. No 1609:406.37–38. Schilling, *Martin Luther*, 390. Cf. Schilling's WA Br reference is WA Br 5. No 1584, June 15, 1530. In the WA Br 5, however, there is no letter of Luther sent to Melanchthon on June 15, 1530. Luther wrote Melanchthon a letter on June 5, 1530 (No. 1584; WA Br 5:350–51), but the letter does not contain the quoted sentence.

275. AE 41:165 WA 50:642.31–32.

[Ps. 116:3; 2 Sam. 22:6; Ps. 9:13; 86:13; Isa. 9:2; Matt. 4:16; Luke 1:79; Ps. 49:15]. But [this was not] by means of their sacrifices or by the works of the little sacrificing priests—those most wicked, completely impure, utterly godless men who have nefariously sold their Masses for money and scoffed at God and men with their "worked works."

Finally, this purgatory [that I still profess] is *not a made-up purgatory* (as theirs is), asserted on the basis of human opinions (even if they are the fathers'), but *something real* which is all too serious a matter for those who, with the prophets and all the saints *in the school of Christ*, learn this harsh lesson: 'He brings down to hell and brings back; He kills and He makes alive' [1 Sam. 2:6]. But I have said enough elsewhere about the Papists' false purgatory.[276]

Luther contends that purgatory he still professes is "something real" (*res ipsa*), and repudiates that the opponents' notion of purgatory is "a made-up purgatory" (*fictum purgatorium*). Luther's use of the term "purgatory" in this context may be a figure of speech, or it may indicate that he did not deny the use of the term "purgatory" itself,[277] or that he simply recalls his redefined definition of purgatory as a foretaste of hell in this life. No matter what type of usage it may be,[278] it indisputably refers to existential *tentatio*, differentiated from a postmortem condition. This subject—"true purgatory" (*verum purgatorium*)[279]—in the theology of the cross is the indispensible life-long lesson that Christians learn in "the school of Christ" (*schola Christi*).[280]

---

276. AE 67:305–6; WA 38:653.20–33. Brackets in original. Emphases added. Here Luther's *Sermon Annotations* resonates with the *Dictata* on Ps. 69:16 regarding the subject of foretasting hell in this life. See "Luther's *Anfechtung* as a Foretaste of Hell in the *Dictata* and the *Explanations*" and "Revisiting Luther's Notion of a Foretaste of Hell—the Cross" in this chapter.

277. See "Already in 1518" in chapter 3.

278. Robert Rosin comments that Luther continued to keep on using technical terms if the use of a term is still valid, or at least if it does not create an issue. Rosin, "Humanism, Luther, and the Wittenberg Reformation," 91–104. In this case, Luther's use of the term "purgatory" in comparison is rather intentional for clarification.

279. AE 12:387; WA 40II:436.24.

280. AE 67:305; WA 38:653.29.

CONCLUSION: *THEOLOGIA CRUCIS* AS LUTHER'S THEOLOGICAL FRAMEWORK

Attempting to answer the final questions: "Why is it significant to examine Luther's view of purgatory despite his denial of purgatory? What was Luther's intention and purpose in treating the subject of the punishments of purgatory in the *Explanations*, and how did he steer it?" this chapter demonstrated that Luther uses his hermeneutical principle of the theology of the cross, and applies it to the subject of postmortem purgatory, contending that indulgences marketed for the souls in purgatory are not only a deceptive and harmful device to Christians with a misplaced security of peace, but also a symbolic icon to the theology of glory which not only neglects the cross of suffering but also removes it from the faith and life of Christians. With the bridal image of union with Christ, and adopting it to his theology of faith, Luther affirms the notion of joyous exchange, on the one hand, and God's alien work of a Christian's conformity to the image of the crucified Christ, on the other. He asserts that souls in purgatory are conformed to the image of the crucified Christ as Christians bear the cross of suffering in faith. In this way, Luther *with one stone* in his hand—that is, "the theology of the cross"—*kills two birds*—the contemporary practices of indulgences, on the one hand, and the scholastic theology behind the promotion of the sales of indulgences in the sphere of the theology of glory, on the other. Furthermore, with the same means, Luther not only defends his theology and propositions on the punishments of purgatory, but also refutes the opponents' claims concerning purgatory and their biblical reference. In undertaking this theological campaign of the Reformation, Luther corroborates his view of purgatory—his theological interpretation of a postmortem condition of torment—in the framework of the theology of the cross.

6

Reflection on the Subject

> We think that *Paradise* and *Calvary*,
> *Christ's* Cross, and *Adam's* tree, stood in one place;
> Look, Lord, and find both *Adams* met in me;
> As the first *Adam's* sweat surrounds my face,
> May the last *Adam's* blood my soul embrace.
>
> —John Donne

INQUIRIES, ANSWERS, AND SIGNIFICANCES

Martin Luther, whose theology is anchored in justification by faith alone, did not reject the doctrine of purgatory until 1521/22. Nor was his rejection simply based on reckoning that the notion of purgatory is incompatible with the axiom of the evangelical doctrine of justification. Luther's view of purgatory exhibits his theological understanding of suffering as the cross, and how inextricably integrated it is into his theologies of justification and of the cross.

On a brief overview of the history of purgatory, I claimed that the practices of prayers for the dead do not prove or presuppose the existence of purgatory, and that the notion of purgatory consolidated with prayers for

Reflection on the Subject

the dead began to appear in Late Antiquity in the Western Church. With the question of why it took so long for Luther to deny purgatory, I compared the documents published in 1521/22 and the *Recantation* of 1530, and challenged the assumption that Luther held the notion of postmortem purgation even in 1528 but denied both the notion of post-mortem purgation and the formal doctrine of purgatory in conjunction with the publication of his *Recantation* in 1530. Based on the terminology employed in those documents, I also claimed that Luther's rejection of the doctrine of purgatory first occurred in 1521/22 followed by his dismissal of the notion of postmortem torment in 1525/26. In the former, we observed three reasons of Luther's attacks on the doctrine, which show a striking parallel to his *Recantation*: first, the doctrine extensively associated with the authority of the pope is lies and deceit; second, purgatory is not an article of faith; and third, no one is a heretic for denying purgatory.

As far as Luther's notion of purgatory is concerned, the chapter highlighted the following five points: first, there are two turning points in Luther's view of purgatory: one in 1521/22, and the other in 1525/26; second, at the first turning point, Luther differentiates his notion of purgatory as postmortem torment from the formal doctrine of purgatory; third, following his two discoveries in early 1520—the gospel condemned and burned with John Huss' death at the stake, and Lorenzo Valla's *Refutation*, Luther rejected the doctrine based on his conviction that the papacy is the Antichrist; consequently, Luther was condemned under the bulls *Exsurge Domine* (June 10, 1520) and *Decet Romanum Pontificem* (January 3, 1521) in addition to the earlier condemnation under the bull *Cum postquam* (November 1518); fourth, Luther's notion of purgatory shifted from postmortem torment to existential sufferings, but his theological view of suffering as the cross remained throughout his works; and fifth, in a similar vein, regardless of his rejection of the doctrine of purgatory, Luther continued to support for individual prayers for the dead.

Concerning the second major question: "How could Luther hold both purgatory and justification by faith alone?" we reviewed the subject of Luther's Reformation breakthrough, including recent developments in scholarship. With the premise that a series of Luther's theological discoveries continued in a process of development towards maturity, the first of which occurred before the *Dictata*, I claimed that in this process Luther integrated the notion of purgatory into his theology of justification. In so doing, Luther distinguished the two correlated effects of the alien righteousness of

God: the *instantaneous* effect with respect to forgiveness, and the *continual* effect in progress that corresponds to the removal of sin, the latter of which played a key role with respect to the notion of purgatory and his theology of justification.

In this framework, we discussed four significances of the continual effect, particularly with respect to Luther's reasoning on purgatory in the *Explanations* of 1518: first, the continual effect anticipates the final destination or completion (i.e., a journey to heaven); second, it also involves faith and love, not as qualitative virtues, but as a gift of God and its fruit in a *continual* growth; that is, faith grows only in bearing the cross, and one enters heaven only through the cross of tribulations; third, it not only implies the frailty of faith but also signifies the imperfect righteousness of faith which necessitates God's imputation; and fourth, Luther perceives purgatory as the cross of souls. In brief, faith and the cross of suffering ought not to be separated, for one—justified by faith alone—bears the cross of *Anfechtung* so as to grow in faith until reaching the final destination.

With the final question: "What was Luther's intention and purpose in treating the subject of the punishments of purgatory in the *Explanations*, and how did he steer it?" I attempted to answer it with a claim that Luther's view of purgatory exhibits his theological understanding of suffering as a foretaste of hell and the cross, his theological insight that appears in the form of the theology of the cross. That is, in the *Explanations* of 1518 Luther articulates his view of purgatory in the framework of the theology of the cross.

From the comparative examinations between the *Dictata* and the *Explanations* regarding the notion of suffering as a foretaste of hell, it is found that Luther's notion precedes his acquaintance with Tauler's sermons. Concerning the inquiry of what particular role Tauler plays in Luther's disputations since Tauler was referenced to the notion of a foretaste of hell in this life, I argued that Luther's use of Tauler was to represent a tradition of German theology in defense of both the Wittenberg theology and Luther's propositions on the subject of the punishments of purgatory, and to dispute the opponents' criticism of Luther, as well as their scholastic tradition and their biblical reference to purgatory. As for Luther's notion of a foretaste of hell in this life, which is embedded in the theology of the cross presented in the *Heidelberg Disputation* of 1518, I also claimed that the same perspective was already addressed in the *Dictata* with a warning against the notion of peace and security that neglects and avoids suffering (e.g., the illustration of a bird's nest). Analogously, in the *Explanations* Luther discusses the punishments of purgatory in light of the notion of a foretaste of hell in the framework of the theology of the cross. Finally, after 1525/26 Luther's use of the term "purgatory" and his discussion about postmortem torment decreased significantly, but he addressed the subject occasionally, for instance, in the *Confession* of 1528, and another instance, in his 1530 *Recantation* criticizing the doctrine of purgatory. Regardless, Luther never dismissed his notion of suffering as the cross.

LUTHER'S REFORMATION BREAKTHROUGH AND HIS VIEW OF PURGATORY

If Luther's Reformation breakthrough is seen strictly as a specific event that prompted his full conviction of the pope being the Antichrist (1520), and if Luther's view of purgatory is treated from this particular perspective, it may be arguably said that there is a correlation between the first turning point of Luther's view of purgatory (1521/22) and his Reformation breakthrough. This view, although it may seemingly be agreeable to a certain extent, *isolates* a series of Luther's foundational theological discoveries and development that include the twofold—instantaneous and continual—effect of the alien righteousness of God *from* the events in 1520 and the paradigm shift in his view of purgatory in 1521/22. In other words, Luther's theological discoveries up to 1520 must be taken into consideration to give a full account of the shift of his view of purgatory. On the other hand, if Luther's Reformation breakthrough is considered as a gradual development or transition toward maturity, his rejection of the doctrine of purgatory in 1521/22 was then a consequential event not only from his full conviction of the pope being the Antichrist by discovering the gospel condemned and burned at the stake with John Huss and also by reading Lorenzo Valla's *Refutation*, but also based on his foundational theological discoveries and development up to that point. In this perspective, Luther's view of purgatory, as well as his theological discoveries and development, can be seen as part of the *whole process* in his Reformation breakthrough.

Luther's view of purgatory further clarifies the scholarly discussion about continuity and discontinuity between the young and mature Luther in the development of his theology of justification in general, and his understanding of the righteousness of God in particular. For Luther, there is no ambiguity or variation in the notion that without perfect spiritual health no one can enter the blissful eternal destination, which is the first half of *continuity*, and that the righteousness of faith—the incipient righteousness—is imperfect as healing for sin has begun and its completion—of removing sin—is still yet to come, which is the second half of *continuity*. From 1525/26 onwards, however, which marks the second turning point in Luther's view of purgatory, a significant shift is noticeable in his perspective. God by his imputation reckons the imperfect righteousness of faith as perfect righteousness, for instance, which is the first half of *discontinuity*, and the soul at death peacefully rests in the promise of God, and no longer suffers torment, which is the second half of *discontinuity*. As demonstrated, when Luther's view of purgatory is discussed within the framework of continuity and discontinuity in Luther's young and mature theology, it reveals that the former—being a minor subject in his theological agenda—has been *a missing piece* in viewing the whole picture of Luther's theology and way of thought.

PASTORAL LUTHER ON THE NOTION OF PURGATORY

With his attacks on the formal doctrine of purgatory in 1521/22, Luther could have dismissed the notion of postmortem tormenting purgation wholesale. Instead, he provided pastoral care and guide for the Christians who under the influence of late medieval religiosity sought theological explanations and pastoral guide. Luther's letter to von Amsdorf as well as his sermons in 1521/22, which shows a striking parallel with his 1530 *Recantation* particularly in his attacks on the formal doctrine of purgatory, is an example that exhibits pastoral Luther who asserted that it is not necessary to believe in purgatory, for it is not an article of faith, nor is anyone a heretic because of denying it. Luther's assertion aimed to liberate the Christians who were captivated under the doctrine of purgatory and concerned about their departed loved ones and their belief in purgatory. Another example is the omission of phrases involving the term "purgatory" in the later editions of the devotional booklets between 1524 and 1525 including the *Personal Prayer Book* and *A Meditation of Christ's Passion*. These omissions are Luther's purposeful prearrangement to guard his fellow Christians from the doctrine of purgatory.

Moreover, Luther's theological interpretation of suffering as the cross shows pastoral Luther, whose theological orientation differentiates doing theology from a scholastic tradition that theorizes theology in a metaphysical notion or speculation. At the second turning point in 1525/26, Luther could have dismissed the notion of postmortem torment but did not discard that of suffering of foretasting hell in this life, or his redefined notion of purgatory—*Anfechtung*—in 1521/22. Not using the term "purgatory," Luther retained the notion of suffering as an integral part of his theology which he gained from his initial discovery before the *Dictata*, the notion of the cross of *tentatio* in the school of Christ for teaching and guiding his fellow Christians.

SUGGESTIONS FOR FURTHER RESEARCH

This book addressed, to a certain extent, a progress in Luther's view of the intermediate state of the soul from a tormenting condition to peaceful rest. Admitting lack of knowledge and information from the Scripture, Luther did not intend to elaborate the subject in detail, but treated it only insofar as adopting the expression of the Scripture and attempted to articulate it.

The two turning points in Luther's view of purgatory are significant in this respect. In 1521/22, Luther inclined to concur with von Amsdorf that the intermediate state of the soul in faith is the state of *rest in peace*, but he did not seem to *fully* grasp this concept until 1525/26. In the *Explanations*, for instance, Luther states that souls in purgatory commit sin continuously as long as they fear punishments and pursue their will (i.e., seeking for rest) instead of God's will. At the Leipzig Debate Luther criticizes Eck for his ignorance of the theology of the cross when Eck asserts that the souls are at rest in peace in purgatory. Furthermore, in the *Heidelberg Disputation*, Luther claims that the Christian life is hidden in God; likewise, in the *Dictata*, Luther asserts that true rest is hidden in suffering.

The *Recantation* exhibits completely the opposite view of Luther on the intermediate state of the soul. With the notion of "rest from their labor" in Revelation 14:13, Luther asserts that those who die in the Lord are blessed and rest in peace. Whoever believes in Christ is not condemned but "righteous, blissful, and holy."[1] In a similar vein, in his *Sermon Annotations on St. Matthew* Luther addresses the state and condition of the departed souls, and while admitting no particular knowledge available with respect to the nature of peace in Christ after death, Luther affirms the soul's peaceful state in Christ. Also, in the *Lectures on Genesis*, Luther criticizes

---

1. AE 61:229; WA 30II:376.29.

law-oriented pastoral care of the Roman Church for "afflicted consciences," and accentuates instead the promise of the gospel that true rest and consolation are found in absolution:

> the pope consigns afflicted consciences to purgatory and makes no certain promise about their salvation but demands contrition, confession, and satisfaction, if perhaps God may be appeased and reconciled by such means . . .[2]
>
> I absolve you from your sins in the name of Christ, who died for you and rose again, and said: 'Because I live, you will live also' (John 14:19). This is solid and firm consolation. In it alone the godly can find rest.[3]

Perhaps until 1525/26, and if not, until 1521/22, Luther's theological orientation of the theology of the cross might have resulted in paying no attention to the aspect of comfort and peace, to a certain degree, as far as the intermediate state of the soul is concerned. Also, as mentioned in chapter 3, for Luther the term "purgatory" always denotes a condition of torment, not peaceful rest. As his statement in the *Lectures on Genesis* notes, the significant shift in Luther's view of the intermediate state seems to be fundamentally rooted in his emphasis on the *effect* of the gospel—the forgiveness of sin.

This raises a couple of questions: At what point does such a noticeable change emerge? When does Luther's view of the effect of the gospel—forgiveness—develop significantly, and what would it be like if this is examined in view of Luther's notion of the postmortem "rest in peace"? It might be sometime after the first turning point in 1521/22, while this conjecture does not imply that Luther did not understand the effect of the gospel before 1521/22, and presumably between the second turning point in 1525/26 and the publication of the *Recantation* of 1530. These questions of Luther's view of the intermediate state of the soul and the effect of the gospel require further research.

Finally, how interested was Luther, as John Stephenson poses a question, in the subject of the intermediate state of the soul? Compared to the major subjects such as justification, the righteousness of God, Sacraments, grace, forgiveness, and the cross and suffering, Luther spared his breath in this regard partly because the Scripture explicitly addresses heaven and hell only. The gravity of the notion of purgatory at the time of Luther should

---

2. AE 8:189; WA 44:717.11–13. On Gen 48:21.
3. AE 8:189; WA 44:717.18–19.

Reflection on the Subject

not be minimized, however, as it was deeply embedded in late medieval religiosity and took a key role in the penitential system of the High and Late Middle Ages. Concerning Luther's dismissal of the notion of postmortem torment and his full adoption of the notion of peaceful state of the soul, which did not occur until 1525/26, I posed a question as to whether Luther's theological orientation in the theology of the cross resulted in paying no due attention to the peaceful state of the soul until 1525/26, and if not, until 1521/22. This question requires further research on Luther's notion of the intermediate state of the soul, particularly between 1521/22 and 1525/26. In addition, an investigation may be required to see if there is any development or shift in Luther in applying his theology of the cross—his principal methodology and perspective—before and after 1525/26.

Afterword

MORE REMARKABLE THAN THE speed with which Min Hwan Kim acquired fluency in English on his move to Canada from his native Korea in the mid-1990s is the marked ability he displayed, already during his seminary training and in his early years of ordained service, to process and articulate complex theological data. As he once explained over the phone how he had used an array of scripture passages in discussion with a parishioner who had exceeded Lutheran limits in her zeal for the Zionist cause, I sat musing, "I couldn't think theologically on my feet like that, especially in a second language." The publication of Chaplain Kim's slightly edited doctoral treatise signals the arrival of a powerful intellect on the scene of Canadian Lutheranism in particular and North American Christendom in general. As his former teacher and good friend of many years, I hope that he is given much opportunity to make his mark in research, in teaching, in writing, and not least in the area of ecumenical dialogue and inter-church debate.

Luther scholars can be a myopic bunch, deeply immersed in the writings and thoughts of the sixteenth-century German Reformer but curiously unconcerned about what preceded, accompanied, and followed him on the great canvas of Christendom. Dr. Kim shows a certain kinship with the great English Luther scholar Gordon Rupp, who was one of the two examiners involved in my own doctoral viva, in placing Luther against the background of universal historic Christendom in general and of Western Christendom in particular, and in his awareness of how Luther might be called on as an interlocutor in contemporary systematic debates. Of especial merit is Kim's endeavor to understand the dispute on indulgences that began in the fall of 1517 against the grand backcloth of the age-old awareness of the Church as the death-defying communion of saints and of the

Afterword

complex reality of the whole understanding and practice of "penance" on which, as Lutherans see it, "indulgences" as remission of canonical penalty feature as a carbuncle.

With Luther himself, Kim is aware that skirmishes on indulgences were a sideshow in the great debate on soteriology and ecclesiology that involved all sides active in the Reformation(s) of the sixteenth century. The chapter in which he masterfully sets forth what all is involved in Luther's so-called "Reformation breakthrough" demonstrates his mastery of a mass of literature and his skill in being able to penetrate beyond timeworn slogans and tired clichés in order to make Luther, one of the "soloists" who as Jaroslav Pelikan put it stand out from the ordinary "choir members" of the Church's theologians, a potential participant in twenty-first-century theological, pastoral, and spiritual formation.

Kim's account of Luther's distinctive and developing understanding of Purgatory fills a hitherto glaring lacuna of monographs on all manner of aspects of the Reformer's thinking and will serve a useful secondary purpose in demonstrating to the Luther scholars of tomorrow how to put in order and make sense of the unfolding testimony of a scholar who, unlike Calvin, declined to offer a systematic account of his thought in a single major opus.

I hope Kim's first foray into published Luther scholarship finds many readers and that opportunity will be provided him to occupy theological podiums and to engage in scholarly discourse both oral and written. As he shares and expounds upon the research here set forth, I hope he will address the wider issue of Luther's treatment of 'life after death' in general (curiously, as Lyndal Roper has pointed out, Luther displays relatively little interest in the topic) and also consider how, as the Reformer understood purgatory in overwhelmingly punitive terms, his theology might relate to the purificatory function of purgatory as articulated by Catherine of Genoa in the sixteenth century and by Joseph Ratzinger in the last generation.

Whether he sticks to the narrow field of Luther scholarship or branches out more widely in the area of systematic and historical theology, it is to be hoped that Dr. Kim's powerful mind and articulate voice will make a valuable contribution to the Church and Academy of our time.

John R. Stephenson
St Catharines, Ontario
Saturday May 4, 2024

Appendix

Responses to the Doctrine of Purgatory

BIBLICAL REFERENCES

It is fair to acknowledge that in response to pastoral and theological inquiries and speculations concerning the intermediate state of the soul, biblical references to postmortem conditions were sought to provide theological premise and rationale while the sources are limited. In the interim, the notion of purgatory was conceived and received as a tradition until the peak of high traffic in indulgences. It is equally fair to comment that the subject of biblical references to the doctrine of purgatory has raised a controversy and drawn a dissecting border between the pro-purgatorial and the anti-purgatorial positions within Christendom. Is purgatory biblical? Does Scripture address the subject of purgatory explicitly? These questions, in fact, underline the queries into the limits of the biblical canonicity since no consensus has been achieved on the subject, particularly between the Roman Catholics and the Protestants, except for Lutherans and Anglicans, on the Apocrypha. While Lutherans acknowledge the fourteen books of the Old Testament Apocrypha—not as the canonized books, but for edification—as Luther included them in *Die Bibel oder die ganze Heilige Schrift des Alten und Neuen Testaments* (1534), the Council of Trent (1546) affirmed canonicity of the twelve books excluding First and Second Esdras,[1] and the

---

1. Lueker, *Lutheran Cyclopedia*, 40–41.

Appendix

Protestants—except for Lutherans as well as Anglicans based on a reference to Jerome—reject the books of the Old Testament Apocrypha.

Particular are three major references to the doctrine of purgatory (e.g., 2 Maccabees 12:39–45; Matthew 12:32; and 1 Corinthians 3:13–15) which facilitated specific concerns of the subject matter in its own thematic parameter. 2 Maccabees 12:39–45 is the major reference to the practice of prayers and sacrifices for the dead. The text contains the story of Maccabeus' offering of a sacrifice by sending two thousand drachmas to Jerusalem for the same number of Israelites killed, as well as his prayers for them.[2] The major concern regarding this text is the canonicity of the book itself. Doubt was thrown on this as early as Jerome, whose Jewish informants did not have the books in their Hebrew texts. While both 1 and 2 Maccabees were composed in Greek, Latin, and Syriac, the second book was first written in Greek.[3] Second Maccabees has been considered as part of the Sacred Scriptures in the Eastern Church, but in Protestant circles in general—except for Lutherans and Anglicans alike—it is known only as the Apocrypha.[4] In addition to the dispute on the canonicity of 2 Maccabees, no canonical Scripture describes the practice of offering the Eucharistic Sacrifice so that the dead might be freed from their sins.[5] Nor did Gregory the Great consider 2 Maccabees as a canonical book; it was only for edification, with which Jerome and Cyprian concurred.[6] Regardless, 2 Maccabees played a key role in being a reference to the late medieval doctrine of purgatory, particularly with respect to prayers and sacrifices for the deceased and was an optional reading in Requiem Masses.[7]

Matthew 12:32 is the major reference to promoting and expediting the notion of the postmortem forgiveness of sin. The passage was popularly cited as a premise to justify a logical reasoning on the subject (e.g., Gregory the Great[8] and Albertus Magnus[9]). At the center stands among

---

2. 2 Macc. 12:39–45. María, *Chronicles-Maccabees*, 596–97.

3. Weiser, *The Old Testament*, 391.

4. Kaiser, *Introduction*, 407.

5. Chemnitz, *Examination*, Pt 4, Topic 3, Sec. 1. C.2, 235.

6. Gregory, *Moral.*, Bk.18, quoted in Chemnitz, *Examination*, Pt 4, Topic 3, Sec. 1. C.2, 237–38.

7. Ratzinger, *Eschatology*, 233.

8. *Dial* 4, 39, quoted in Chemnitz, *Examination*, Pt 4, Topic 3, Sec. 1. C.2, 341

9. Albertus Magnus, *Commentarii in IV Sententiarum*, Bk 4. Dist 21. Art 4. 865-66. See also Le Goff, *Birth of Purgatory*, 260–61.

other biblical references 1 Corinthians 3:13–15, directing to the "authentic heart of the doctrine" and "its rationale," as Benedict XVI comments.[10] This particular text, however, has recently drawn the attention of the Roman Catholic scholarship in a new perspective to defining purgatory.

RECENT ROMAN CATHOLIC SCHOLARSHIP ON PURGATORY

In the Latin Church, the doctrine of purgatory is traditionally associated with the concept of punishment as a consequence of venial sins, as well as penalty for mortal sins forgiven, due to the incompleteness of penance in this life. Recent scholarship within Roman Catholic circles, however, reorients the doctrine with reference to the concept of purification (e.g., union with Christ) rather than that of punishment in view of satisfaction,[11] and claims the christological aspect of purgatory. Benedict XVI acknowledges this new development and adopts Joachim Gnilka's assertion[12] that "this testing fire [in 1 Corinthians 3:15] indicates the coming Lord himself,"[13] and defines purgatory not in reference to satisfaction but to the state of purification. He states that "purgatory is not . . . some kind of supra-worldly concentration camp where man is forced to undergo punishment in a more or less arbitrary fashion. Rather is it the inwardly necessary process of transformation in which a person becomes capable of Christ . . ."[14]

In this respect, the encounter with Christ works both judgment and salvation, which is a "painful transformation 'as through fire'" but "a blessed pain."[15] Drawing a final remark, he notes: "If one presupposes a naively objective concept of Purgatory, then of course the text [of Scriptures] is silent. But if, conversely, we hold that Purgatory is understood in a properly Christian way when it is grasped christologically, in terms of the Lord himself as the judging fire which transforms us and conforms us to his own glorified body; then we shall come to a very different conclusion."[16] Here Benedict XVI notes that the text of Scriptures is silent about the "objective

10. Ratzinger, *Eschatology*, 228.
11. Rausch, *Systematic Theology*, 284.
12. Gnilka, *1st Kor 3, 10–15*, quoted in Ratzinger, *Eschatology*, 228–33.
13. Ratzinger, *Eschatology*, 228.
14. Ratzinger, *Eschatology*, 230.
15. Benedict XVI, *Spe Salvi*, 47, quoted in O'Callaghan, *Christ Our Hope*, 308.
16. Ratzinger, *Eschatology*, 229.

concept" of purgatory, and presents purgatory with respect to the state of purification. Yves Congar, Hans Urs von Balthasar, and Giovanni Moioli also adopt this new perspective in reference to Christ's passion and death.[17]

In addition, Karl Rahner in "The Life of the Dead" alludes to the opinion that it is inappropriate to reckon the intermediate state as "a defined doctrine." The intermediate state should be conceived as a "cultural amalgam, a little harmless piece of mythology," he argues.[18] Concerning the biblical references to the doctrine, Rahner calls into question finding a biblical reference to the doctrine of purgatory. He claims: "There is not much to be got out of Scripture, whether of the Old or New Testaments, *particularly if we may hold the opinion that prayers for the dead do not necessarily imply a doctrine of purgatory*."[19]

The process of purgation takes place *in this life*, particularly through pains at death that individuals experience. He thus asserts, "These pains are purifying and constitute the essence of 'purgatory' . . . Purgatory takes place in death itself."[20] Finally, Zachary Hayes approaches the doctrine in a metaphorical sense, and asserts that the notion of purgatory itself indicates "the need for further maturation" rather than the other world in a literal and geographical sense.[21]

The new christological aspect of purgatory differentiates the concept of postmortem conditions from the medieval penitential satisfaction. It does not conceive purgatory as a postmortem place per se. It is rather a *condition* of the soul as in "a state of growth and purification of love after death."[22]

RESPONSES OF THE PROTESTANT CHURCH

Among the Protestants, only two Reformers—Luther and Calvin—and C. S. Lewis and Jerry Walls will be reviewed. In the *Ninety-Five Theses* of 1517, Luther called into question the indulgences employed in the medieval

---

17. O'Callaghan, *Christ Our Hope*, 308.

18. Rahner, "The Life of the Dead," *Theological Investigations* 4:353, quoted in Phan, *Eternity in Time*, 122–23.

19. Rahner, *Theological Investigations* 19:182–83, quoted in Phan, *Eternity in Time*, 124; emphasis added.

20. Rahner, *Theological Investigations* 19:187, quoted in Phan, *Eternity in Time*, 126–28.

21. Hayes, "The Afterlife," 72–75.

22. Nichols, *Death and Afterlife*, 172.

penitential practices.²³ While upholding his theology of justification, he did not oppose the practice of praying for the dead, nor did he deny the notion of purgatory. Instead, in 1521/22 he redefined purgatory from a place of suffering *hereafter* to such sufferings as tasting hell *in this life*, rejecting the formal doctrine of purgatory, on the one hand, and continuing to retain the notion of purgatory as postmortem torment but only for few souls, on the other. In 1525/26, as far as the intermediate state of the soul is concerned, Luther dismissed the notion of postmortem torment, and conjectured the postmortem state of the soul as rest in peace drawn from Scripture. In 1530, the year that the Augsburg Confession was presented to Charles V, Luther published *A Recantation*.

In the *Institutes of the Christian Religion* of 1536, Calvin criticized the Latin doctrine as "the fictitious purgatory of the Papists,"²⁴ and that penitential satisfaction is the "parent of indulgences."²⁵ For Calvin, just as for other Reformers in general except for Luther, the doctrine of justification by faith alone *is* the foundational rationale for his rejection.²⁶ Regarding the biblical references to the doctrine, Calvin argued that the subject of Matthew 12:32 is not satisfaction for but guilt of sin; therefore, the text is irrelevant to a purgatorial punishment of satisfaction. Calvin underlined that the text addresses the remission of sins in a manner of amplification.²⁷ By reason of canonicity, he intentionally avoided discussing 2 Maccabees 12:39–45 so as not to give misimpression as if he concurred on the notion that it is a canonical book.²⁸ He also argued that the fire in 1 Corinthians 3:13–15 is to be understood as a metaphor in reference to the "examination of the Holy Spirit," or to the Holy Spirit that tests everyone.²⁹ Finally, Calvin *repudiated* prayer for the dead, and contended that such a practice has no biblical foundation.³⁰

---

23. Luther had a great impact on Zwingli not only of the theology of justification by faith alone but of the subject of indulgences. Hall, "Ulrich Zwingli," 358.

24. Calvin, *Institutes*, Bk 3. Ch 5. Sec 6.

25. "The dogma of satisfaction the parent of indulgences. Vanity of both." "From this dogma of satisfaction that of indulgences takes its rise." Calvin, *Institutes*, Bk 3. Ch 5. Sec. 1.

26. Walls, *Purgatory*, 41–42.

27. Calvin, *Institutes*, Bk 3. Ch 5. Sec. 7.

28. Calvin, *Institutes*, Bk 3. Ch 5. Sec. 8.3.

29. Calvin, *Institutes*, Bk 3. Ch 5. Sec. 9.5.

30. Calvin, *Institutes*, Bk 3. Ch 5. Sec. 10.

Appendix

Not all Protestants disapprove of the notion of purgatory, however. In *Letters to Malcolm: Chiefly on Prayer*, C. S. Lewis, for instance, affirms his personal prayers for the dead, and avouches himself as an adherent to a pious belief in purgatory, not as a doctrine, but as his personal reasoning and conviction based on the grace and goodness of God. For Lewis no concurrence with other Protestants seemed to be felt necessary on this subject.[31] Of this particular initiative, Jerry Walls is currently a leading proponent who believes in purgatory, "not as a dogma but as a theological proposal." He proposes it "in an ecumenical fashion" with five theological aspects for consideration: first, hermeneutics is considered the fundamental issue of the subject; second, compatibility of the doctrine of purgatory with the doctrine of justification by faith alone can be feasible in a sanctification model of purgatory; third, a human responsibility is required in "a process of moral transformation"; fourth, issues concerning personal identity need to be addressed with respect to the process of moral transformation; and finally, there is a theological concern of "postmortem grace and probation." With his theological proposal, Walls underlines the goodness of God in which "a second chance for repentance" would be available in "an eschatological setting."[32]

RESPONSES OF THE ORTHODOX CHURCH

The Western and the Eastern Churches did not find a point of agreement on the subject of postmortem purgation except the general values and utility of suffrages which include prayers for the dead.[33] Discussions between the Western and the Eastern Churches on the subject of purgatory began in the thirteenth century (1231) at the meeting of Friar Bartholomew (Latin) and George Bardanes (Greek), which was reported to Patriarch Germanus II (d. 1240, Patriarch of Constantinople).[34] Controversy soon began

---

31. Lewis, *Letters to Malcolm*, 137–43, especially 138–41. According to Jerry Walls, Lewis's personal belief in purgatory was based on his theological understanding, particularly of Christ's atonement in soteriology. Christ is the "perfect penitent," but not the penal substitution for humankind. Each individual must do repentance as required in this process although the goal will never be achieved by human efforts. Walls, *Purgatory*, 153–75.

32. Walls, *Purgatory*, 123–52, 177–81.

33. Ratzinger, *Eschatology*, 219. See also Pozo, *Theology of the Beyond*, 470.

34. Larchet, *Life After Death*, 212–16, 226. See also Trumbower, *Rescue for the Dead*, 171–74.

in 1252 when an anonymous Dominican published *Tractatus contra Graecos*; subsequently, when Innocent IV in his official letter (1254) addressed postmortem purification and the efficaciousness of the prayers of the living for the dead[35] together with his wish to obtain an agreement from the East on the subject of purgatory.[36] The Second Council of Lyons (1274, two decades after the second centennial anniversary of the Great Schism) affirmed the Latin position, and at the Council the letter of Nicaean Emperor Michael Paleologus (d. 1282) was also presented, whose formula was the same as the "Profession of Faith" by Clement IV in 1267.[37] The Emperor's letter, however, made no mention of a purgatorial fire, nor was there a notion of purgatory conceived as a place.[38] At the Council of Florence (1439), the Latin position was reaffirmed, and the Greeks' responses to the Latin doctrine were presented.[39]

At the Council of Florence Mark of Ephesus (d. 1444) presented the position of the Orthodox Church on the subject, and his points are summarized in two main documents: the *Orthodox Catechism* of Meletios Pigas (d. 1601) in the Patriarchate of Alexandria (Vilna, 1596) and the *Confession of Faith* of Dositheus (d. 1707) in the Patriarchate of Jerusalem (1690). Meletios summarizes Mark of Ephesus' critical comments on the Latin position: first, due to Christ's "total and full satisfaction," no subsequent or secondary satisfaction is required for post-baptismal sins; second, it is solely for "a pedagogical and prophylactic purpose" that the confessor imposes the sacramental penance; third, after receiving the sacramental absolution, no burden of painful satisfaction should remain; fourth, neither punitive nor satisfactory quality for sin should be implied in the sacramental penance and the trials of this life; fifth, with regard to repentance and its fruits, there is no need for "a satisfactory compensation for sin"; sixth, for the sake of Christ's sacrifice a full remission is granted to those who died even without paying a full penance; seventh, according to the Scriptures (e.g., Luke 16:22–28), either the bosom of Abraham (e.g., Lazarus) or hell (e.g., the rich man) are the only postmortem conditions for the souls; and finally the doctrine of purgatory is "superfluous and akin to Origenism."[40]

---

35. *CCDD*, 838:278.
36. Ombres, *Theology of Purgatory*, 44.
37. A brief editorial note on May 7–July 17, 1274, *CCDD* 281.
38. *CCDD* 856:283. See also Ombres, *Theology of Purgatory*, 44.
39. *CCDD* 1304–6:336.
40. Larchet, *Life After Death*, 199.

Appendix

In addition, Meletios repudiates in the *Orthodox Catechism* biblical references claimed by the Latin Church for the doctrine: first, Matthew 5:26, for instance, does not imply the notion of purgatory, but refers to the sufferings in hell; second, 2 Maccabees 12:43–45 does not support, rather destroys, the doctrine of purgatory, for the sacrifice in the passage is not for the "expiation of a venial sin" but for "a serious sin of idolatry committed by people who died impenitent"; third, as far as the concept of fire in 1 Corinthians 3:13–15 is concerned, it refers, not to the fire of purgatory, but to "a fire of trial" by which both the good and the evil will be tested; and finally concerning Matthew 12:32 where it addresses that certain sins "will not be forgiven either in this age or in the age to come," it simply means that "the sin against the Holy Spirit will never be forgiven."[41]

In addition, noteworthy are the following critical differences between the Western and the Eastern Churches presented in Dositheus' *Confession of Faith*: first, other than paradise and hell, the Eastern Church does neither admit nor accept the notion of a third world; second, the concept of fire is theocentric in which God himself is "the purifying fire" for perfect salvation (e.g., redemption, refreshment, remission, and reconciliation); third, all "peccadilloes," or venial sins, are remitted at death; fourth, it is absurd to claim that within the distinction between guilt and penalty, pain remains while guilt is remitted, for all pains due to sins are "blotted out by repentance or priestly absolution";[42] and finally, as far as the Eastern Church's stance on the relationship between the living and the dead is concerned, the Church's prayers for the dead are necessary from the moment of death.[43]

Throughout discussions and debates between the two churches, the Eastern Church confirmed the position that the Roman doctrine of purgatory has no basis either in Scripture or in the works of early fathers. Prayer for the dead is the single item that both Churches commonly acknowledged, to a certain extent; nonetheless, the Eastern Church did not agree to the Western Church's claim that prayers for the deceased imply and prove the doctrine of purgatory.[44] From the perspective of the East, the notion of a purgatorial fire is merely imaginative.[45] Furthermore, the Roman doctrine of purgatory is in essence rooted in the theories of satisfaction and

---

41. Larchet, *Life After Death*, 200.
42. Larchet, *Life After Death*, 200–202.
43. Larchet, *Life After Death*, 205.
44. Larchet, *Life After Death*, 174–75.
45. Bartmann, *Purgatory*, 155–56.

expiation developed after Augustine, and papal authority is also deeply tied to the doctrine and its practices.[46] In evaluating the Latin doctrine of purgatory, Larchet's succinct comment is worth noting: "the doctrine of purgatory can be seen as being in agreement with the post-Augustinian orientation of Latin Theology."[47]

---

46. Larchet, *Life After Death*, 177–78.
47. Larchet, *Life After Death*, 176.

Bibliography

Abelard, Peter. *Peter Abelard's Ethics: An Edition with Introduction, English Translation and Notes by D. E. Luscombe.* Oxford: Clarendon, 1971.

Aland, Kurt, ed. *Martin Luther's Ninety-five Theses: With the Pertinent Documents from the History of the Reformation.* Translated by C. M. Jacobs. Revised by Harold J. Grimm. St. Louis: Concordia, 1967.

Albertus Magnus. *Commentarii in IV Sententiarum (Dist. I–XXII).* Opera Omnia: Ex Edition Lugdunensi Religiose Castigate 29. Paris: Ludovicum Vivès, 1890–1899.

Althaus, Paul. *The Theology of Martin Luther.* Translated by Robert C. Schultz. Philadelphia: Fortress, 1966.

Ambrose. *Funeral Orations by Saint Gregory Nazianzen and Saint Ambrose.* Translated by Roy J. Deferrari. The Fathers of the Church 22. New York: Fathers of the Church, 1953.

Anderson, Gary A. *Charity: The Place of the Poor in Biblical Tradition.* New Haven: Yale University Press, 2013.

Aquinas, Thomas. *Supplementum Indices. Appendix ad Supplementum Tertiae Partis Summa Theologiae.* ST 5. Matriti: Biblioteca de Autores Cristianos, 1952.

Augustine of Hippo. *The City of God.* Translated by Marcus Dods. New York: Random House, 1950.

Bailey, Lloyd R., Sr. *Biblical Perspectives on Death.* Overtures to Biblical Theology. Philadelphia: Fortress, 1979.

Bainton, Roland H. *Here I Stand: A Life of Martin Luther.* A Hendrickson Classic Biography. Peabody: Hendrickson, 1950.

Barry, William T., trans. *Enchiridion of Indulgences: Norms and Grants.* New York: Catholic Book, 1969.

Barth, Hans-Martin. *The Theology of Martin Luther: A Critical Assessment.* Minneapolis: Fortress, 2013.

Bartmann, Bernhard. *Purgatory: A Book of Christian Comfort.* Translated by Dom E. Graf. London: Burns, Oates & Washbourne, 1936.

Bayer, Oswald. *Martin Luther's Theology: A Contemporary Interpretation.* Translated by Thomas H. Trapp. Grand Rapids, Michigan: Eerdmans, 2008.

———. *Living By Faith: Justification and Sanctification.* Translated by Geoffrey W. Bromiley. Grand Rapids: Eerdmans, 2003.

Bibliography

———. *Promissio: Geschichte der reformatorischen Wende in Luthers Theologie*. Forschungen zur Kirchen- und Dogmengeschichte 24. Göttingen: Vandenhoeck & Ruprecht, 1971.

Bede. *Bede's Ecclesiastical History of England*. Translated by A. M. Sellar. London: Bell, 1907. The Project Gutenberg Ebook. https://www.gutenberg.org/ebooks/38326.

———. *Bede the Venerable: Homilies on the Gospels Book One, Advent to Lent*. Translated by T. Martin and David Hurst. Cistercian Studies 110. Kalamazoo, MI: Cistercian, 1991.

Bellarmine, Robert. *Purgatory: The Members of the Church Suffering*. Translated by Ryan Grant. Post Falls: Mediatrix, 2017.

Beutel, Albrecht. "Luther's Life." In *CCML* 3–19.

Borth, Wilhelm. *Die Luthersache (causa Lutheri) 1517–1524: Die Anfänge der Reformation als Frage von Politik und Recht*. Historische Studien 414. Lübeck: Matthiesen, 1970.

Bovey, Alixe. "Death and the afterlife: how dying affected the Living." In *The Middle Ages*. Published April 30, 2015. https://www.bl.uk/the-middle-ages/articles/death-and-the-afterlife-how-dying-affected-the-living.

Brecht, Martin. *Martin Luther*. 3 vols. Translated by James L. Schaaf. Minneapolis: Fortress, 1993–1999.

Brown, Peter. *Augustine of Hippo: A Biography*. London: Faber & Faber, 1988.

Bysted, Ane L. *The Crusade Indulgence: Spiritual Rewards and the Theology of the Crusades, c. 1095–1216*. History of Warfare 103. Leiden: Brill, 2015.

Calvin, John. *Institutes of the Christian Religion*. https://ccel.org/ccel/calvin/institutes/institute s.i.html.

Canadian Conference of Catholic Bishops. *Catechism of the Catholic Church*. Ottawa: Canadian Conference of Catholic Bishops, 1992.

Carey, Phillip. "Luther and the Legacy of Augustine." In *Remembering the Reformation: Martin Luther and Catholic Theology*, edited by Declan Marmion, Salvador Ryan, and Gesa E. Thiessen, 37–54. Minneapolis: Fortress, 2017.

Carlsmith, Christopher. "Education in Early Sixteenth-Century Europe." In *Martin Luther in Context*, edited by David M. Whitford, 22–29. New York: Cambridge University Press, 2018.

Catherine of Genoa. *Purgation and Purgatory: The Spiritual Dialogue*. Translated and notes by Serge Hughes. Classics of Western Spirituality. New York: Paulist, 1979.

Chemnitz, Martin. *Examination of the Council of Trent*. Translated by Fred Kramer. 4 vols. St. Louis: Concordia, 1971–1986.

Clark, Robert Scott. "*Iustitia Imputata Christi*: Alien or Proper to Luther's Doctrine of Justification?" *Concordia Theological Quarterly* 70 (2006) 269–310.

Connolly, Hugh. *The Irish Penitentials: and Their Significance for the Sacrament of Penance Today*. Portland, OR: Four Courts, 1995.

Cross, F. L., and E. A. Livingstone, eds. *Oxford Dictionary of the Christian Church*. 3rd ed. London: Oxford University Press, 1997.

Cross, Richard. *Communicatio Idiomatum: Reformation Christological Debates*. London: Oxford University Press, 2019.

Cunliffe-Jones, Hubert, ed. *A History of Christian Doctrine*. Edinburgh: T. & T. Clark, 1978.

Daley, Brian E. *The Hope of the Early Church: A Handbook of Patristic Eschatology*. New York: Cambridge University Press, 1991.

Daniel, David P. "Luther on the Church." In *OHMLT*, 333–52.

Bibliography

Delumeau, Jean. *History of Paradise: The Garden of Eden in Myth and Tradition*. Translated by Matthew O'Connell. New York: Continuum, 1995.

Dieter, Theodor. "Luther as Late Medieval Theologian: His Positive and Negative Use of Nominalism and Realism." In *OHMLT*, 31–48.

Dragseth, Jennifer Hockenbery. *The Devil's Whore: Reason and Philosophy in the Lutheran Tradition*. Studies in Lutheran History and Theology. Minneapolis: Fortress, 2011.

Dudley, Martin. "The Sacrament of Penance in Catholic Teaching and Practice." In *Confession and Absolution*, edited by Martin Dudley and Geoffrey Rowell, 56–90. Collegeville, MN: Liturgical, 1990.

Duttenhaver, Krista. "Suffering and Love: Martin Luther, Simone Weil, and the Hidden God." In *The Global Luther: A Theologian for Modern Times*, edited by Christine Helmer, 96–112. Minneapolis: Fortress, 2000.

Ebeling, Gerhard. *Luther: An Introduction to His Thought*. Translated by R. W. Wilson. Philadelphia: Fortress, 1970.

Eusebius. *The Ecclesiastical History of Eusebius Pamphilus, Bishop of Caesarea, in Palestine*. Translated with an Introduction by Christian F. Cruse. Grand Rapids: Baker, 1995.

Evangelische Verlagsanstalt. *From Conflict to Communion*, Lutheran–Roman Catholic Common Commemoration of the Reformation in 2017: Report. 5th ed. Leipzig: Evangelische Verlagsanstalt, 2017.

Evener, Vincent. "Wittenberg's Wandering Spirits: Discipline and the Dead in the Reformation." *Church History* 84 (2015) 531–55.

Fabisch, Peter, and Erwin Iserloh, eds. *Dokumente zur Causa Lutheri (1517–1521)*. Corpus Catholicorum 41–42. Münster: Aschendorff, 1988–1991.

Fabri, Johann. *Antilogiarvm Martini Lutheri Babylonia*. Augustae Vindelicorum: Weyssenhorn, 1530. https://reader.digitale-sammlungen.de/en/view/bsb00021164?=page,1.

Ferdinandy, Michael de. "Charles V, Holy Roman Emperor." In *Encyclopaedia Britannica*. https://www.britannica.com/biography/Charles-V-Holy-Roman-emperor.

Flogaus, Reinhard. "Luther versus Melanchthon? Zur Frage der Einheit der Wittenberger Reformation in der Rechtfertigungslehre." *Archiv für Reformationsgeschichte—Archive for Reformation History* 91 (2000) 6–46.

Forde, Gerhard O. *On Being a Theologian of the Cross: Reflections on Luther's Heidelberg Disputation, 1518*. Grand Rapids: Eerdmans, 1997.

Francke, Kuno. "Medieval German Mysticism." *Harvard Theological Review* 5 (1912) 110–20.

Frantzen, Allen J. *The Literature of Penance in Anglo-Saxon England*. New Brunswick, NJ: Rutgers University Press, 1983.

German, Brian Thomas. "Martin Luther's First Psalm Lectures and the Canonical Shape of the Hebrew Psalter." PhD diss., University of St. Michael's College, 2014. https://tspace.library.utoronto.ca/bitstream/1807/67632/1/German_Brian_T_201411_PhD_thesis.pdf.

Giselbrecht, Rebecca A. "Hulrych Zwingli." In *Martin Luther in Context*, edited by David M. Whitford, 257–64. New York: Cambridge University Press, 2018.

Gnilka, Joachim. *Ist Kor. 3, 10–15 ein Schriftzeugnis für das Fegfeuer? Eine Exegetische-historische Untersuchung*. Düsseldorf: n.p., 1995.

Gorman, Michael J. *Cruciformity: Paul's Narrative Spirituality of the Cross*. Grand Rapids: Eerdmans, 2001.

Bibliography

Gregory the Great. *Dialogues.* https://www.tertullian.org/fathers/gregory_04_dialogues_book4.htm.

Griffith, Susan B. "Medical Imagery in the 'New' Sermons of Augustine." In *Augustine, Other Latin Writers: Papers presented at the Fourteenth International Conference on Patristic Studies held in Oxford 2003*, edited by Frances M. Young et al., 107–12. Studia Patristica 43. Leuven: Peeters, 2006.

Hall, Basil. "Ulrich Zwingli." In *A History of Christian Doctrine*, edited by Hubert Cunliffe-Jones, 353–70. Edinburgh: T. & T. Clark, 1978.

Hall, Douglas John. "The Theology of the Cross." In *Encounters with Luther: New Directions for Critical Studies*, edited by Kirsi I. Stjera and Brooks Schramm, 73–80. Louisville: Westminster John Knox, 2016.

Hamm, Berndt. "Martin Luther's Revolutionary Theology of Pure Gift without Reciprocation." *Lutheran Quarterly* 29 (2015) 125–61.

———. *The Early Luther: Stages in a Reformation Reorientation*. Translated by Martin J. Lohrmann. Grand Rapids: Eerdmans, 2014.

Hayes, Zachary. "The Afterlife: Death, Judgment, Purgatory, and Heavens, and Hell." In *Reclaiming Catholicism: Treasures Old and New*, edited by Thomas H. Groume and Michael J. Daley, 72–78. Maryknoll, NY: Orbis, 2010.

Hebblethwaite, Margaret, and Kevin Donovan. *The Theology of Penance*. Theology Today 20. Butler, WI: Clergy Book Service, 1979.

Helmer, Christine, ed. *The Global Luther: A Theologian for Modern Times*. Minneapolis: Fortress, 2000.

Hendrix, Scott H. *Luther and the Papacy: Stages in a Reformation Conflict*. Philadelphia: Fortress, 1981.

Hinlicky, Paul. *Luther vs. Pope Leo: A Conversation in Purgatory*. Nashville: Abingdon, 2017.

Hoffman, Bengt R. *Theology of the Heart: The Role of Mysticism in the Theology of Martin Luther*. Edited by Pearl Willemssen Hoffman. Minneapolis: Kirk House, 1998.

Huss, John. *De Ecclesia: The Church*. Translated by David S. Schaff. Westport, CT: Greenwood, 1976.

Iserloh, Erwin. *The Theses Were Not Posted: Luther Between Reform and Reformation*. Introduction by Martin E. Marty. Boston: Beacon, 1968.

Jonas, Justus, Michael Coelius, et al. *The Last Days of Luther*. Translated and annotated by Martin Ebon. Introduction by Theodore G. Tappert. Garden City, NY: Doubleday, 1970.

Jones, Claire Taylor. Review of *Der 'Frankfurter' / 'Theologia Deutsch': Spielräume und Grenzen des Sagbaren (Frühe Neuzeit 201)* by Lydia Wegener. *Medieval Mystical Theology* 26 (2017) 157–59.

Kaiser, Otto. *Introduction to the Old Testament: A Presentation of Its Results and Problems*. Translated by John Sturdy. Minneapolis: Augsburg, 1977.

Karant-Nunn, Susan C. "Martin Luther on Death and Dying." *Oxford Research Encyclopedia of Religion*. https://doi.org/10.1093/acrefore/9780199340378.013.341/.

Kelly, Anthony. *Eschatology and Hope*. Theology in Global Perspective. Maryknoll, NY: Orbis Books, 2006.

Kittelson, James. "Luther and Modern Church History." In *CCML*, 259–71.

Knowles, David. "From Gregory the Great to Charlemagne. Rome and Constantinople." In *A History of Christian Doctrine*, edited by Hubert Cunliffe-Jones, 231–41. Edinburgh: T. & T. Clark, 1978.

Bibliography

Kohnle, Armin. *Reichstag und Reformation: kaiserliche und ständische Religionspolitik von den Anfängen der Causa Lutheri bis zum Nürnberger Religionsfrieden.* Heidelberg: Gütersloher, 2001.

Kolb, Robert. "Luther on the Theology of the Cross." In *The Pastoral Luther: Essays on Martin Luther's Practical Theology,* edited by Timothy J. Wengert, 33–58. Minneapolis: Fortress, 2017.

———. "Luther's Theology of the Cross Fifteen Years after Heidelberg: Lectures on the Psalms of Ascent." *Journal of Ecclesiastical History* 61 (2010) 69–85.

———. *Martin Luther: Confessor of the Faith.* Oxford: Oxford University Press, 2009.

Koslofsky, Craig. *The Reformation of the Dead: Death and Ritual in Early Modern Germany, 1450–1700.* Early Modern History: Society and Culture. New York: St. Martin's, 2000.

Köberle, Adolf. *The Quest for Holiness: A Biblical, Historical, and Systematic Investigation.* Translated by John C. Mattes. Minneapolis: Augsburg, 1938.

Köstlin, Julius. *The Theology of Luther in Its Historical Development and Inner Harmony.* 2 vols. Philadelphia: Lutheran Publication Society, 1897.

Larchet, Jean-Claude. *Life After Death according to the Orthodox Tradition.* Translated by G. John Champoux. Orthodox Research Institute. New Hamsphire: Rollinsford, 2012.

Le Goff, Jacques. *The Birth of Purgatory.* Translated by Arthur Goldhammer. Chicago: University of Chicago Press, 1984.

Lea, Henry Charles. *A History of the Inquisition of the Middle Ages.* Russell Scholars Classic Editions 1. New York: Russell & Russell, 1958.

Leppin, Volker "Luther's Roots in Monastic-Mystical Piety." In *OHMLT,* 49–61.

———. "Luther's Transformation of Medieval Thought: Continuity and Discontinuity." In *OHMLT,* 105–14.

———. *Martin Luther: The Late Medieval Life.* Translated by Rhys Bezzant and Karen Roe. Grand Rapids: Baker Academic, 2017.

Levy, Ian C. "The Leipzig Disputation: Masters of the Sacred Page and the Authority of Scripture." In *Luther at Leipzig: Martin Luther, the Leipzig Debate, and the Sixteenth-Century Reformations,* edited by Mickey L. Mattox et al., 115–44. Studies in Medieval and Reformation Traditions 218. Leiden: Brill, 2019.

Lewis, C. S. *Letters to Malcolm: Chiefly on Prayer.* London: Bles, 1964.

Lindberg, Carter. "Prierias and His Significance for Luther's Development." *Sixteenth Century Journal* 3 (1972) 45–64.

———. "There Will Be No Poor Among You: The Reformation of Charity and Social Welfare." In *The Protestant Reformation of the Church and the World,* edited by John Witte Jr. and Amy Wheeler, 139–60. Louisville: Westminster John Knox, 2018.

Loewenich, Walther von. *Martin Luther: The Man and His Work.* Translated by Lawrence W. Denef. Minneapolis: Augsburg, 1986.

Lohse, Bernhard. *Martin Luther: An Introduction to His Life and Work.* Translated by Robert C. Schultz. Philadelphia: Fortress, 1986.

———. *Martin Luther's Theology: Its Historical and Systematic Development.* Translated by Roy A. Harrisville. Minneapolis: Fortress, 1999.

Lueker, Erwin L., ed. *Lutheran Cyclopedia.* St Louis: Concordia, 1954.

Lull, Timothy F., and Derek R. Nelson. *Resilient Reformer: The Life and Thought of Martin Luther.* Minneapolis: Fortress, 2015.

Luther, Martin. "Articuli Smalcaldici (1537)." In *Concordia Triglotta: Libri Symbolici Ecclesiae Lutheranae,* edited by F. Bente, 453–529. St. Louis: Concordia, 1921.

Bibliography

MacCulloch, Diarmaid. *The Reformation*. New York: Penguin, 2005.

María, José, ed. *Chronicles-Maccabees: The Books of 1 and 2 Chronicles, Ezra, Nehemiah, Tobit, Judith, Esther and 1 and 2 Maccabees in the Revised Standard Version and New Vulgate*. Dublin: Four Courts, 2003.

Marshall, Peter. *1517: Martin Luther and the Invention of the Reformation*. Oxford: Oxford University Press, 2017.

McGinn, Bernard. *The Harvest of Mysticism in Medieval Germany*. New York: Herder & Herder, 2005.

McGrath, Alister E. *Luther's Theology of the Cross: Martin Luther's Theological Breakthrough*. 2nd ed. Malden, MA: Wiley-Blackwell, 2011.

McNeill, John T., and Helena M. Gamer. *Medieval Handbooks of Penance: A Translation of the Principal* libri poenitentiales *and Selections from Related Documents*. Records of Western Civilization. New York: Columbia University Press, 1990.

Meyer, Kuno. "An Old Irish Treatise: De arreis." *Revue Celtique* 15 (1894) 485–98.

Moltmann, Jürgen. *The Crucified God: The Cross of Christ as the Foundation and Criticism of Christian Theology*. Translated by R. A. Wilson and John Bowden. London: SCM, 1974.

Moreira, Isabel. *Heaven's Purge: Purgatory in Late Antiquity*. Toronto: Oxford University Press, 2010.

Morwood, James, ed. *Oxford Latin Desk Dictionary*. Rev. ed. Oxford: Oxford University Press, 2005.

Ngien, Dennis. *Luther's Theology of the Cross: Christ in Luther's Sermons on John*. Eugene, OR: Cascade Books, 2018.

———. *The Suffering of God According to Luther's* Theologia Crucis. Vancouver, BC: Regent College Publishing, 2005.

Nichols, Terence. *Death and Afterlife in the Christian Tradition: A Theological Introduction*. Grand Rapids: Brazos, 2010.

Oberman, Heiko A. *Luther: Man Between God and the Devil*. Translated by Eileen Walliser-Schwarzbart. New Haven: Yale University Press, 1990.

———. *The Harvest of Medieval Theology: Gabriel Biel and Late Medieval Nominalism*. Cambridge: Harvard University Press, 1963.

———. *The Reformation: Roots and Ramification*. Translated by Andrew Colin Gow. Grand Rapids: Eerdmans, 1994.

O'Callaghan, Paul. *Christ Our Hope: An Introduction to Eschatology*. Washington, DC: Catholic University of America Press, 2011.

Olivier, Daniel. *The Trial of Luther*. Translated by John Tonkin. St. Louis: Concordia, 1978.

Ombres, Robert. *Theology of Purgatory*. Theology Today Series 24. Butler: Clergy Book Service, 1978.

O'Reggio, Trevor. "A Re-examination of Luther's View on the State of the Dead." *Journal of the Adventist Theological Society* 22 (2011) 154–70.

Ozment, Steven E. "An Aid to Luther's Marginal Comments on Johannes Tauler's Sermons." *Harvard Theological Review* 63 (1970) 305–11.

———. *Homo Spiritualis: A Comparative Study of The Anthropology of Johannes Tauler, Jean Gerson and Martin Luther (1509–1516) in The Context of Their Theological Thought*. Studies in Medieval and Reformation Thought 6. Leiden: Brill, 1969.

———. *The Age of Reform (1250–1550): An Intellectual and Religious History of Late Medieval and Reformation Europe*. New Haven: Yale University Press, 1980.

Bibliography

Packull, Werner O. "Luther and Medieval Mysticism in the Context of Recent Historiography." *Renaissance and Reformation* n.s. 6.2 (1982) 79–93. https://www.jstor.org/stable/43444352/.

Palmer, Paul F. *Sacraments and Forgiveness: History and Doctrinal Development of Penance, Extreme Unction and Indulgences*. Sources of Christian Theology 2. Westminster, MD: Newman, 1959.

Papal Encyclicals Online, s.v. "Exsurge Domine: Condemning the Errors of Martin Luther, Pope Leo X—1520." https://www.papalencyclicals.net/leo10/l10exdom.htm.

Pasulka, Diana Walsh. *Heaven Can Wait: Purgatory in Catholic Devotional and Popular Culture*. Toronto: Oxford University Press, 2015.

Paulson, Steven. "Luther's Doctrine of God." In *OHMLT*, 187–200.

———. *Luther's Outlaw God*. 3 vols. Lutheran Quarterly Books. Minneapolis: Fortress, 2018–2021.

Paulus, Nikolaus. *Geschichte des Ablasses im Mittelalter*. Vol. 1. Paderborn: Schöningh, 1922.

Phan, Peter C. *Eternity in Time: A Study of Karl Rahner's Eschatology*. Toronto: Associated University Press, 1988.

Plass, Ewald M., ed. *What Luther Says: A Practical In-Home Anthology for the Active Christian*. 1959. Reprint, St. Louis: Concordia, 1994.

Podmore, Simon D. *Struggling with God: Kierkegaard and the Temptation of Spiritual Trial*. Cambridge: James Clarke, 2013.

Poschmann, Bernhard. *Penance and the Anointing of the Sick*. Translated and revised by Francis Courtney. Montreal: Palm, 1964.

Pozo, Candido. *Theology of the Beyond*. Translated by Mark A. Pilon. 5th ed. Madrid BAC. Staten Island, NY: Fathers and Brothers of the Society of St Paul, 2009.

Price, Richard. "Informal Penance in Early Medieval Christendom." *Studies in Church History* 40 (2004) 32–33

Rahner, Karl. *Main in the Church*. Vol. 2 of *Theological Investigations*. Translated by Karl-H. Kruger. Baltimore: Helicon, 1963.

Ratzinger, Joseph. *Eschatology: Death and Eternal Life*. 2nd ed. Translated by Michael Waldstein. Translation edited by Aidan Nichols. Dogmatic Theology. Vol. 9. Washington, DC: Catholic University of America Press, 1988.

Rausch, Thomas P. *Systematic Theology: A Roman Catholic Approach*. Collegeville, MN: Liturgical, 2016.

Reeves, Michael. *The Unquenchable Flame: Discovering the Heart of the Reformation*. Nashville: B&H, 2009.

Reinhardt, Kurt E. *My Light and My Salvation*. Fort Wayne, IN: Redeemer, 2008.

Rex, Richard. *The Making of Martin Luther*. Princeton: Princeton University Press, 2017.

Rittgers, Ronald K. "How Luther's Engagement in Pastoral Care Shaped His Theology." In *OHMLT*, 462–70.

———. "Penance and Indulgences." In *Martin Luther in Context*, edited by David M. Whitford, 85–91. New York: Cambridge University Press, 2018.

———. *The Reformation of Suffering: Pastoral Theology and Lay Piety in Late Medieval and Early Modern Germany*. Oxford Studies in Historical Theology. New York: Oxford University Press, 2012.

Roper, Lyndal. *Martin Luther: Renegade and Prophet*. New York: Random, 2017.

Rosin, Robert. "Humanism, Luther, and the Wittenberg Reformation." In *OHMLT*, 91–104.

Bibliography

Rupp, Gordon. *Luther's Progress to the Diet of Worms*. New York: Harper Torchbooks, 1964.

———. *The Righteousness of God: Luther Studies*. London: Hodder & Stoughton, 1968.

Saak, Erick Leland. *Luther and the Reformation of the Later Middle Ages*. Cambridge: Cambridge University Press, 2017.

Salkeld, Brett. *Can Catholics and Evangelicals Agree about Purgatory and the Last Judgment?* New York: Paulist, 2011.

Scaer, David P. "The Concept of *Anfechtung* in Luther's Thought." *Concordia Theological Quarterly* 47 (1983) 15–30.

Schilling, Heinz. *Martin Luther: Rebel in An Age of Upheaval*. Translated by Rona Johnston. Oxford: Oxford University Press, 2017.

Schürmann, Reiner. "Meister Eckhart." In *Encyclopaedia Britannica*. https://www.britanica.com/biography/Meister-Eckhart.

Schwarz, Hans. *Eschatology*. Grand Rapids: Eerdmans, 2000.

———. *True Faith in the True God: An Introduction to Luther's Life and Thought*. Translated by Mark William Worthing. Minneapolis: Augsburg, 1996.

Schwarz, Reinhard. *Martin Luther: Lehrer der christlichen Religion*. 2nd ed. Tübingen: Mohr Siebeck, 2016.

Shaffern, Robert W. *The Penitents' Treasury: Indulgences in Latin Christendom, 1175–1375*. Scranton: University of Scranton Press, 2007.

Slenczka, Notger. "Luther's Anthropology." In *OHMLT*, 222–32.

Standorth, Maxwell, trans. *Early Christian Writings: The Apostolic Fathers*. Revised translation, introduction, and new editorial material by Andrew Louth. 1968. Reprint, Toronto: Penguin, 1987.

Stayer, James M. *Martin Luther, German Saviour: German Evangelical Theological Factions and the Interpretation of Luther, 1917–1933*. Montreal: McGill-Queen's University Press, 2000.

Steinmetz, David Curtis. *Luther and Staupitz: An Essay in the Intellectual Origins of the Protestant Reformation*. Duke Monographs in Medieval and Renaissance Studies 4. Durham: Duke University Press, 1980.

Stephenson, John R. "Luther's Eucharistic Writings of 1523 to 1528." PhD diss., Durham University, 1982. http://etheses.dur.ac.uk/7695/.

———. "The Reformation of Repentance." *Lutheran Theological Review* 29 (2017) 57–67.

Sterponi, Laura. "Reading and Meditation in the Middle Ages: *Lectio Divina* and Books of Hours." *Text & Talk* 28 (2008) 667–89.

Swanson, Robert N. *Indulgences in Late Medieval England: Passports to Paradise?* Cambridge: Cambridge University Press, 2007.

Tanner, Norman P., ed. *Decrees of the Ecumenical Councils*. 2 vols. Washington, DC: Georgetown University Press, 1990.

Tauler, John. "Johannes Tauler." World Heritage Encyclopedia Edition. Project Gutenberg Self-Publishing Press. http://self.gutenberg.org/articles/eng/Johannes_Tauler/.

———. *The Sermons and Conferences of John Tauler of the Order of Preachers, surnamed "The Illuminated Doctor," Being His Spiritual Doctrine*. Translated by Walter Elliott. The first complete English translation with introduction and index. Brooklin Station: Apostolic Mission House, 1910.

Taylor, Larissa Juliet. "God of Judgment, God of Love: Catholic Preaching in France, 1460–1560." *Historical Reflections* 26 (2000) 247–68. https://www.jstor.org/stable/41299175.

Bibliography

Tentler, Thomas N. *Sin and Confession on the Eve of the Reformation*. Princeton: Princeton University Press, 1977.

Thiel, John E. *Icons of Hope: The "Last Tings" in Catholic Imagination*. Notre Dame: University of Notre Dame Press, 2013.

Thiemann, Ronald F. "Luther's Theology of the Cross: Resource for a Theology of Religions." In *The Global Luther: A Theologian for Modern Times*, edited by Christine Helmer, 228–46. Minneapolis: Fortress, 2000.

Thompson, W. D. J. Cargill. "The 'Two Kingdoms' and the 'Two Regiments': Some Problems of Luther's *Zwei-Reiche-Lehre*." *Journal of Theological Studies* 20 (1969) 164–85. https://www.jstor.org/stable/23960585.

Trumbower, Jeffrey A. *Rescue for the Dead: The Posthumous Salvation of Non-Christians in Early Christianity*. Oxford Studies in Historical Theology. Toronto: Oxford University Press, 2001.

Vercruysse, Jos E. "Luther's Theology of the Cross at the Time of the Heidelberg Disputation." *Gregorianum* 57 (1976) 523–48. https://www.jstor.org/stable/23575620.

Viladesau, Richard. *The Triumph of the Cross: The Passion of Christ in Theology and the Arts, from the Renaissance to the Counter-Reformation*. New York: Oxford University Press, 2008.

Vogelsang, Erich. *Der angefochtene Christus bei Luther*. Arbeiten zur Kirchengeschichte 21. Berlin: de Gruyter, 1932.

———, ed. *Der junge Luther*. Luthers Werke in Auswahl 5. Berlin: de Gruyter, 1955.

———. "Weltbild und Kreuzestheologie in den Höllenfahrtsstreitigkeiten der Reformationszeit." *Archiv für Reformationsgeschichte—Archive for Reformation History* 38 (1941) 90–132. https://doi.org/10.14315/arg-1941-jg07.

Walls, Jerry L. *Purgatory: The Logic of Total Transformation*. Toronto: Oxford University Press, 2012.

Weiser, Artur. *The Old Testament: Its Formation and Development*. New York: Association, 1964.

Welker, Michael. "The European Reformation: Advocacy of Education and Liberation." In *The Protestant Reformation of the Church and the World*, edited by John Witte Jr. and Amy Wheeler, 89–103. Louisville: Westminster John Knox, 2018.

Wengert, Timothy J. *Luther's Ninety-Five Theses: With Introduction, Commentary, and Study Guide*. Minneapolis: Fortress, 2015.

Westhelle, Vitor. "Communication and the Transgression of Language in Martin Luther." In *The Pastoral Luther: Essays on Martin Luther's Practical Theology*, edited by Timothy J. Wengert, 59–84. Minneapolis: Fortress, 2017.

———. "God against God: Luther the Theologian of the Cross." In *The Alternative Luther: Lutheran Theology from the Subaltern*, edited by Else Marie Wiberg Pedersen, 275–96. Lanham, MD: Lexington, 2019.

———. "Luther's *Theologia Crucis*." In *OHMLT*, 156–67.

Whitford, David M. *Luther: A Guide for the Perplexed*. New York: T. & T. Clark, 2011.

———, ed. *Martin Luther in Context*. New York: Cambridge University Press, 2018.

Wicks, Jared, trans. and ed. *Cajetan Responds: A Reader in Reformation Controversy*. Washington, DC: Catholic University of America Press, 1978.

———. *Luther and His Spiritual Legacy*. Wilmington, DE: Glazier, 1983.

———. *Man Yearning for Grace: Luther's Early Spiritual Teaching*. Veröffentlichungen des Instituts für Europäische Geschichte Mainz 56. Wiesbaden: Steiner, 1969.

BIBLIOGRAPHY

———. "Martin Luther's Treatise on Indulgences." *Theological Studies* 28 (1967) 481–518. https://journals.sagepub.com/doi/pdf/10.1177/ 004056396702800302.

Woodbridge, Russell S. "Gerhard Westerburg: His Life and Doctrine of Purgatory and the Lord's Supper." PhD diss., Southeastern Baptist Theological Seminary, 2003.

Wriedt, Markus. "Luther's Theology." Translated by Katharina Gustiavs. In *CCML*, 86–119.

Wright, N. T. *For All the Saints? Remembering the Christian Departed*. New York: Morehouse, 2003.

———. *Surprised By Hope: Rethinking Heaven, the Resurrection, and the Mission of the Church*. New York: HarperCollins, 2008.

Zwingli, Hulrych. *No. 305: Zwingli's Sixty-seven Articles*. Christian History Institute. https://christianhistoryinstitute.org/study/module/zwinglis-sixty-seven-articles.

Subject Index

Abelard, Peter, 31
absolution, x, 21–22, 27–29, 69, 128, 130n243, 194, 205–6. *See also* the Office of the Keys
accounts, visionary, 15, 17, 20
afterlife, 15–17, 20n46, 23
Albertus Magnus, 200
Albrecht of Magdeburg, 38
Alexander II, Pope, 29
Alighieri, Dante, 14n13, 25n77
Althaus, Paul, 84nn288–89, 176n216, 177n230
Ambrose of Milan, 18
analogy of: fire and iron, 122n193; healing, 103–5, 108n103, 109, 113, 121, 128; health, 132, 136; journey, 119–21; leaven, 107n96, 113–14, 117, 123, 135; marriage, 111, 131. *See also* joyous exchange; sleep, 82n275, 83
Anfechtung(en), xi, 6, 44, 98–100, 102n66, 104–6, 115, 124–25, 127–28, 137–38, 140–41, 144–51, 154–55, 159–70, 172, 176, 180–86, 190, 193. *See also* a foretaste of hell; suffering; *tentatio*
antichrist, 9, 35, 37, 63, 78–81, 86, 88–89, 91, 95n27, 96nn29–30, 126, 140, 189, 191
antiquity, 8, 12–13, 15, 20, 21n54, 32, 189
apokatastasis, 14. *See also* Origen
Aquinas, Thomas. *See* Thomas Aquinas

Augsburg, 41, 67, 152; *Apology of Augsburg Confession*, 33; *Augsburg Confession (Confessio Augustana)*, 68, 203; Diet of Augsburg. *See* Diet
Augustine of Hippo, 13, 16, 18, 20, 31–32, 34, 47, 79, 95n24, 99n45, 101, 153, 169n168, 207; *Confessions*, 13n10, 16
Aurifaber, Johannes, 65, 153
authority, 20n46, 26, 127n216; of councils, 77; of the judgment of reason and/or experience, 144n4, 159–63, 164, 181; of the pope, 12, 29n102 (papal absolution), 39, 40n10, 45, 77, 80, 86, 89, 95, 189, 207; of the Scripture, 53, 80, 157n101, 158, 161–62; of tradition, 158–63, 181

Bainton, Roland H., 78n254
Bayer, Oswald, 1, 92, 94, 136n285
Bede, the Venerable, 8, 12, 19–20, 22
Bellarmine, Robert, 43
Benedict XVI, Pope, 8, 19, 142, 201. *See also* Joseph Ratzinger
Boniface VIII, Pope, 30
Bugenhagen, Johannes (Pommeranus), 65

Cajetan, Thomas de Vio, 45n46, 47–48, 80, 128
Calvin, John, 8, 198, 202–3

Subject Index

Catherine of Genoa, 14, 198
Charles V (Holy Roman Emperor), 67n200, 78, 203
Chemnitz, Martin, 133n255
Chrysostom, John, 23–24
Clement IV, Pope, 205
Clement VI, Pope, 29, 40n10
Clement VII, Pope, 62
commemoration, 17, 19
communion of saints, 17–19, 23, 197. See also *ecclesial continuum*
confession(s), 12, 23, 28–29, 68n208, 89, 104n78, 128, 132, 152n69, 194. See also Augsburg; Dositheus; Luther: works
consolation(s), 24, 69, 124n205, 194
continuity, xi, 7–8, 9, 57, 95, 97n32, 120, 139–41, 191–92.
cross. See Luther: theology of the cross; purgatory: as the cross
culpa, 28, 31n122. See also sin; *poena*
cure, 65–66, 104, 118, 121
Cyprian of Carthage, 13, 18n34, 200

Damascene, John, 23
Day: All Souls', 19; All Saints', 19, 41n19, 69n215
death, xi, 3n5, 9, 13, 15–18, 19, 22–23, 26–28, 33n136, 35, 48, 50n95, 58–59, 61n154, 65–67, 69n215, 82nn274–75, 84–85, 89, 92, 95n27, 106, 111–15, 117–19, 121, 126, 133–37, 139, 141, 144–47, 150–53, 156n98, 171, 175–77, 183n255, 185, 189, 192–93, 197–98, 202, 206
devil(ish), 41n17, 61, 68, 69n212, 69n215, 105n82, 114, 115
Diet: of Augsburg (1518), 47, 109, 128; of Augsburg (1530), 65, 67n200; of Worms (1521), 77
dilemma, confessional, 96
discontinuity, 7–8, 9, 57, 97n32, 139–41, 191–92
Dositheus (Patriach of Jerusalem, d. 1707), *Confession of Faith*, 206
doubts about: canonicity of 2 Macc, 200; the pope as the antichrist, 80, 95n27, 96n30, 140, 161, 163; purgatory/scriptural references for purgatory, 2, 70n217, 85, 87, 161

ecclesial continuum, 17, 33. See also communion of saints
Eck, Johann, 43, 48–51, 56, 72, 79–81, 86, 139, 174, 176–77, 193
Eckhart, Meister von Hochheim, 152, 154n79
ecumenical councils: of Chalcedon, 106n87; of Ephesus II (431), 106n87; Lateran IV, 29, 30; Lateran V, 162; of Clermont, 29; of Florence (1431–45), 21, 24n69, 25, 26, 27n85, 157n102, 205; of Lyons II, 21, 157n102, 205; of Trent, 25–27, 68, 199; Vatican Council I, 25–27; Vatican Council II, 26–27
Eucharistic Sacrifice, 18, 25, 200
Eudes of Châteauroux, 25
evangelical, 33, 58, 62, 64–65, 79, 94, 96, 137, 138n299, 188
existential, 2–3, 38, 54, 62, 70, 73, 78, 85, 88–89, 92, 137n292, 140–41, 144–48, 151, 159, 162, 165, 175, 182, 185–86, 189

Fabri, Johann, 67
faith, ix–xi, 2, 4–5, 9, 17, 25–26, 27n85, 33–35, 37, 39, 43n28, 46–48, 50–51, 53, 55–57, 61–62, 64–65, 68–69, 71, 75–78, 84nn290–91, 85, 89, 91–93, 97, 99–100, 102–4, 107–41, 144, 146, 153n72, 155, 159n115, 164–65, 167–68, 169n168, 172–78, 180, 183, 185, 187–90, 192–93, 203–6; article(s) of, 39, 47, 50, 53, 55–57, 62, 64, 75–78, 80, 132n252, 189, 192
fear, 44, 46, 51–52, 59, 66, 84–85, 87n301, 92, 101n59, 106, 117, 121n188, 125–26, 133, 134n261, 135–36,

220

Subject Index

139–41, 144–45, 147, 157n103, 158, 160n119, 165, 185n271, 193
forgiveness, 5, 30, 65–66, 92, 103–14, 119–20, 127–28, 130–31, 141, 148, 155n89, 190, 194, 200
Francis I (emperor), 32n131
Francis of Assisi, 30
Francis of Mayron, 32
Frederick III (the Wise), 40, 68
Frederick, Johann (Magnanimous), 68
Freedom, 47, 48n77, 53, 125n125, 156–57. *See also* Luther: works

Gansfort, Johan Wessel, 42, 72n225
gospel, ix, 7, 9, 56, 65–66, 69, 79, 81, 84n289, 89, 95n27, 107n96, 112–17, 120, 123–24, 127, 132n252, 147, 163, 189, 191, 194
Great Schism, 12, 25, 205
Gregory I (the Great), 16, 18, 20, 28, 32, 200

heal: heal(ing/ed), 97, 103–9, 113–14, 118, 120–21, 127–28, 132, 133n258, 135, 141, 149, 192; healer, 65; health(y), 65, 104–6, 120–21, 132, 134, 136, 139, 191. *See also* analogy
hell: a postmortem place, 16, 22–24, 49–50, 59, 161, 194, 205–6; condition/punishments of, 14, 20, 22n62, 24, 46, 50, 136, 146, 157n103, 158, 160nn118–19, 162, 164, 166, 206; a foretaste of/tasting pains of, 4–6, 10, 35, 44, 46–47, 49, 52, 54, 60–61, 67, 78, 92, 98, 143, 145n19, 146, 148–52, 157n101, 159, 160n119, 163–65, 168, 171, 175–86, 190–91, 193, 203. *See also anfechtung*, suffering, and *tentatio*
Henry of Segusio, 31
heretic, 34, 45, 48, 53, 56–57, 63–64, 77, 88, 158, 189, 192
heresy, 6, 9, 64, 79
Hincmar of Rheims, 28
holiness, 65

Honorius III, Pope, 30
Hugh of Pisa, 31n122
Hugh of St. Cher, 29
Huss, John, 9, 35, 78–79, 89, 95n27, 189, 191

idolatry, 69, 206
illness, 147, 121n186
imputation, 97, 104–7, 111, 113, 116–24, 135, 141, 190, 192. *See also* righteousness
indulgence(s), x, 2n2, 6, 8, 12, 21, 23, 27–33, 35, 39–40, 45–48, 55, 57, 80, 125, 130, 132, 162–63, 171–72, 187, 197–99, 202–3; crusade indulgence(s), 27 29, 31, 40; Jubilee indulgences, 30, 62. *See also* Luther: works
Innocent III, Pope, 29
Innocent IV, Pope, 25, 157n102, 205
intercession(s), 18, 24–25, 28, 31, 34, 71n220, 126

John VIII, Pope, 29
Jonas, Justus, 62
joyous exchange, 65, 102, 103n71, 108n103, 111, 117, 129, 131, 155, 178, 187. *See also* analogy
justification by faith alone, 1–2, 4–7, 9, 35–36, 89, 92–93, 95–141, 155, 168, 177–78, 188–91, 194, 203–4

Karlstadt, Andreas Rudolf Bodenstein von, 3n5, 41–42, 48n77, 54

Larchet, Jean-Claude, 8, 12, 82n274, 207
law(s), x, 27, 80, 126, 182n250; and gospel, 65, 84n289, 103, 113, 114n143, 115–18, 120, 123–24, 127, 178, 194
Le Goff, Jacques, 13, 16, 23n64, 25n77, 27
Leipzig Debate, 2, 7, 34n141, 43, 47–51, 57, 59, 72, 76n245, 78–80, 86n296, 87, 121n28, 123, 126, 138n295, 157n102, 174, 177n224, 193
Leo IX, Pope, 29
Leo X, Pope, 2, 45, 47–48, 52n101, 81

221

Subject Index

Link, Wenzel (Wenzeslaus Linck), 80, 81n270

love(d), x, 5, 9, 14, 19, 26n80, 43n28, 46, 51–52, 60n150, 87n301, 88, 92–93, 98, 100, 120, 123–26, 131–41, 145n13, 153, 157, 159n115, 164, 166, 176–79, 184–85, 190, 192, 202

Luther, Martin: theology of, 1–2; theology of the cross, 5–6, 10, 35, 141, 143, 162, 168, 170–87, 190–91, 193–95; lectures: *First Lectures on Psalm (see Dictata)*; on *Galatians (1516/17, printed in 1519)*, 59, 70n217, 103, 140; on *Galatians (1531/35)*, 7, 107n96, 114–19, 121n118, 123; on *Romans*, 7, 46, 50, 93–94, 98n36, 102–9, 123, 154–55, 173; letter, *to Nicholas von Amsdorf*, 7, 51, 53–54, 56, 60, 73, 77, 83, 159n116, 192–93; sermon(s): *Annotations on St Matthew*, 7, 44n35, 66–68, 84, 185–86; *de Poenitentia*, 7, 47, 48n69, 94, 109–10, 129; *on the Christmas Day*, 7, 50n93, 51, 55, 73, 77; *on the Gospel for the Epiphany*, 7, 33, 44n34, 50n93, 51, 56–58, 60, 68n203, 73, 75–77; *on the Gospel of St John*, 7, 65–66, 74, 110n118; *on Indulgences and Grace*, 45, 125n208, 133n260; *on Two Kinds of Righteousness*, 7, 103n71, 110–19, 129; with the theme of three stages, 7, 107–9; works: *Adoration of the Sacrament*, 7, 58; *Against Latomus*, 7, 113–14; *Bondage of the Will*, 74, 149n49; *Catechism*: Large, 112; Small, 112, 135; *Commentary on Psalm*, 65n192, 145n13; *Confession Concerning Lord's Supper*, 4n8, 7, 33, 61–62, 66, 68, 70, 72, 74, 82n276, 89, 183, 191; *Defense and Explanation of All the Articles*, 7, 41, 50n93, 51–55, 73, 75, 77, 86–87, 132n252, 150n60, 151, 154, 159–60; *Dictata*, 7–10, 43n29, 92, 94–95, 96n30, 99–102, 103n73, 105n82, 107n96, 121n184, 123, 134n264, 140, 143, 148–52, 155, 160, 168–71, 174n199, 179–80, 182, 186n276, 189–90, 193; *Disputation and Defense of Brother Martin Luther against the Accusations of Dr. Johann Eck*, 48; *Disputation Concerning Justification*, 7, 9, 110n120, 118–20, 121n186, 124n197; *Disputation on the Power and Efficacy of Indulgences*, 2n2, 32. See also *Ninety-five Theses*; *Explanations of the Ninety-five Theses*, 2, 4–5, 7, 9–10, 34–36, 42n24, 43n30, 45–49, 52, 66, 72, 78, 84–85, 87n301, 90, 92–93, 103n71, 109, 121n188, 123–24, 126–45, 148–52, 154, 156–58, 159n117, 160, 162, 167, 171, 174, 176, 180–83, 185n271, 186n276, 187, 190–91, 193; *Freedom of a Christian*, 7, 81n272, 103n71, 110n115, 134; *Heidelberg Disputation*, 10, 45n48, 131, 143–44, 151, 155n91, 155n93, 171–72, 173n191, 173n194, 175, 177, 190, 193; *Instruction on Several Articles*, 48; *On the Misuse of the Mass*, 71; *Ninety-five Theses*, x, 2, 38n2, 38n4, 39, 44–45, 47, 88, 93, 95, 125, 125n208, 127n216, 130, 155n91, 171–72, 185n270, 202; *Notes on Ecclesiastes*, 3, 7, 60–61, 73, 84; *Personal Prayer Book*, 7, 58–59, 86, 97n32, 192; *Recantation of the Doctrine of Purgatory*, 3–5, 7, 35, 37–38, 57, 62–64, 66, 70–77, 82, 86, 91, 183, 189, 191, 193–94, 203; *Smalcald Articles*, 68–69; works, other: *Christiano lectori Martinus Lutherus S.*, Foreword, 42n22; *Meditation on Christ's Passion*, 7,

Subject Index

58–59, 86, 97n32, 184n261, 192; *Preface and Glosses to Two Bulls of Pope Clement VII on the Jubilee Indulgence*, 62n162

magisterium, 25
mammon, 64
Mantua, 68
Mark of Ephesus, 8, 24, 205
martyrdom, 28, 156n98
martyrs, 28, 164
mass for the dead, 18
Maximilian I (emperor), 47–48
Melanchthon, Philip, 62, 91, 97, 185
money, 65n192, 67, 186
motu, 97, 100–101, 104. *See also simul*
mystic(s), 108n103, 152, 154n79, 168n164, 181
mystical, 65, 71, 97n33, 143, 152, 166, 168, 169n169, 170, 173n197, 183
mysticism, 71, 101n59, 111, 120n183, 137n292, 138n298, 154n79, 155, 165, 169n171

notional(ly), 65, 146

Oberman, Heiko A., 8, 39n4, 94, 96, 98n35
Office of the Keys 28, 39, 47n69, 69, 136n285, 162. *See also* absolution
omnipotence, 75
Origen(ism), 14, 16–17, 205
Ozment, Steven, E., 143, 151n65

papacy, 9, 35, 37, 69n212, 80–81, 86–90
papal bulls: *Ad dominici gregis curam*, 68; *Cum postquam*, 48, 189; *Decet Romanum Pontificem*, 9, 52, 57, 81, 189; *Exsurge Domine*, 9, 51, 57, 78, 81, 91, 95, 96, 128, 189; *Inter Sollicitudines*, 62; *Pastoris aeterni*, 62
papists, 56, 67, 69, 76, 185–86, 203
pastoral(ly), x, 8, 10, 12, 14–16, 20–23, 54, 56–59, 66, 87–88, 125, 192–94, 198, 199
Paul III, Pope, 68

penance, 8, 12, 20, 26, 28, 31, 128, 132, 137n289, 138n299, 152n69, 182n254, 198, 201, 205; canonical, 21–23; Celtic/tariff(ed), 12, 21–22, 28; remission of, 28. *See also* sacrament
penitential: practice(s), 17, 21n53, 28, 202–3; system, 12, 20, 23–24, 32–33, 195; theology, 52n102
Peter of Osma, 31, 32n130
physician, 65, 121
Picardi of Bohemia, 34, 72, 85
piety, late medieval, 39–40, 98. *See also* religiosity
poena, 28. *See also* sin; *culpa*
pontifical, 25, 29n102, 32.
post-Augustinian, 12, 32, 207
power: of baptism, 112; of indulgences, 2n2, 32; of the Office of the Keys, 28, 162; of the pope, 39, 40n10, 49, 55, 79n260, 80, 86, 89, 97n32, 125; of sin, 91, 115; (ordinate) power of God, 81, 100n52, 175; (absolute) power of God's hidden will, x, 4–5, 58, 72, 74, 82n276
prayer(s): *ectenia*, 17; for the dead, 8, 11–13, 16–25, 31–34, 39, 49n87, 56, 63n172, 70n218, 71n220, 188–89, 200, 202–6; for the dead in the ancient Coptic liturgy, 17–18; Gallican, 18
Prierias, Sylvester Mazzolini, 45, 47, 79–80
promise(s): of Christ, 103, 111, 122, 130–32; faith in, 109; of forgiveness, 104–5, 110, 127, 131; of God, 85, 104, 129, 138, 140, 192; of the gospel, 194; the word of, 128; of salvation, 69
promptuaria, 13
purgare, 13
purgation: process of, 202; progression of, 71; postmortem, 3–4, 8, 12–14, 17, 19–20, 22–23, 25–26, 32–33, 35, 50, 70, 71n219, 74, 75, 157n102, 189, 192, 204

Subject Index

purgatory: belief in, 16, 35, 47–48, 53, 55, 57–58; biblical reference, 6, 10, 39, 47, 49, 52–53, 60–61, 64, 70, 78, 143, 150, 157n101, 160–61, 187, 190, 199–206; condition/place, postmortem, x, 3, 6, 8–9, 13–14, 19, 23–25, 32, 39, 52, 54, 57, 60, 122, 125; as the cross, 5, 9, 92–93, 137–39, 142–87; denial/rejection of, 9, 35, 37, 43, 54–57, 61, 66, 70–88; emergence of the formal doctrine of, 25–27; existence of, 11, 34, 47–48, 53, 58; Luther's redefinition of, xi, 5, 35, 38, 43n28, 44, 54, 67, 70, 85, 92, 160, 186, 193, 203; punishment(s) of/in, 4, 5, 6, 9, 10, 35, 44, 46, 48, 50, 54, 133, 136, 158, 203; sanctification model of, 14, 204; satisfaction model of, 14; terminology, 43n28, 44, 89; true/real, 67–68, 186; turning point in Luther's view: first, 72–73; second, 73–75

purification: with respect to persecution and suffering, 13, 137n292, 150; a place of, 20n46, 72n225; postmortem, 4, 27, 42, 71–72, 74, 86, 150, 205; the state of, 201–2; as union with God, 201

Rahner, Karl, 8, 202
Ratzinger, Joseph, 198. *See also* Benedict XVI, Pope
Reformation breakthrough, 4, 7, 8n12, 10, 92–96, 189, 191–92, 198
refrigerium, 18
relationship: inner-churchly, 12, 21; of the living and the dead, 17, 19, 25, 33, 206. *See also* ecclesial continuum
religiosity: commercial, 40; late medieval, 40. *See also* piety
rest in peace, 5, 18, 38, 50–51, 57, 60, 63, 66, 69–70, 82–85, 89, 101, 121, 124, 133, 139–40, 169–70, 192–94, 203

righteousness, 46, 110, 112n128, 114, 118–19, 122, 130, 134, 172; beginning of, 101, 104, 106–7, 120–21; referring to Chist, 102n68, 114, 115n153, 120; Christ's, 65, 103, 110–12, 121–22, 129–31, 140, 168n163; of faith, 93, 108–9, 116–17, 120, 123–24, 135, 190, 192; of God, 95, 97, 99–108, 113n136, 121, 191, 194; external/alien righteousness of God, 5, 9, 110–20, 189, 191; external/alien righteousness, continual effect of, 5, 9, 93, 97, 100, 103, 107–8, 111–14, 117, 119–25, 131–41, 178–79, 190–91; external/alien righteousness, instantaneous effect of, 5, 9, 92, 97, 107, 111–13, 120, 123, 141, 178–79, 190–91. *See also* Luther: works

Sacrament: of the Altar, 61, 66; of Baptism, 5, 21, 107, 111–12, 118–21, 132n252, 136n285, 179; of Penance, 52n102, 94
salvation, x, 14, 31, 52n102, 65–66, 69, 86, 102, 107n96, 111, 113, 116, 127–28, 132, 137, 138n299, 139–40, 157, 163–65, 170n172, 172, 175–78, 194, 201
sanctification, 14, 91–92, 97, 102n68, 136n285, 184, 204
satisfaction, 14, 17, 23–24, 28, 33, 48, 52n102, 65–66, 72n225, 87n301, 126, 133, 134n261, 139, 194, 201–3, 205–6
scholastic(s/ism), 6, 10, 23, 32, 35, 46n51, 102–3, 104n78, 133, 143, 158–59, 161n125, 162, 181–83, 187, 190, 193
self-accusation, 99
Shultz, Hieronymus, of Brandenburg, 38n2
sick, 28, 65, 105, 128.
Simon of Cremona, 31
simul, 84n289, 91, 97, 101–2, 105–6, 112–13, 119, 135. *See also motu*

Subject Index

simul iustus et peccator, 84n289, 101, 112, 119, 135
sin(s): confession of, ix–x; post-baptismal, 20n46, 21, 30, 132n252, 205; remission of, 16–18, 28–31 (penalty and guilt), 40, 119, 128n228, 203; removal of, 5, 92, 103–4, 107–8, 113–14, 118–20, 123, 132n252, 139, 141, 190; remove(d), 103, 104n78, 111–12, 118, 179
Sixtus IV, Pope, 29, 31
Smalcald Articles. See Luther: works
Smalcald League, 68
soul: three types of dying, 66, 84, 124, 133; intermediate state of, 38, 41, 82–83, 193–95, 199, 203; (a)sleep, 60–61, 63n172, 71, 73, 82–85, 140. *See also* analogy
Steinmetz, David Curtis, 7
Stephan VIII, Pope, 29
suffering(s), x, 5–6, 9–10, 13–14, 28, 35, 38–39, 44, 47–48, 52n102, 58n139, 59–62, 68, 76, 89, 92, 99, 105n82, 123–26, 131–34, 137–41, 142–87, 188–95, 203, 206. *See also anfechtung*; a foretaste of hell; *tentatio*
suffrages, 17, 23–25, 32, 204

Tauler, John, 6, 10, 43n28, 108n103, 143, 151–68, 181–82, 190
tentatio, 15, 44, 52, 54, 61–62, 67–68, 72–73, 78, 88–89, 92, 99–100, 124–25, 127–28, 138, 140, 146, 173, 183–86, 193. *See also anfechtung*; a foretaste of hell; suffering(s)

Tertullian of Carthage, 13
Tetzel, John, 30, 44–45
Theodosius the Great (Roman emperor, d. 395), 18
Thomas Aquinas, 13, 24, 161
tradition: of German theology, 6, 10, 143, 158, 160n118, 163, 181–83, 190; of scholastic theology, 6, 10, 143, 158, 162, 190, 193
Trajan (Roman emperor, d. 117), 18n37

Urban II, Pope, 29, 40n10

Valla, Lorenzo, 9, 35, 79–80, 95n27, 189, 191
Volta, Gabriele della, 45

Weller, Hieronymus, 66n197
Westerburg, Gerhard, 3, 41
will: divine, 46, 74, 106–7, 126, 133–35, 137, 176–77, 193; hidden, 4–5, 58, 72, 74–75, 82n276, 89; revealed, 74
William of Auxerre, 31
Wimpina, Konrad Koch, 44–45
wisdom: referring to Christ, 102n68; of the cross, 170; experienced, 154, 163, 181, 184; drawn from Scripture, 184; of the world, 162, 169, 170, 184
Wittenberg, x, xi, 6, 10, 38n4, 41–42, 45, 52, 59, 87, 143, 160–61, 183, 190

Zwingli, Hulrych, 41, 203n23
Zwolle, 42

Scripture Index

OLD TESTAMENT

Genesis
2:24	129n235
25:7–10	69n216, 85nn292–94
37:35	149, 150n59
41:1–7	150n60, 160n120
48:21	69n213, 194n2

Deuteronomy
28:65	53n107

1 Samuel
2:6	67, 150n58, 175

2 Samuel
22:6	67, 186

Psalms
2:5	53n107
2:10	100n50
4:4	99n50
5–7	64n182
6:2–7	53n107
6:12	53n112
9	174n205
9:13	67, 186
18:11	180n243
18:15	127
23	64n182
25	64n182
27	64n182
28:1	158n109
40–42	64n182
49:15	67, 186
51	64n182, 68n204
60:8	150n54
62–63	64n182
66:12	63, 76
69	151n65
69:3	43n29, 180n242, 182n255
69:16	149nn51–52, 150, 179, 180n243, 186n276
71:20	158n109
72:1	105n82
84:3	169, 180n245
86:13	67, 186
88:33	158n109
90:3	118n176
91:7	155n91
92:4	155n91
94:17	158n109
110	65n192
116:3	67, 186
119	183
121:1	145n18
130	64n182
130:1	150n58
141:7	158n109
148–50	64n182

Scripture Index

Proverbs
28:1	53n107

Ecclesiastes
9:5–6	3, 60

Isaiah
9:2	67, 186
28:21	175n213
38:10–20	64n182
38:10	150n58, 158n110
38:13	158n110
17	150n58
53:2	175n210
53:5	107n96

Jeremiah
23:24	146

Jonah
2:3	150n58

Micah
6:8	134n261

NEW TESTAMENT

Matthew
2:1–12	7, 44n34, 50n93, 51, 56n132, 76n239, 77n246, 77n252
4:16	67, 186
4:17	137
5:26	206
6:16–18	69n212
11:25	108n105
12:31	24
12:32	53n112, 200, 203, 206
16:19	69n211
16:28	66, 84
18:7	43n29, 68n203
22:4	166n152, 168n164
23:29–30	65n192
25:31	27
25:41	43n28

Mark
3:29	53n112

Luke
1:79	67, 186
5:3–10	168n166
16:22–28	205
24:32	154n83

John
6–8	65n188
6:58	65
12:32	168n164
14:19	69, 194
15:4–5	110n118
16:13	65n193

Acts
14:22	171

Romans
1:17	107
3:28	118n175
4:7	102n68
5:3	174n199
6	153n72
6:6	137n289
8:23	118
8:26	154n83
8:29	138
8:32	129n235
9:3	46n56
12:1	104n80

1 Corinthians
1:30	102n68
3:10–15	201n12
3:13–15	200–201, 203, 206
3:15	53n112, 64, 76, 201

Scripture Index

11:31	137n289
15:26	27
15:50	132n250

2 Corinthians
12:2	148, 181

Galatians
2	153n72
2:17, 20	153n72
2:21	103n72

Ephesians
5:31–32	129n235

1 Thessalonians
5:21	158

1 Timothy
6:16	180n243

Titus
2:11–15	7, 51, 55
3:4–7/8	7, 50n93, 51, 55, 77n247, 89n306

Hebrews
12:11	174

1 Peter
3:8	166n149

1 John
4:18	52n105, 135–36

Revelation
14:13	50, 63, 66, 193
21:27	52, 132–33, 139
22:11	100, 123

APOCRYPHA

2 Maccabees
12:39–45	200, 203
12:42–45	19
12:43–45	63, 76, 206
12:43	53n112
12:45	49n87